Nāgas

The Tribe and The C

Nāgas

The Tribe and The Cult

R.K. SHARMA

ARYAN BOOKS INTERNATIONAL
New Delhi

NĀGAS: THE TRIBE AND THE CULT

ISBN-81-7305-306-5

Published in **2006** by:
ARYAN BOOKS INTERNATIONAL
Pooja Apartments, 4B, Ansari Road, Darya Ganj, New Delhi-110 002 (India)
Tel.: 23287589, 23255799; Fax: 91-11-23270385; E-mail: aryanbooks@vsnl.com

Computer Typeset and Printed in India at
ABI Prints & Publishing Co., New Delhi

PREFACE

Nāgas, the snake-worshipping non-Āryan tribe of Ancient India occupy an important place in Indian history. To a student of Indian history, it appears as if there lay a complete veneer of belief in the divinity of the Nāgas and of the Nāga racial blood over the length and breadth of India. From Kashmir, Tibet or Nepal to the Malabar Coast in the South; from Gujarat to Bengal and Assam; from Śrī Laṅkā to Jāvā, Sumātrā and Cambodia, there are very few places indeed where we do not meet frequently with individual or local names of which the word 'Nāga' forms a part, or where the ruling dynasty is not believed sometimes to have been associated with a Nāga clan. The subject, however, is difficult as it is interesting, for, on deeper investigation, it is found that intricacies associated with Nāga problem in Indian history are too many. It is precisely for this reason that distinguished scholars like James Fergusson, H. Oldenberg, E.W. Hopkins, Kern, Oldham, M. Winternitz, Prazyluski, Monier Williams, James Hastings, J.Ph. Vogel, K.P. Jayaswal, T.V. Mahalingam, etc have worked on a few of the varied aspects of the Nāga history and cult. Their works are well known. Within past few decades, works like Dr. P.K. Maity's *Historical Studies in the Cult of Manasā* (Calcutta, 1966), Dr. S.N. Rajaguru's *Nāga Itihāsa* (in Oriya), (Bhubaneswar, 1958), H.L. Kosare's *Prāchīn Bhāratātil Nāga* (in Marathi) (Nagpur, 1989), Dr. Naval Viyogi's *Nāga the Ancient Rulers of India – their Origin and History* (Delhi, 2002), Dr. S.C. Panda's *Nāga Cult in Orissa* (Delhi, 1986), etc along with sporadic research papers published in different journals have engaged attention of the learned world. A peep into these investigations would reveal that each one of the scholars mentioned above has approached the Nāga history or the cult from one or the other specific point of view only. A systematic critical history of the Nāgas based on reliable evidences and presented in chronological order is the need of the hour and it is precisely to fulfil this need that the present study has been taken up.

The history of each Nāga dynasty bristles with controversial problems, particularly relating to its origin, the different houses, their mutual relationship and relations with the contemporary powers. Based on evidences supplied by archaeological and literary sources and accounts of the foreign travellers and writers, discussion on all the problems has been attempted. All efforts have been made to draw attention on each controversial issue with a view to enable the reader to form his own opinion. The work is limited with the time frame bracketed within the earliest times to c. 15th century AD.

The study has been planned as under:

Chapter I entitled 'Nāgas: The Tribe and the Cult' is an attempt to locate the tribe and trace the origin and antiquity of the cult of serpent worship. It has been suggested that the Nāgas appear to have been a totemistic group of people with serpent as their totem. As for the serpent worship, evidences suggest that "Serpent worship in India had nothing to do with the serpent worship either of the non-Āryans or the aborigines of the country and had an independent origin and independent development." It was indigenous and Āryan in Origin.

An important aspect of the history of the Nāgas is its traditional history, the historical value of which cannot be denied. The literary works from the post-Vedic Period onwards, chiefly the *Mahābhārata*, the *Rāmāyaṇa*, the *Purāṇas*, the Jaina literature the Buddhist literature supply accounts of the principal Nāgarājas and their contribution to the history of India. A critical account of the traditional history of the Nāgas has been attempted in Chapter II.

That Magadha was a seat of power of the Nāgas from the times of the epics till the rise of the Nandas is the subject matter of discussion in Chapter III entitled 'The Nāgas of Magadha'. This is followed by a period of oblivion in the history of the Nāgas till we find them ruling in the region of Vidishā-Padmāvatī-Kāntipurī and Mathurā during the period c. 1st century BC to AD 350. Their history, mainly based on the *Purāṇas* and the latest numismatic evidences has been critically discussed in Chapter IV.

An independent Chapter V is devoted to the Bhāraśiva Nāgas who played a dominant role in driving the Kuṣāṇas out of the country. Were the Bhāraśivas really paramount sovereigns? Were they solely responsible for the overthrow of the Kuṣāṇas? All these and hotly debated allied issued have been made subject of critical discussion in this chapter.

The next chapter provides an account of the Nāgas in the "History of Kashmir". The contributions of the Kārkoṭa Nāga dynasty finds a special treatment.

Between c. 8th and 15th century AD there was revival of the Nāga power in Bastar, Kawardha and Bhatgaon region of Central India. Most likely they were successors of the Nāgas of Vidishā-Padmāvatī-Kāntipurī, whose revival after their southward migration took place after a long interval of several centuries. Chapter VII is devoted the history of these Nāga dynasties.

An overview of the Nāga association with Śrī Laṅkā, South India, Deccan, East India and Greater India has been attempted in Chapter VIII.

In summarising the findings the concluding Chapter IX throws light on the intricacies associated with the Nāga problem in Indian history.

A select Bibliography and good number of plates follow the conclusion.

The author is grateful to the Indian Council of Historical Research, New Delhi, for providing Senior Fellowship to him for two years to complete major portion of this work which formed its project entitled 'Nāgas of North India: A Political Study.' Thanks are also due to Shri Rajendra Tiwari, Chairman, Mahakoshal Shiksha Prasar Samiti, Jabalpur; Dr. Ashutosh Srivastava, Secretary, Mahakoshal Shiksha Prasar Samiti, Jabalpur and Smt. Abda Firdausi, Principal, C.P. Mahila Mahavidyalaya, Jabalpur. All of them came to the rescue of the author in providing necessary facilities in their institution to conduct this project smoothly. With valuable and timely assistance given by Dr. (Smt.) Rachna Mehrotra and Dr. Sanjay Mehrotra, it was possible to present this work in a well-typed form and get-up within time limit. The author is thankful to them. Also, it will be a failure on the part of the author if he does not adequately thank his wife Smt. Sarla Sharma whose sustained interest and ceaseless inspiration helped him to complete this work as early as possible.

Jabalpur
21st January; 2006

R.K. Sharma

CONTENTS

ABBREVIATIONS

ABIA	:	*Annual Bibliography of Indian Archaeology*, Leiden.
ABORI	:	*Annals of the Bhandarkar Oriental Research Institute*, Pune.
AG	:	Grade, M.B., *Archaeology in Gwalior*, 2nd ed., Gwalior, 1934.
AI	:	*Ancient India* – The Bulletin of the Archaeological Survey of India, New Delhi.
AIOC	:	*All India Oriental Conference.*
AMMK	:	*Ārya-Mañju-Śrī-Mūlakalpa.*
AR	:	*Asiatic Researches.*
ARIE	:	*Annual Report of India Epigraphy.*
ASIAR/ARASI	:	*Archaeological Survey of India, Annual Report.*
BDCRI	:	*Bulletin of the Deccan College Research Institute*, Pune.
Bhandarkar	:	Bhandarkar, D.R., A List of the Inscriptions of Northern India in Brāhmī and its derivative scripts form about 200 A.D. Appendix to Epigraphia Indica, Vols. XIX-XXIII.
BMC, AI	:	*Catalogue of Indian Coins in the British Museum – Ancient India.*

CAI	:	Cunningham's *Coins of Ancient India.*
CASIR/ASR	:	Cunningham's *Archaeological Survey of India Reports,* Vols. I-XXIII.
CCIMC	:	*Catalogue of Coins, Indian Museum,* Calcutta.
CCNP	:	Trivedi, H.V., *Catalogue of Coins of the Nāga Kings of Padmāvatī.*
CHI	:	*Cambridge History of India.*
CII	:	*Corpus Inscriptionum Indicarum.*
CL	:	Bhandarkar, D.R., *Carmichael Lectures.*
CLAR	:	*Cousens' List of Antiquarian Remains in C.P. and Berar,* Calcutta, 1897.
CMI	:	Cunningham's *Coins of Medieval India.*
CPMC	:	*Chronology of Punch Marked Coins,* Varanasi, 1966.
DKA	:	*The Purāṇa Text of the Dynasties of Kali Age* by F.E. Pargiter.
DDPN	:	*Dictionary of Pāli Proper Names* (Malalasekara)
DV	:	*Divyāvadāna*
EC	:	*Epigraphia Carnatica.*
EI	:	*Epigraphia Indica.*
EHI	:	*Early History of India.*
ERE	:	*Encyclopaedia of Religion and Ethics.*
GAR	:	*Annual Adminsitration Reports, Archaeology Department,* Gwalior State.
Hiralal List	:	Hiralal, R.B., *Inscriptions in C.P. and Berar,* Nagpur, 1932.
IA/Ind. Ant.	:	*Indian Antiquary.*
IAR	:	*Indian Archaeology-A Review.*
IC	:	*Indian Culture.*
IHQ	:	*Indian Historical Quarterly.*
IMC	:	Smith, V.A., *Catalogue of the Coins in the Indian Museum,* Calcutta.
INC	:	*Indian Numismatic Chronicle.*
INHAC	:	*Indian Numismatics, History and Culture* (Dr. P.L. Gupta Fel. Vol.), Delhi, 1992.

JA	:	*Journal Asiatique.*
JAOS	:	*Journal of American Oriental Society.*
JAHRS	:	*Journal of the Andhra Historical Research Society.*
JASB	:	*Journal of the Asiatic Society of Bengal.*
JBBRAS	:	*Journal of the Bombay Branch of the Royal Asiatic Society.*
JOBRS	:	*Journal of the Bihar Orissa Research Society.*
JESI	:	*Journal of the Epigraphical Society of India.*
JIH	:	*Journal of Indian History.*
JMPIP	:	*Journal of Madhya Pradesh Itihasa Parishad.*
JNSI	:	*Journal of the Numismatic Society of India.*
JOHRS	:	*Journal of the Orissa Historical Research Society.*
JOR	:	*Journal of Oriental Research,* Madras.
JRAS	:	*Journal of Royal Asiatic Society.*
JRAS, GB	:	*Journal of the Royal Asiatic Society, Great Britain and Ireland.*
JRAS (NS)	:	*Journal of the Royal Asiatic Society* (New Series).
JRASB	:	*Journal of Royal Asiatic Society,* Bengal.
JUPHS	:	*Journal of the U.P. Historical Society.*
KA	:	*Kauṭilya's Arthasastra.*
MAR	:	*Annual Report of the Mysore Archaeological Department.*
MASI	:	*Memoirs of the Archaeological Survey of India.*
MBI	:	Dwivedi, H.N., *Madhya Bhārat Kā Itihās,* Gwalior, 1956.
ME	:	*Man and Environment,* Pune.
MER	:	*Mysore Epigraphy Reports.*
MPSG	:	Sharma, R.K., *Madhya Pradesh Ke Purātattva Kā Sandarbha Grantha,* Bhopal, 1974.
MS	:	Marshall and Foucher, *Monuments of Sanchi,* 3 Vols., Delhi, 1940.
MUH	:	Patil, D.R., *Monuments of Udayagiri Hills.*
MV	:	*Mahāvaṁsa,* ed., W. Geiger.
ND	:	*Numismatic Digest.*
NIA	:	*New Indian Antiquary,* Bombay.

PASB	:	*Proceedings of the Asiatic Society of Bengal.*
PHAI	:	*Political History of Ancient India* by H.C. Ray Chaudhuri.
PIHC	:	*Proceedings of Indian History Congress.*
QJMS	:	*Quarterly Journal of the Mythic Society.*
RAJ	:	*Rājataraṅgiṇī* of Kalhaṇa (ed.) and tr. by Stein.
SBE	:	*Sacred Books of the East.*
SC	:	*Science and Culture.*
SII	:	*South Indian Inscriptions.*
VRIA	:	Mirashi, V.V., *Vakāṭaka Rajvansh Kā Itihāsa Tathā Abhilekh*, Nagpur.

LIST OF ILLUSTRATIONS

17. Indor (Guna Dist.): Nāga.
18. Ujjain (M.P.): Nāgarāja.
19. Gwalior Fort: Pārśvanātha (upper part).
20. Khajuraho: Kṛṣṇa Janma.
21. Tewar (Jabalpur Dist.): Nāgī (c. 11th cent. AD).
22. Hinglajgarh (Mandsaur Dist.): Śiva-Kalyānasundara.
23. Hinglajgarh (Mandsaur Dist.): Viṣṇu.
24. Hinglajgarh (Mandsaur Dist.): Pārvatī (c. 10th cent. AD).
25. Hinglajgarh (Mandsaur Dist.): Padmāvatī.
26. Hinglajgarh (Mandsaur Dist.): Kubera.
27. Badami, cave No. 4: Bāhubalī (late 6th cent. AD).
28. Badami, cave No. 3: Viṣṇu seated on Śeṣa.
29. Barhut: Southern Gate: Nāga king.
30. Barhut: Railing: Nāgarāja Elāpata worshipping Bodhi tree.
31. Barhut: Nāgarāja.
32. Sanchi, Eastern Toraṇa: Miracle of serpent (c. 1st cent. BC).
33. Sanchi, Eastern Toraṇa: Scenes from Uruvilva, Victory over Nāga etc.
34. Sanchi, Eastern Toraṇa: Nāgarāja.
35. Ajanta, Cave No. 20: Standing Nāga Dvārapāla (AD 462-480).
36. Ajanta, Cave No. 2, Porch: Nāgarāja (c. 2nd half of 5th cent. AD).
37. Mathura Museum: Nāga standing (c. 1st cent. AD).
38. Mathura-Yamuna river bed: Nāga (c. 3rd cent. AD).
39. Mathura (Bhuteśvara): Nāga deity, dt. yr. 52.
40. Mathura (Bhadar Village): Bhūmi Nāga flanked by two Nāgīs.
41. Mathura (Chargaon): Nāga (c. 184 AD).
42. Mathura (Kukaryam): Balarāma (c. 5th cent. AD).
43. Deogarh (Jhansi Dist.): Viṣṇu's Gajendra-mokṣa panel.
44. Deogarh (Jhansi Dist.): Nāga image (c. 5th cent. AD).
45. Deogarh (Jhansi Dist.): Viṣṇu on Śeṣa (AD 500-525).
46. Deogarh (Jhansi Dist.): Viṣṇu Anantaśayana (AD 500-525).
47. Deogarh (Jhansi Dist.): Seated Pārśvanātha (c. 9th cent. AD).
48. Indore Museum: Ambikā.
49. Sagar (M.P.): Nāga couple (c. 11th cent. AD).
50. Papet (Sagar M.P.): Nāgī standing in Varada-Mudrā (c. 13th cent. AD).

1

NĀGAS: THE TRIBE AND THE CULT

The term 'Nāga' is a Sanskrit word meaning snake. It also means a 'hill' or a 'mountain'.[1] Since early men lived in natural caverns and caves in the hills, it may probably be presumed that those that lived in these places be named as Nāgas. Attempts at deriving the word from 'Nagna', meaning naked have also been made.[2] Evidently, the primitive tribes did not use clothes and remained naked. The word may also mean an elephant; but there does not appear to have been any close connection between that animal and men as between snakes and men to justify the latter to be named after it. A better explanation of the word is found in the cult of Serpent worship. This cult had been widespread in ancient India. From evidences available this cult beyond doubt is a universal cult.[3] The Vedas, the oldest literature in India, describe the antagonism between the Āryans and Dasyus and associate the latter with serpents.[4] In post-Vedic early Sanskrit literature the Nāgas are referred to as a class of semi-divine beings with their bodies half-man and half-snake and classed along with other semi-divine beings like the Kinnaras, Gandharvas, Yakṣas, etc. They are described as possessing immense wealth, living in luxurious and magnificient cities in the nether regions enjoying eternal happiness and bliss, and leading sensual lives with their women noted for their enrapturing beauty and charm. They are also described as a class of *gaṇas* in heaven attending on the gods. Side by side with such descriptions we find them described also as human beings living in different parts of the country. The *Purāṇas* divide the nether world into seven regions of which the first four were occupied by *Daityas* or *Dānavas* and the rest by the Nāgas. The lowest region *Pātāla* is vividly pictured in the *Viṣṇu Purāṇa* and *Padma Purāṇa*.[5] Different accounts are also found about the existence of the *Pātāla*.[6]

Really speaking, the Nāgas appear to have been a totemistic people with the serpent as their totem. The word 'totem' belongs to the languages of the Ojibwas, a tribe of the Algonkin stock living near Lake Superior in North America. It serves as a symbol or device of a gens or tribal division by which it is distinguished from other such divisions. The totemistic devices belong to the animal kingdom such as for instance, the wolf, the bear, the fish and the snake, birds, vegetables like corn, potato, the tobacco plant, natural objects like the sun, earth, sand, salt, sea, snow, ice, water, rain, etc.[7]

Describing the nature of the totem Sir J.G. Frazer says: "A totem is a class of natural phenomena or material. Object – most commonly a species of animals or plants – between which and himself the savage believes that a certain intimate relation exists. The exact nature of the relation is not easy to ascertain; various explanations of it have been suggested, but none has yet won general acceptance; whatever it may be, it generally leads the savage to abstain from killing or eating his totem if his totem happens to be a species of animals or plants. Further the group of persons who are knit to any particular totem by this mysterious tie commonly bear the name of the totem, believe themselves to be of one blood, and strictly refuse to sanction the marriage or cohabitation of members of the group with each other. This prohibition to marry within the group is generally called by the name of exogamy. Thus totemism has commonly been treated as a primitive system, both of religion and of society. As a system of religion, it embraces the mystic union of the savage with his totem; as a system of society it comprises the relations in which men and women of the same totem stand to each other and to members of other totemistic groups....Whether the two sides, the religious and social, have always co-existed, or are essentially independent is a question which has been variously answered. Some writers – for example, Sir John Lubbock and Mr. Herbert Spencer, have held that totemisms began as a system of society only, and that the superstitious regard for the totem developed later, through a simple process of misunderstanding. Others, including J.F. Mc Lennan and Robertson Smith, were of opinion that the religious reverence of the totem is original and must at least have preceded the introduction of exogamy."[8] Primitive society was a network of totemistic groups and each of them had an emblem like an animal or a plant. In course of time the totemistic groups themselves came to be called by the name of their totem. Thus one finds, for instance, totemistic groups in India being called Vānaras (the monkey tribe), the Ajas (the goat tribe), the Vṛṣṇis (the ram tribe), the Garuḍas (the kite tribe), the Matsyas (the fish tribe) and Nāgas (the serpent tribe).[9] Thus the Nāgas can be considered to be a people associated with the serpent, at times tracing their descent from it, bearing it on their crest, banners, etc.

The origin of the Nāgas is shrouded in obscurity and offers one of the complicated problems of the history of ancient India. According to some scholars, the Nāgas were originally serpent worshippers, and from the cult name were afterwards themselves known as Nāgas.[10] In this connection the views expressed by James Fergusson in his book *Tree and Serpent Worship* (1868, 2nd ed., 1971) have often been quoted, and have no doubt, exercised considerable influence, but will hardly find any adherents among scholars today. According to him the Nāgas were serpent worshipper, an aboriginal race of Turanian stock inhabiting Northern India, who were conquered by war-like Āryans. Fergusson positively declares that neither the Āryans nor the Dravidians were serpent worshippers, and, in order to maintain his thesis, he even asserts that "any traces of serpent worship that may be found in the Vedas or early writings of the Āryans must be either interpolations of a later date or concessions to the superstitions of the subject races." Buddhism, which replaced serpent worship, he qualifies as "little more than a revival of the coarser superstitions of the aboriginal races." Vogel has rightly pointed out that "these are strange and baseless theories."[11]

A few scholars have asserted that serpent worship as an organized cult had its origin among the Scythians of Central Asia, who spread it throughout the world.[12] They were in the habit of using the serpent as a national symbol.[13] In this connection it has also been suggested that the Proto-Dravidians who came to India spoke a language similar to that of Scythians by which, in modern terminology, was meant the Finno Ugrian family of languages.[14] This view originated with the 19th century authority on Dravidian languages, Caldwell, and was also held by Professor T. Burrow of Oxford. On the other hand, S.C. Roy and others have suggested that the Proto-Dravidians were early immigrants of the Mediterranean race and that they contributed to the snake cult in India.[15]

Thus the theories regarding the origin and the spread of the cult are at variance and none can be accepted with certainty; moreover, snake worship was widely prevalent in the human world (for details, see *Encyclopaedia of Religion and Ethics*, Vol. XI, pp. 399ff). The claim of the Scythians cannot stand for two reasons – firstly, the theory that they brought snake worship to India depends only on superficial similarities between Dravidian and Finno-Ugrian languages, and there is no historical evidence for an invasion of Central

Asians. The latest archaeological and genetic findings have proved that the Āryan invasion/migration theory in second millennium BC is a myth.[16] Secondly, there is no trace of the general cult of the serpent in Central Asia except the use of the snake as an ornament or symbol.[17] Lubbock believed in independent local origin of serpent worship at different places and times, arising naturally out of the common instincts of terror, fear and wonder at the activities and apparently supernatural power of the reptile.[18] Similarly Frazers' maxim that 'homogeneity of belief' shows 'homogeneity of race'[19] is rejected by A.C. Haddon on the ground that common beliefs and practices may have independent origins, due to the fundamental and essential uniformity of human thought and imagination.[20] In the present state of our knowledge the theory of the local origin of snake cults in various parts of the world seems to be the firmest based and to carry most conviction. Thus "primitive religious characteristics are human, not racial."[21]

The Nāgas were a powerful and widespread people of more than usual importance, who appear to have been in the occupation of different parts of India from very early times. It is not known by what name they were known before they came to be called Nāgas in Sanskrit. 'Nāga' in Dravidian language is known as *'pāmbu'* or *'pāvu.'* Probably the name *'Pāvā'* mentioned as one of the cities of Northern India, and the capital of the Mallas, at the time of the Buddha (*Pārāyaṇavagga, Sutta Nipāta*, SBE,X, p. 180); (*Mahāvamsa*, IV, 17-19), had retained the older name of the tribe inhabiting it, namely, the Nāgas. It is quite possible that as the name *'Mīnas'* was changed to *'Matsyas,'* the *'Kudagas'* to *'Vānaras'* (Heras, "Mohenjo Daro, The People and the Land", *Indian Culture*, III, pp. 708, 715), so also, the *'Pāvas'* (meaning the snakes) was changed to the Nāgas, later on, by the Āryans, and the 'snake men' came to be called Nāgas in course of time by the Sanskritists.

A few finds that have been unearthed at Harappa are of much interest in as much as they throw light on the place of the serpent in the religious life of the contemporary people. Among them is a faience tablet where a seated deity is worshipped by a kneeling man on either side of it. Behind each worshipper is seen a cobra with head raised and hood expanded, evidently showing that it was also joining in the adoration of the god.[22] Besides that have been found painted pottery with the reptile occasionally painted on it, the carved figure of a snake and a clay amulet figuring a reptile before a low stool, on which appears to be an offering, probably of milk.[23] There has also been found an amulet at Harappa displaying the figure of Garuḍa flanked by two Nāgas. The above finds point to the fact that the serpent was associated with worship among the Indus Valley people though not necessarily being objects of worship themselves, as Keny points out,[24] and there must have been in that region people with the Nāga totem.

From the account contained in the *Mahābhārata* that the Nāgas, who were the children of Kāśyapa and Kadrū, reached after encountering much heat, storm and rain, the land of Ramaṇīyaka which lay across the sea, it is considered that the Nāgas migrated to that country, which has been sought to be identified with Egypt.[25] They are said to have been led by a Garuḍa chief. Whether this theory be acceptable or not, it is interesting to note that the Pharaohs of Egypt were in some way associated with the hawk or Garuḍa and serpent.

As for the question whether the Nāgas were Āryans or non-Āryans, much has been written and most of the scholars are of opinion that they (the Nāgas) were a Dravidian people inhabiting the northern part of India before the immigration of the Āryans to India.[26] Without entering into the controversy of the Āryan immigration theory, which, as pointed out above, has been proved to be a myth by latest researches, it may be pointed that the Nāgas were not a non-Āryan people just because of their worshipping the snake which was their totem and not necessarily an object of worship. They were a non-Āryan tribe whether they worshipped snake or not. Snake as a totem of a tribe and snake as an object of worship are two different factors. Adoption of the former need not necessarily imply adoption of the latter. This is amply proved in the entire history of Ancient India where the ruling tribes/dynasties adopting the totem of Nāgas were not necessarily Nāga worshippers and non-Āryans.

During Ancient India, most of Northern India was being inhabited by the Nāgas.[27] The *Ṛgveda* finds a place for Vṛitra and Tugra.[28] The *Mahābhārata* is full with the description of the exploits of many Nāga kings. The great epic opens with the historical persecution of the Nāgas under king Takṣaka residing in the great Khāṇḍava forest in the valley of the Jumna near Indraprastha or Old Delhi.[29] In fact there were several very powerful kings of the Nāga tribe, the best known being Śeṣa or Ananta, Vāsuki, Takṣaka, Karkoṭaka, Kāśyapa, Airāvata, Kauravya and Dhṛatarāṣṭra, all born of Kadrū.[30] Dhṛatarāṣṭra, the foremost of all the Nāgas,[31] alone had twenty-eight thousand Nāgas as his followers.[32] References do not lack even in the *Jātakas* to prove the existence of the Nāgas in North India.[33] The great kings of the Ikṣvāuku Dynasty were the ancient Nāgas of Pataliputra.[34] The Bharatas were also included among the snake races.[35] The great king Yayāti, father of the equally great king Puru, was the son of the Nāga Nahuśa and the maternal grandfather of Aṣṭaka.[36] The five Pāṇḍava brothers were the grandsons of the grandson of the Nāga named Āryaka (Arka).[37] There is no wonder then that Arjuna should marry the Nāga princess Ulūpī.[38] The Yādavas were also Nāgas. Not only was Kuntī, the mother of the five Pāṇḍava heroes, the paternal aunt of Kṛṣṇa,[39] but even the latter was a direct descendant of the Nāga chief Āryaka (Arka), who was the great-grandfather of Vasudeva, the father of the Yādava king.[40] Even his elder brother Baladeva is represented as having his head covered with many huge snakes,[41] which is rightly said to be the canopy to distinguish great Nāgarājas.[42] Baladeva is said to be a portion of the Nāga Śeṣa,[43] which means that either he was a relative of the great Śeṣa Nāga or that he was as powerful as the great Nāga king named Śeṣa. And as Kaṁsa, the maternal uncle of these two Nāga heroes of the Yādava clan, was the son-in-law of the Bārhadratha king Jarāsandha of Magadha,[44] we see that even Magadha had Nāgas as her rulers in her ancient dynasty, namely, the Bārhadrathas.

According to the *Purāṇas* the Bārhadrathas of Magadha were succeeded by the Pradyotas, who in turn, were followed by the Śiśunāgas.[45] And so many authors have rightly said that in the Śiśunāgas, Magadha had a Nāga dynasty to rule over her.[46] The word Śiśunāga itself is very significant. After the fall of the Bārhadratha Dynasty, which was a Nāga dynasty, there came into power another dynasty known as the Pradyota Dynasty. But this dynasty, which was absolutely different than its preceding Nāga dynasty, was again defeated by the Śiśunāga Dynasty, which, as its name shows, was a Nāga dynasty. Thus Nāgas came to power once more, after a short break during the period of the Pradyotas. These Śiśunāgas were the followers of the earlier Nāgas of the Bārhadratha Dynasty. And so after their coming to power once more they were known as Śiśunāgas or 'Junior'(*śiśu*) Nāgas being the followers of the earlier senior Nāgas, viz., the Bārhadrathas. The Buddhist tradition about the origin of Śiśunāga, the founder or rather the restorer of the Śiśunāga as being protected by a Nāgas,[47] furthur proves that he was a Nāga.[48]

Even Chandragupta Maurya is said to have belonged to the Nāga race.[49] And the people with whom Alexander I came into contact after crossing the Indus, were the Nāgas.[50]

According to the *Purāṇas*, King Bimbisāra of Magadha was the great-great-grandson of Śiśunāga.[51] And it was during his reign that the Buddha preached and propagated his faith. By this time Magadha was already influenced by Āryan culture; and Buddhism was a revolution against this Āryanism. The Śiśunāgas, according to the *Purāṇas*, were "degenerate Kṣatriyas."[52] This was due to the hatred of the Brahmins towards the non-Āryans Nāga people of Magadha. The changing of the origin of the name Nālanda as derived from a Nāga of the same name, to that as 'na+alam+da', applied to a king for his "charity without intermission,"[53] seems to be another proof of the Āryan intentions to do away with the old traditions of the Dravidian people. And probably it is for this hatred and persecutions that we hear the following words of a Nāga : "so wretched is the state of a Nāga that we deem it impossible to attain to a good birth."[54] The stories of Pūrṇabhadra's *Pañchatantra* and *Kathāsaritsāgara*, regarding marriages between the Nāgas and the Brahmins,[55] are a proof of the contact between the people of both races. With all this, it would not be out of place for the Buddha to revolt against Brahmanism. Buddha revolted, being a patriot of his race. He was a great man of the Nāgas. Accordingly, the *Pārāyaṇavagga* of the *Sutta Nipāta* refers to him as a Nāga.[56] Some scholars, thus, are perfectly right in stating that the Buddha was of a Nāga lineage.[57] He was naturally on friendly terms with the Nāga people who played such a prominent part in the legends relating to the life of the Buddha. Even at his death, Nāga kings are said to have claimed a share of his relics, and built stupas over them.[58] And as shown on the Sanchi and Amaravati stupas, it is not surprising that Buddha's teachings should be accepted by the Nāgas[59] belonging to his own non-Āryan stock.[60] The representation of the Buddha with a hooded Nāga only means that he was a great and respectable personality of the Nāga people, similar to Balarāma, as we have already seen. Even as regards Jainism, the Nāga is almost always found in Jaina temples as an object of worship, but definitely subordinate to the Tīrthaṅkara to whom the temple is dedicated.[61] Supārśva, the seventh and Pārśva the twenty-third Tīrthaṅkara of the Jainas, also, as can be seen from their representations with hooded Nāgas, belonged to the tribe of the Nāgas. Great as they were they were, always represented with the canopy of the many hooded Nāgas, like the Buddha and Balarāma.

The population of Magadha and its neighbourhood, where the Buddha spent the greater part of his life, was then, as in earlier times, and in later times largely made up of Nāga tribes.[62] And it was owing to the Āryan migration that they were forced to expand into the Deccan, South India, and Ceylon.[63] The downfall of the Nāgas was, it seems quite natural, due to the downfall of Buddhism. It was the inducement or compelling of the Āryans to the non-Āryan Buddhists for the latters' adoption to Hinduism, that probably led to the fatal downfall of the Nāgas from the history of North India.[64]

If the Nāgas did not get their denomination from Nāga-worship, what was the origin of their name, and what was their cult like?

Even at present, in spite of their not worshipping the Nāgas, there are, in the immediate neighbourhood of Manipur, in Assam, numerous tribes of aboriginal people called Nāgas.[65] The Rajas of Manipur are said to have descended from the Nāgas.[66]

The derivation of the name of the Nāgas is due to the fact that they had the serpent (Nāga) as their national or racial or tribal emblem or *lāñchana*.[67] At present the serpent-gods are worshipped in northern India, "not as dangerous reptiles," or "as mere symbols, but as the deified rulers of an ancient people."[68] Through a *lāñchana* one "feels that he is in intimate though mysterious association with the whole species"[69] of that particular symbol. "The ancestral character of the totem accounts for the association with it of the ideas of protection, which is based on the existence of a fraternal relationship between the totem and all the individual belonging to a particular group of kin. The totem as a badge or symbol, therefore represents the group of individual, dead or alive, towards whom a man stands in a fraternal relation, and the protection of whom he is therefore entitled to, so long as he performs all the obligations on his part which flow from the existence of that relationship".[70]

Amongst the non-Āryan Nāgas "were included various tribes and that these were distinguished by different totems or sub-totems. But the Nāga was common to all."[71] And in Lāñchanism lies the fundamental idea of a 'badge of fraternity' or a 'symbol of gens'. And so a person would look on the *lāñchana* "first with interest, then with respect, and at length with a sort of awe".[72] And, accordingly, in course of time, these Nāga-people "became identified with serpents and the result has been a strange confusion in the ancient myths between serpents and human beings; between the deity and emblem of the Nāgas and the Nāgas themselves."[73]

Keeping the above facts in our mind what can we say about the first positive evidence of Nāga worship in India. Fergusson[74] and Sir Charles Elliot[75] mention Nāga worship as existing in the pre-Āryan Period. But their assertions are mere conjectures not based on any positive evidences. The pre-Āryan cult of snake worship can even be denied on philological ground. As the word 'Nāga' is purely a Sanskrit term, it cannot be said to have been in existence before the period of the Āryans, though the tribe with snake as totem did exist. It must have been known by different denominations of which we know nothing. In other words, we may state that though the Nāgas did exist even in early times, still serpent worship as such did not exist at that time.

Then what is the earliest positive evidence of serpent worship in India? Scholars have tried to prove the existence of serpent worship among the Harappans. But as pointed out above, these do not necessarily prove that the Nāga was an object of worship. Rather the Nāgas are represented as worshipping some supreme deity or they were the totem of devotees who worshipped the god of the seal. Sometimes the serpents are placed in a position where they are shown as protecting the situation concerned. The maximum conclusion that can be drawn is that the people with Nāga totem were involved in religious life of the contemporary people and as their importance as protector could not be undermined, they are represented on the seals. However, a better picture emerges with the rise of the Āryans.

At this point it is necessary to point out that in the light of the latest archaeological finds, Āryans are no more considered as different from the Harappans.[76] From the point of view of religion three-fold divisions have been evisaged, i.e., (1) Harappans of the Indus Valley who have been identified with early Āryans. They were Śiva-Śakti worshippers; (2) The Ṛgvedians of the Sarasvati Valley and Lothal, Panis, the great traders of Patal, i.e., Surkotada-Dholavira of the Kachchha region. They were predominantly fire-worshippers; (3) Later Āryans of Haryana and Punjab represented at Dhadheri-Bhagwanpura respectively. They were characterized by their typical burial practices.

If picture of snake-worship by the Harappans, i.e., early Āryans is vague, it emerges clearly during the period of the *Ṛgveda* and Later Vedic literature. The concept originated with the war between Indra and Vṛtra who is conceived of as having the form of *ahi* (serpent). It developed to the notion of 'Ahi-Budhnya' (the serpent of the deep), reference to which has been made twelve times in the *Ṛgveda* itself. This 'Ahi-Budhnya' is a divine-being, and is invoked to 'rejoice' and "gladden the hearts of his worshippers." His blessings are desired 'as a boon for suppliants.' (*Uta nohirbudhnyo mayaskah, śiśuṅ no pipyuṣīva veti Sindhuh*"-vide Griffith's Ṛv. Bk. 1, Hymn 186, verses 5 and 6).

In *Ṛgveda*, Ahi-Budhnya has been always mentioned in association with Viśvadevas. Similarly he is mentioned with Aja-Ekapād (five times), Apāṁ Napāt (three times), Savitri (two times), Samudra (three times). Ahi-Budhnya is thus an atmospheric deity and in some of the texts, he is mentioned among the 'divinities of middle or aerial region'.

Ahi-Budhnya is also allegorically connected with Agni-Gārhapatya in later Vedic texts like *Vājasaneya-Samhitā* (5, 33), *Aitereya-Brāhmaṇa* (3, 36), *Taittirīya-Brāhmaṇa* (1, 1, 10, 3), etc. Agni has been also compared to a 'raging-Ahi' (Ṛv. I, Hymn 79, verse I). The name of 'Ahi-Budhnya' has also been used as a name for Rudra as well as of Lord Śiva in post-Vedic literature (vide Vogel's, *Indian Serpent Lore*, pp. 3-4).

In almost all the post-Vedic literature, wherever Ahi-Budhnya has been mentioned (also in *Yajurveda* and *Atharvaveda*), he has been mentioned as a semi-divine being with great respect and devotion, and here was the germ of the 'serpent-worship' in the Vedic Period.

It will be interesting to note here certain passages from *Taittirīya Saṁhitā*:[77]

Namo astu sarpebhyo ye ke che prithvimanu, Ye antarikse ye divi, tebhyah sarpebhyo namah, Ye do rochane dive, ye va suryasya rasmisu, Yesam apsu sadah kritan, tebhyah sarphebhyo namah, Ye isavo yatudhananam, ye va vanaspatim ranu, Ye va vatesu serate, tebhya sarphebhyo namah.

Obviously here salutations have been paid to those "divine snakes who inhabit the earth, the firmament, heaven in the rays of the sun, who reside in the water, who are the arrows of the Yātudhanas who inhabit the trees, and who sleep in the hollows of the trees etc."

In the *Taittirīya-Brāhmaṇa* there are certain passages where sacrificial offerings have been made to the divine serpents.[78]

Idam sarpebhyo havirastujusta, Asresa yesamanuyanti chetah........
Tebhyah sarpebhyo madhumojjuhomi etc.

Again, in the Aśvamedha sacrifice, certain portions of the horse are offered to the divine serpents. Offerings of curds and barley and made to them by the gods who seek their help to conquer their cousins, the *Asuras*. (T. Brāh. III, I, IV, Śloka-7).

It is, however, in the *Āśvalāyana Gṛihya-sūtra* that the 'divine-serpents' have been for the first time termed as 'Nāga.' 'Sarpa-bali' or sacrifice to the serpents, is distinctly laid down here and the ritual has been described in detail in this *sūtra*. In the *Pāraskara Gṛihya-sūtra*, '*Sarpadevajana*' or divine serpents are invoked, offered 'pāyasa' and requested to wash and comb themselves, put unguents in their eyes, and garlands on their necks. In this way they are worshipped with all due formalities: "*Anjanam-Kajjalam loukika-dipodbhavam souviram veti*"....... (*Pāraskara Gṛihya sūtra*, Kāṇḍa II, Kaṇḍikā 14, Śloka 17). Similar passages also occur in the *Hiraṇyakeśin Gṛihya-sūtra*.

It is interesting to note here that in one of the *ślokas* of *Pāraskara Gṛihya-sūtra* (Kāṇḍa II, Kaṇ. 15, Śloka 2), *'pāyasa'* has also been offered to God Indra, Aja-Ekapād, and Ahi-Budhnya. The *śloka* is as follows:

Payasam-Indra-Sarpayitva-a-pupanscha-a pupah ... stirtva-a-ajya bhaga, vistva-a-a-jya-huti juhoti-Indrayena-a-Aja Aikapada-Ahir Budhnya-yaya- prousthapadabhyascheti.

From these passages scholars have ventured to advocate that the worship of serpent the India, had originated in the Vedic Period. "Serpent worship in the Ṛgveda had nothing to do with the serpent worship either of the non-Āryans or the aborigines of the country and had an independent origin and independent development."[79] It was indigenous and Āryan in origin.

REFERENCES

1. cf. Vedas giving picture of Dasyu hill-forts. Obviously there must have been cave-dwellers in Ancient India.
2. Hiralal, R.B., "The Nāgas of Central India," in *Maharaja College Magazine*, Vizayanagaram, Vol. V, p. 2
3. Hastings, *Encyclopaedia of Religion and Ethics*, Vol. XI, pp. 399-423.
4. *Ṛgveda*, I. 32.5.8; 52, 10. I.; 61-8, I,; 80, I, 103-7.
5. *Viṣṇu Purāṇa*, tr. Wilson, p. 204. The fourth canto of *Padma Purāṇa,* called *Pātālakhaṇḍa* describes the underworld in detail.
7. C. Staniland Wake, *Serpent Worship and other Essays*, with a chapter on totemism (London, 1888), pp. 267 ff.
8. Risley, *The People of India*, p. 105.
9. Several totemistic tribes with the names of animals are mentioned in the *Ṛgveda*. Hopkins, however, expresses a doubt whether the names of animals point to totemism in the *Ṛgveda* (*JAOS*, 1894, p. cliv).
10. Atkinson, *Himalaya District Gazetteer*, 1884, p. 373.
11. Vogel, J. Ph. *Indian Serpent Lore*, Reprint ed., 1972, p. 2.
12. Tod, J., *Annals and Antiquities of Rajasthan*, London, 1914, p. 86, *ERE*, Vol. XI, p. 412.
13. *QJMS*, Vol. 16, p. 193; *ERE*, Vol. XI, p. 412.
14. E.J. Rapson (ed.), *The Cambridge History of India*, Vol. I, p. 594, *QJMS*, Vol. 16.
15. *Proceedings and Transactions of 7th All-India Oriental Conference*, 1935, pp. 203ff; *QJMS*, Vol. 16, p. 199.
16. Shivaji Singh, "Redefining the Rigvedic and Harappan connections," in *Man and Environment*, Vol. XXVI, No. 1, 2001, pp. 93-98.
17. *ERE*, Vol. XI, p. 412.
18. Lubbock, *The Origin of Civilization and the Primitive Condition of Man*, p. 269.
19. *QJMS*, Vol. 16, p. 197.
20. Haddon, *The Wonderings of Peoples*, p. 10
21. Hopkins, *The History of Religions*, p. 16.
22. Marshall, *Mohanjodaro and the Indus Civilization*, III, pl. CXVI, CXVIII.
23. Earnest Mackey, *The Indus Civilization*, p. 83; Heras H, *Studies in Proto-Indo Mediterranean Culture*, p. 364, fig 219.
24. Keny, L.B., "The Nāgas in Magadha", *JBORS*, Vol. XXVIII, pt. II, pp. 160-61.
25. Heras, H., *op. cit*, pp. 363-6.
26. Oldham, *The Sun and the Serpent*, pp. 31, 36, 44, 160-61, 165; Banerji Sastri, *Asura India*, pp. 92, 96; Fr. Heras, "Mohenjodaro the People and the land," *Indian Culture*, III, p. 719; Srinivasachari, *IHQ*, III, p. 520; Atkinson, *op cit.*, pp. 280-81, 373; Hewitt, "The Notes on the History of Northern India," *JRAS*, 1889, p. 218; Wheeler, *History of India*, I, pp. 147, 441; II, p. 630; Slater, *Dravidian Element in Indian Culture*, p. 56; Menon, *Dravidian Culture and its Diffusion*, p. 80; Dikshitar, *Proc. Seventh AIOC*, p. 244; Ghosh, "An Introduction to the Study of Antiquities

found at the Pataliputra Excavation," The 8th All-India Oriental Conference, p. 267; Banerji, *Hellenism in Ancient India*, p. 83; Ayyar, "The Ancient History of Magadha," *Indian Antiquary*, XLV, p. 10; Chaṇḍa, *Indo-Aryan Races*, p. 77; Fausboll, *Indian Mythology*, p. 1.

27. *Mahābhārata*, Ādi Parva, III. 130; Banerji Sastri, *op cit.*, p. 95; Oldham, *op cit.*, p. 55; Beal, *Buddhist Records of the Western World*, I., pp. 20, 144; Oldham, "The Nagas," *JRAS*, 1901, pp. 461-73.
28. *Rg. Veda*, I, 33, 15; VI. 20,8 : VII, 19. X, 49, 4.
29. *Mahābhārata*, Ādi Parva, LII-LVIII.
30. *Ibid.*, Ādi Parva, XXXV, 5-16; LXVII, 75; LXVI, 40-41.
31. *Ibid.*, Virāṭa Parva, III, 30; Hewitt (*JRAS*, 1889, pp. 291-292) mistakes this Nāga Dhṛatarāṣṭra for the brother of Pāṇḍu. He even goes to the extent of committing mistake by calling Jarāsandha of Magadha as the son of Dhṛatarāṣṭra.
32. *Ibid.*, Ādi Parva, III, pp. 137-38.
33. Fausboll, *op cit.*, VI (Bhūridatta Jātaka), p. 158.
34. Hewitt, *History and Chronology of the Mythmaking Age*, p. 362.
35. Hewitt, *JRAS*, 1889, p. 290.
36. *Mahābhārata*, Ādi Parva, LXXXVII, pp. 42, 44; Udyoga Parva, XVII, pp. 17-23.
37. *Ibid.*, Ādi Parva, CXXXVII, pp. 34-35.
38. *Ibid.*, Ādi Parva, CCXXXIV, pp. 13-32.
39. *Ibid.*, Udyoga Parva, CXXXI, 50; CXL, 10; XC, 1,90.
40. *Ibid.*, Ādi Parva, CXXXVIII, 34-35, cf. Slater, *op cit.*, p. 55; Banerji Sastri, *op cit.*, p. 95; Oldham, *op cit.*, p. 78.
41. *Ibid.*, Anuśāsana Parva, CCLI, 56.
42. Oldham, *op cit.*, p. 79.
43. *Mahābhārata*, Ādi Parva, LXVIII, 152; Anuśāsana Parva, CCLI, 59.
44. *Ibid.*, Sabhā Parva, XIV, 31-32, 49.
45. Pargiter, *Ancient Indian Historical Tradition*, p. 286.
46. Fergusson, *op cit.*, p. 60; Banerji Sastri, "The Nāgas," *Annals of the Bhandarkar Oriental Research Institute*, XVIII, p. 347; Hewitt, *op cit.*, pp. 354-362; Hewitt, *History and Chronology of the Mythmaking Age*, p. 590; Mehta, *Pre-Buddhist India*, p. 66; Wake, *op cit.*, p. 141.
47. Bigandet, *Legend of Gautama*, II, p. 115; Turnour's Introduction to the *Mahāvamsa*, p. XXXVII.
48. According to the Buddhist legend a courtezan bore a child to a Lichchhavi king; but the child proved an abortion and so being put into a basket was thrown on a dungheap. A Nāgarāja, the tutelar of the city, encircled it with its folds and sheltered it with its hood. The people made a noise "*Su, Su*" to frighten and drive away the snake. They found, afterwards, into the basket, the abortion, matured into a male child which was named, for the above incident, *Su-su-nāga* (Śiśunāga). Some scholars (Srinivaschari and Aiyanagar, *History of India*, I., p. 51), though proving the Nāga element of the Śiśunāgas, wrongly explain it by holding that Śiśunāga meant Śeṣanāga.

49. Hewitt, *JRAS*, 1890, p. 432.
50. Oldham, *op cit.*, p. 113.
51. Pargiter, *Dynasties of the Kali Age*, p. 21.
52. Jayaswal, "The Saisunaka and Maurya Chronology," *JBORS*, I, p. 114 (fn.)
53. Beal, *op cit.*, II, p. 167.
54. *Divyāvadāna*, XXIV, p. 345 (ed. Cowell and Neil): "तादृषः सुदुष्ठनागो यद् वयं सुगतिगमनं अपि न संभावयामः।"
55. Vide, Vogel, *op cit.*, pp. 174-176.
56. *Sutta Nipāta*, p. 203 (Pali Text Society): "तं तं नमस्सामि समच्च नाग।"
57. Oldham, *op cit.*, p. 181; Wake, *op cit.*, pp. 92, 141.
58. *Mahā Parinibbāṇa Suttanta*, VI, 28; Beal, *op cit.*, II, p. 41.
59. Fergusson, *op cit.*, p. 61.
60. According to Menon, it was the top-knot of the Buddhists which represented the hood of the Nāga: *Dravidian Culture and its Diffusion*, p. 82.
61. Fergusson, *op cit.*, p. 70.
62. *Mahābhārata*, Ādi Parva, III, 136; cf. Oldham, *op cit.*, p.146; Dalton, *Descriptive Ethnology of Bengal*, pp. 165-66.
63. Srinivaschari, "The Ancient Tamils and the Nāgas," *Indian Historical Quarterly*, III, p. 520.
64. Oldham, *op cit.*, p. 147; Menon, *op cit.*, pp. 88-89. Mr. Menon is of the opinion that the Nāgas "in common with many of the Buddhists in India became merged with the Ceras and were gradually absorbed in the Hindu fold."
65. Vide, Fergusson, *op cit.*, pp. 61, 192.
66. Hudson, "The native tribes of Manipur," *Journal of the Anthropological Institute*, XXX, pp. 302-304; Fergusson, *op cit.*, p. 61.
67. Mazumdar, *History of the Bengali Language*, pp. 32, 39; Dikshitar, *op cit.*, p. 248; W. Crooke, *Popular Religion and Folklore in Northern India*, II, p. 148; Atkinson, *op cit.*, 1884, pp. 373-74; Oldham, *op cit.*, pp. 30, 184, 206; Will Durant, *Story of Civilization*, p. 402; Wheeler, *History of India*, I, pp. 146-47.
68. Oldham, *op cit.*, p. 85; Wake, *op cit.*, pp. 96, 97, 272, 275.
69. Sir John Lubbock, *Origin of Civilization*, p. 199.
70. Wake, *op cit.*, p. 275.
71. Oldham, *op cit.*, pp. 47, 48. In the above two quotations, it would have been more proper to use the word *lāñchana* instead of 'totem', for, as seen above, the ancient Nāgas never worshipped their tribal symbol. Totemism is different from lāñchanism.
72. Wake, *op cit.*, p. 264.
73. Wheeler, *op cit.*, I, pp. 146-47.
74. *op cit.*, p. 114; *History of Indian Architecture*, I, p. 43.
75. *Hinduism and Buddhism*, I, p. 103.
76. For details, see, Joshi, J.P., "Harappan Civilization as seen at the close of the twentieth century," in: *Man and Environment*, Vol. XXV, No. 1, 2000, pp. 15-30.

77. *Anandasram Sanskrit Series*, No. 42, *Kāṇḍa* IV, *Prapatha* 2, *Anuvatta* 8, p. 2791.
78. *Tr. Brāḥ*, *Kāṇḍa* III, *Pr.* I, *Anu* I, *Śloka* V and VI, pp. 2 and 3, *Bibliotheca Indica*, Vol. III.
79. Mukherjee, U.N., "Nāga Worship in Ancient India and its references in Vedic Literature," in *Proceedings, Indian History Congress*, 1961, Delhi.

2

TRADITIONAL HISTORY

Our sources for the traditional history of the Nāgas from post-Vedic Period onwards are mainly the *Mahābhārata,* the *Rāmāyaṇa,* the *Purāṇas*, the Jaina literature, the Buddhist literature and other literary works. We come across references to the principal Nāgarājas and their contributions to the history of the Nāgas. About the historical value of traditional accounts opinion is divided among scholars, some showing excessive scepticism about them and some others taking everything said in them as wholly historical. But the truth lies midway between the two diametrically opposite views. Though it is true that the *Purāṇas* and the Epics contain much which may be difficult to accept as historical "it is absurd to suppose that fiction completely ousted the truth." Some of the statements contained in them are now being confirmed by archaeological, epigraphic and numismatic evidence.

During this period the term Nāga is also known by a few other synonymous expressions like 'Pannaga', 'Sarpa', 'Uraga', 'Bhujañga', and 'Ajagara'. Their habitat is said to have been *Nāgaloka* in the bowels of the earth which was endless (*aparyanta*) crowned with hundreds of different kinds of palaces, houses, towers and pinnacles (*anekavidhaprāsāda harmyavala bhīneryūha*) and strewn with wonderful pleasure-grounds large and small (*unccāvacakrīḍāśdascarya sthānāvakīrṇa*). It was also called *pātāla* which was one of the seven regions of the netherland extending over thousands of *yojanas*. The *Pātāla*, also called *Rasātala* or *Niraya*, was the abode of happiness and attraction. According to the *Viṣṇu Purāṇa*, sage Nārada, who visited it felt that it was more delightful than Indra's heaven. He is said to have exclaimed: "what can be compared to *Pātāla* where the Nāgas are decorated with brilliant and beautiful and pleasure shedding jewels; who will not delight in *Pātāla* where the lovely daughters of the *Daityas* and *Dānavas* wander about fascinating even the most austere; where the rays of the sun diffuse light and not heat by day; and where the moon shines by night for illumination not for cold; where the sons of Danu, happy in the enjoyment of delicious viands and strong wines, know not how time passes? There are beautiful groves and streams and lakes where the lotus blows; and the skies are resonant with the koil's song. Splendid ornaments, fragrant perfumes, rich unguents, the blended music of the lute and pipe and tabor; these and many other enjoyments are the common portion of the *Dānavas, Daityas* and snake-gods who inhabit the region of *Pātāla*.[1] The capital of *Pātāla* was Bhogavatī, so called probably because it was a place of perpetual enjoyment. The word, it may be mentioned in passing, means also 'snake's coil.' According to the *Mahābhārata* it was a subterranean realm and Takṣaka, who had seized the jewel left on the ground by Uttanka glided into *Pātāla* through a fissure.[2] The region was not easily accessible, though there were a few entrances into it. One of them in Kashmir, the *Kathāsaritsāgara* informs us, was made by Maya.[3] Another was the cave of Namuci which Raṇāditya, an ancient king of Kashmir, was believed to have entered "after passing through the waters of the Chandhabhāgā." He is said to have gained sovereignty over the underworld (*pātālaiśvarya*), the realm of the *Daityas* and the *Dānavas*. The location of the *Pātāla* in the lower portions of the Punjab and Sindh is supported by a few other pieces of evidence. The Greek historian Arrian mentions a maritime city, Pātāla, which was visited by the Macedonian general Alexander.[4] The different branches of the family of the Sindas who ruled over parts of the Deccan claim in a number of inscriptions to have descended from an eponymous founder of the family called Sinda who flourished in the region of the Sindhu.

But some other accounts make one think if the Pātāla was not located in some other part of the country. According to the *Mahābhārata*,[5] young Bhīma who had been administered poison along with food by Duryodhana and dropped into the Ganges entwined by creepers went deep into the waters and glided into *Pātāla* where he was bitten by Nāgas (snakes) and thus cured of the effects of the poison administered to him. Again while in the course of the *tīrthayātrā* Arjuna was one evening performing his ablutions in the Gangādvāra he is said to have been taken away by the Nāga nymph Ulūpī to *Pātāla*, where, after the performance of his evening rites he succumbed to the charms of the Nāgī and married her.[6] From these mythological stories it appears that *Pātāla*, referred to above, lay to the east of the Ganges and on the other side of Hastinapura, and was the country of the Nāga people. While describing the descent of the Ganges from Heaven as a result of Bhagīratha's penance the *Pātāla* is located at the mouth of the sacred river.[7] From these references to *Pātāla* it appears that the country of the Nāgas lay in the upper and lower reaches of the Gangetic area, regions lying close to water courses. The Nāgas seem to have been spread over the Assam country also, as may be seen from some references to them in medieval inscriptions as also the existence of Nāga tribes in the region even now.

But according to a few other accounts *Pātāla* can be tried to be located somewhere else also. The descriptions contained in a few *Purāṇas* and the *Mahābhārata* show that among the nine divisions of India one was that of the Nāgas, and it was in the western part of the country, with Virūpākṣa, the Nāga demi-god as its guardian.[8] Jīmūtavāhana, who was the deliverer of the Nāgas from Garuḍa and who was living in the Malaya mountain, is said to have offered himself on behalf of Śankhacūḍa as prey to him when he had gone to Gokarṇa, the abode of Śiva for his last prayers. Gokarṇa is a well known religious centre in Kanara.[9] The *Rāmāyaṇa* would have us believe that the *Rasātala* lay in the midst of the ocean and Rāvaṇa, the lord of Laṅkā, had won a victory over the Nāgas by taking their city Bhogavatī.[10] From another reference to Bhogavatī in the same epic it seems to be associated with the abode of Agastya. Sugrīva while sending an army of Vānaras under Hanumān to the south in search of Sītā says: "There is the mountain named Kuñjara, lovely to the eyes and to the heart where the dwelling of Agastya has been fashioned by Viśvakarman. There is his divine house (*śaraṇa*) of gold adorned with various gems, a *yojana* wide and ten *yojanas* high. There is the town Bhogavatī, the abode of snakes, with large roads, invincible, guarded on all sides by terrible serpents sharp-fanged and great of poison, wherein dwelleth Vāsuki, the very dreadful king of snakes."[11] It is traditionally believed that the abode of Agastya was the Podiyil hill in the southern extremity to the Western Ghats. According to the *Mahābhārata* also Bhogavatī was situated in the southern region and was ruled by Vāsuki, Takṣaka and Airāvata.[12] Perplexingly enough Bhogavatī is also mentioned as the name of a river and is sought to be identified with the river Sarasvatī near Kurukṣetra. Thus the word would indicate probably a city (the city of enjoyment-*bhoga*) as also a winding river (*bhoga* meaning also snake's coil). If it meant a river is it not possible that the name could have been applied to the mythical city of the winding ones, i.e., the snakes?[13]

The *Mahābhārata*, the great epic, is singularly rich in myths and sagas relating to the Nāgas. Here we meet the myths related to: The origin of the Nāga race,[14] the Wager of Kadrū and Vinatā,[15] the Rape of Soma by Garuḍa,[16] Śeṣa, the world serpent,[17] how the Nāgas held Council,[18] the hermit Jaratkāru and the snake-maiden Jaratkāru,[19] the Brahmin Uttaṅka and the serpent-king Takṣaka,[20] how King Parikṣit was killed by the Nāga Takṣaka,[21] the serpent-sacrifice,[22] how the boy Bhīmasena was healed of poison by the Nāgas,[23] the story of Arjuna and Utūpī,[24] Arjuna and Aśvasena, the son of Takṣaka,[25] King Nala and Nāga Karkoṭaka,[26] Mātali, the charioteer of Indra, in search of son-in-law,[27] story of the wise and virtuous Nāga Padmanābha who drew the one-wheeled chariot of the Sun-god,[28] how Kṛṣṇa overcame the Nāga Kāliya,[29] how Akrūra beheld the world of serpents.[30] The traditional history that can be squeezed out of the myths is that after the cataclysm of the *Mahābhārata* war political conditions in north-western India appear to have become very much disorganised leading to the rise of the Nāgas in the region. The Paurava king Parikṣit, the grandson of the Pāṇḍava Arjuna, is said to have been ruling over the Kuru kingdom (extending over the region between the river Sarasvatī and the Gaṅgā). According to the *Mahābhārata*, on account of a curse he was killed by Takṣaka, the king of snakes, in spite of elaborate precautions. His son Janamejaya, therefore, performed the *sarpasatra* (snake-sacrifice) in which, through the spell of *mantras*, many snakes fell as oblations into the sacred fire and perished. After all, this is obviously a mythological account of the rise of the Nāgas of Gandhāra and their successful attack of Hastināpur under Parikṣit, who probably died in the course of the resistance he offered. Later his son Janamejaya, who appears to have been a strong ruler, fought against the Nāgas and conquered the capital of Takṣaka, the king of the Nāgas. However, as a result of the intercession of an Āstika, Janamejaya stopped the slaughter of all the Nāgas and their complete extinction. The conquest of the capital of Takṣaka by Janamejaya may be taken as a historical fact for the story of the *Mahābhārata* was recited to him by Vaiśampāyana at that place. To the east of their country lay that of the Pāñchālas, who are believed originally to have been known as the Krivis. In the epic period it was divided into the northern and southern parts. Uttara Pāñchāla, which according to the *Mahābhārata* was wrested from Drupada by Droṇa with the help of the Kurus, had Ahichchhatra for its capital. It was also called Ahikṣetra; but in view of the local legend of Ādi-Rāja who was protected before his elevation to kingship by a hooded cobra while asleep, Ahichchhatra is probably the correct form, meaning 'Serpent Umbrella'. In Ptolemy the place is called Ādisadra.[31] The place has been identified with Rāmnagar in the Bareilly district of Uttar Pradesh.[32] The country of Ahichchhatra according to Hiuen-Tsang was about 3000 *li* in circuit and the capital itself about 17 or 18 *li*. The Buddha is said to have preached there and converted its Nāga king.[33]

Farther east also there were Nāga dynasties. Yayāti, the father of Puru, was the son of Nāga Nahuṣa and the maternal grandfather of Aṣṭaka.[34] The Pāṇḍavas were the grandons of Nāga Āryaka.[35] The Yādavas too were of Nāga origin. Kṛṣṇa was also a Nāga, as may be seen from the fact that his father Vasudeva is said to have been the great-grandson of Nāga Āryaka mentioned earlier.[36] His elder brother Baladeva was considered to be a portion of Nāga Śeṣa.[37]

As already noticed in the preceding chapter the Nāgas appear to have been connected with the Magadha country also. According to the *Mahābhārata* it was the country of Jarāsandha of the Bārhadratha dynasty, who was the father-in-law of Kaṁsa.[38] The country and its city Rājagṛha had Nāga associations. The Śiśunāgas who ruled over Magadha in still later times appear to have been members of a Nāga dynasty and were so called apparently to distinguish them from the Nāga Bārhadrathas to which Jarāsandha belonged. The Buddha and Vardhamāna Mahāvīra were popular religious leaders during their period and the Nāga people of the region appear to have joined the new faiths in large numbers. Among the Nāga followers of the Buddha in Magadha mention may be made of Muchilinda, the Nāgarāja who sheltered the Buddha under the Bodhi tree and Nāgarāja Kāla who predicted the enlightenment of the Buddha.[39] The Nāga of ūrvila was converted after the first sermon.[40] The Nāgas are said to have constructed a bridge across the Ganges between Rājagṛha and Śrāvastī.[41]

The Nāgas had spread in the Malwa region and the adjoining area. Māndhātṛ of the Haihaya dynasty destroyed the Mauneya Gandharvas at the instance of the Nāgas, for the latter had been despoiled by them. But later, the Haihayas overthrew the Kārkoṭaka Nāgas whose habitat appears to have been somewhere in the Narmadā region, and captured Māhiṣmatī from them.[42] The enmity between the Haihayas and the Nāgas appears to have continued long.

Besides occupying parts of western Deccan it seems that the Nāgas were in the occupation of its eastern half also. In the *Rāmāyaṇa* the serpent Śeṣa is said to have had his seat in the East. While deputing his monkey hosts to different directions in search of Sītā, Sugrīva says that in the East they would see such wonders as the Milk Ocean, the white mountain Ṛṣabha standing in the midst of it, the terrible 'mouth of the Mare', and on the north of it the

'Golden Mountain'. "There Oh! monkeys, ye will behold the earth-carrying serpent white like the moon and having eyes wide as lotus leaves, seated on the top of the mountain and worshipped by all gods – the thousand-headed god Ananta, clad in a dark blue garment. A three-headed golden palm-tree, the banner of the great being, placed on the top of the mountain, shineth together with its pedastal."[43] It is mentioned in the Buddhist stories that Nāgarājas, Kṛṣṇa and Gautamka came from their islands in the western ocean to hear the Buddha in Suppātaka.[44] The *Jātakas* mention a Nāga island near Broach and another Kāradyīpa near it.[45] Besides, the Nāgas are said in the epics and *Purāṇas* to have been in many islands across the seas.

Even in later times in the centuries immediately before and after the dawn of the Christian Era there were a number of tribes and dynasties with Nāga associations in different parts of the country. In the north-west were the two large tribes of the Takhis and the Vāhlas or the Bāhlikas. The former are considered to have been of the race of Takṣaka.[46] According to the *Purāṇas* the Bāhilkas ruled as independent kings for thirty years.[47] Nāga rule over considerable parts of Northern and Central India after the decline of the Kuṣāṇa power is amply attested to by epigraphic and numismatic evidence, besides literary references. Nāga dynasties ruled from Vidishā, Kāntipura, Mathurā, Padmāvatī, Taxila, Ayodhyā and a number of other places.[48] We shall discuss their history in detail in a subsequent chapter.

In the Buddhist literature also, in the legendary accounts relating to the life of Śākyamuni, the Nāgas play a prominent part as in Brahmanical lore. However, in the Buddhist stories, there is an aspect which is different from that presented by the Brahmanical literature. In the Buddhist tradition there is an emphasis on the fact that the ancient gods, even Brahmā and Śakra, were inferior and subservient to the Buddha. The same is applied to the Nāgas. The dreaded serpent-demons are generally represented as devout worshippers of the Buddha. Neither gods nor men nor animals can resist the holy influence of the Blessed One: thus the Nāgas too, who in reality combine the nature of these three classes of beings, are won by his word.

In the stories related to the life of the Buddha, the Nāgas figure prominently. From his birth until his final extinction, presence of the Nāgas may be noticed. In the *Lalitavistara* we read that when Queen Māyā had given birth to the future Buddha in the Lumbini garden, there appeared the two Nāgarājas, Nanda and Upananda, who, standing in the air 'half-bodied', and producing two streams of water, cold and warm, bathed the Bodhisattva.[49] The same legend is repeated by Hiuen Tsang, though in a duplicated form.[50] Both these forms of the legend, which also occur in the *Mahāvastu*,[51] are represented in the Buddhist art.

Far more important than Śākyamuni's natural birth is his spiritual birth (*Sambodhi* or *Mahābodhi*) whereby he became the Buddha, 'the Enlightened One'. This great event has become the nucleus of numerous legends which are favourite subjects of literature and art. It is related in the *Lalitavistara*[52] that when Sujātā, the daughter of the village headman of Uruvilvā, had offered the Bodhisattva a golden vessel of milk-rice after his long fast, he went towards the 'river of Nāgas', the Nairañjanā, to refresh his limbs, where the Nāga-daughter brought him a jewelled throne. Seated on this throne he took Sujātā's food and thereafter cast away the golden bowl carelessly into the water. Sāgara, the Nāgarāja, seized it, but Indra in the guise of a Garuḍa tried to rob it but failed. He begged it from the Nāgarāja who offered it and Indra took it to the heaven of the thirty-three gods and instituted the annual 'festival of the bowl'. The precious throne was preserved by the daughter of the Nāgarāja as an object of worship. This episode is well preserved in the sculptured panels at Borobudur.

The Bodhisattva's progress from the river Nairañjanā towards the sacred tree is described as a triumphal march in which a host of heavenly being, including Nāgarāja Kāla or Kālika, accompany him. The incident is related by Aśvaghoṣa in his *Buddhacharita*.[53] The *Lalitavistara*[54] and the *Mahāvastu*[55] too render this episode in proximity. In Indian sculpture, this incident is exhibited in several bas reliefs.

As per *Vinaya Piṭaka*, after the Buddha attained Enlightenment, he spent some weeks in meditation at various places in the neighbourhood of the Bodhi tree. After the end of the second week, he betook himself to the Muchilinda tree where a great cloud rained for seven days. The Buddha was protected by Muchilinda, the serpent-king and this legend is narrated in the *Nidānakathā*,[56] *Lalitavistara*[57] and the *Mahāvastu*[58] and sculptured in Buddhist art.

The *Mahāvastu* also preserves a legend of the Nāgarāja Elāpattra questioning the Buddha.[59] The story is also known in the Tibetan and Chinese sources and recorded by the Chinese pilgrim Fa-Hien.[60] It exists in several Graceo-Buddhist sculptural pieces.

After the Buddha had preached his first sermon in the Deer Park of Varanasi, he returned to Uruvilvā where he had to perform several miracles in order to subdue the fiery Nāga.[61] This legend is well represented in the bas-reliefs of Sanchi and Amaravati.[62]

Number of other legends related to the Nāgas and the Buddha are narrated in different Buddhist literary works. Thus *Mahāvagga*[63] and *Vinaya Piṭaka*[64] mention how a Nāga was ordained as a Buddhist Friar. *Suttavibhaṅga*[65] narrates how the elder Svāgata subdued the Nāga of the Mango Ferry. Participation of the two Nāgarājas, Nanda and Upananda in the Great Miracle performed by the Buddha is recorded in the *Divyāvadāna*.[66] The same work mentions the episode of how the Nāgarājas, Kṛṣṇa and Gautamaka came to hear the Good Law,[67] and also the legend of how the Buddha crossed the river Gaṅgā with the aid of the Nāgas.[68] A story of the Nāgarājas, Girika and Vidyujjvāla, banished by King Bimbisāra is found in *Life of the Buddha* written in Tibetan.[69] *Mahāvaṁsa* and *Dīpavaṁsa* narrate how Mahodara and Chūlodara, the Nāga kings of Ceylon, were reconciled by the Buddha.[70]

The Chinese pilgrim Hiuen Tsang in his travel accounts has referred to some legends which he learnt at places visited by him. At Nagar in Kabul Valley he learnt the story of how the Nāga Gopāla was appointed the guardian of the Buddha's shadow.[71] At Mangalapura, the capital of Udyāna (Swat Valley), he came across a legend of the Nāga Apalāla who was subdued by the Buddha.[72] Another legend which he learnt in the Swat Valley, related to the Śākya youth who married a snake-maiden and became king of Udyāna.[73] The story of the Nāgas' obtaining a share of the Buddha's holy relics, as recorded in *Mahāparinibbānasutta'*[74] is also preserved in the itinerary of Hiuen Tsang.[75] At Rāmagrāma, so the Chinese pilgrim records, was prevalent a legend of how the old stupa of the time of the Buddha, was guarded by the Nāgas.[76] In course of his account of the capital of Kashmir, the Chinese pilgrim relates the legend of the tooth relic of the Buddha which was entrusted to the Nāgas.[77]

The *Jātakas* are another Buddhist literary source which yield as rich a harvest of Nāga lore as does the *Mahābhārata*. In handling the *Jātakas*, a distinction is to be made between those stories which are Buddhist in origin and spirit and those (probably the large majority) which are in reality fables, fairly tales, ballads and romances converted into birth stories and adapted by the Buddhist preachers for the purpose of pious edification. Birth stories of the Buddha related to the Nāgas are contained in the Jātakas, viz., *Ghatāsana Jātaka*[78] containing the story of the Nāga and the birds; *Bakabrahma-Jātaka*[79] with the story of the foolish raftsman and the angry Nāga; *Daddara-Jātaka*[80] having the story of the Dardara, the exiled Nāga; *Kharaputta-Jātaka*[81] narrating how King Senaka received a charm from a Nāgarāja; *Mahāvānija-Jātaka*[82] providing the story of the greedy merchants; *Jarudapāna-Jātaka*[83] with the story of an old well; *Paṇḍara-Jātaka*[84] containing the story of the Nāga Pāṇḍura who let his secret out; *Uraga-Jātaka*[85] telling how a Nāga and a Suparṇa were reconciled through the holy influence of a hermit; *Vidhura-Jātaka,*[86] the *Jātaka* of Vidhura the wise; *Mahāpaduma-Jātaka*[87] with the story of Prince Padma being sheltered by a Nāga; *Sīlānisaṁsa-Jātaka*[88] containing the story of the pious layman and the barber; *Maṇikaṇṭtha-Jātaka*[89] narrating the story of the hermit and the too tender Nāga; *Śaṅkhapāla-Jātaka*[90] providing the story of the virtuous Nāga Śaṅkhapāla; *Champeyya-Jātaka*[91] with the story of the Nāga Champaka who was caught by a snake charmer; and *Bhūridatta-Jātaka*[92] covering the romantic story of the wise and virtuous Nāga Bhūridatta. Plastic representations of these stories may be easily traced in the Buddhist art of India and as well as of those countries where Buddhism migrated.

Jaina literary works too have contributed to the traditional history of the Nāgas. Among the gods in *Pātāla*, according to Jaina cosmogony, there are two main classes, *Bhavanapati* and *Vyantara*. The first group is divided into ten minor divisions. Among them *Nāga Kumāra* is one. The body of its members is white. Their favourite garments are green and on their crown is a serpent's hood as symbol. The *Vyantara* group consists of demons, again of various groups. Of them the black-bodied Mahoraga (the seventh) has the snake tree as his symbol.[93] The *Pārśvanāthacharita* says that while Pārśvanātha, the 23rd Tīrthaṅkara, was engaged in his devotion his enemy caused a great rain to fall upon him. But the serpent Dharaṇīdhara came and as Seva-Nāgari overshadowed his head as with a *chhatra*. In the *Śatruñjayamāhātmya Dharaṇa*, the Nāga king is represented as approaching Pārśva while engaged in his second *kāyotsarga* or profound meditation at Śivapuri in the Kausambaka forest, and holding his out-spread hood (*phaṇa*) over him as an umbrella. It is said that from this the town obtained the name of Ahichcchatra.[94] In Jaina icons, sculptures and paintings, Pārśvanātha is usually represented as one with nine hands, a serpent on the seat and snake hoods over his head and attended by the Yakṣa Dharaṇendra and the Yakṣiṇi Padmāvatī.[95]

The colossal statue of Gomaṭeśvara at Śravaṇa Beḷgola, the greatest monument of the Western Gaṅgā Period, which is about 57 feet high is represented as surrounded by ant-hills from which emerge serpents; and a climbing plant twines itself round both the legs and arms of the statue. With this may be compared two other statues, one at Enur and the other at Karkala both in the South Canara district. The one at Enur which is about 35 feet high is represented as having each hand resting on the hood of a fully formed cobra. A creeper twines round the thighs and arms while the cobra with its hood forms a suppport for each hand. The one at Karkala which is 41 feet 5 inches in height is similar to the one at Śravaṇa Beḷgola with regard to its representation.[96] In all these cases the existence of the ant-hill with which the Nāga is closely associated deserves to be noticed.

According to some legends relating to ancient Madurai the Śramaṇas (Buddhists and Jains) who were envious of the prevalence and popularity of the Śaiva religion in the Pāṇḍya capital created by their incantations and sent out on three occasions three supernatural emissaries in the form of an elephant, a Nāga and a cow for the destruction of Madurai. Lord Sundareśvara of Madurai is said to have petrified these monsters into their present forms of hill called Āṇaimalai, Nāgamalai and Paśumalai.[97] Here the Nāga associated with the Jainas and the Buddhists deserves notice.

The fables and fairy tales of ancient India have also contributed towards building traditional history of the Nāgas. In them too we find the Nāgas playing a major role. The Sanskrit work *Pañchatantra* furnishes two fables which contain elements of primitive sphere of thought. The first of these two tales is that of the gold granting snake and the poor brahmin.[98] The other gives the story of the snake, himself son of human parents, who is wedded to a maiden.[99]

Another important work of the same category is the *Kathāsaritsāgara,* that marvellous collection of tales, which the Kashmirian poet Somadeva completed between the years 1063 and 1081 AD. It was a recast of a much earlier work, Guṇāḍhya's *Bṛhatkathā.* The *Kathāsaritsāgara* narrates the story of how Guṇāḍhya himself was reputed to be the son of a Nāga prince.[100] The tale of King Udayana of Vatsa and the wonderful lute is another one.[101] The story of the jealous Nāga is third in the series.[102] The other similar stories contained in *Kathāsaritsāgara* are: The Nāga who left his secret out,[103] the Curse of a Nāga,[104] and the legend of Jīmūtavāhana.[105] The story of the Curse of a Nāga reminds us of the incantation scene which occurs in Bāṇa's *Harṣacharita.* In the third chapter of this work, the author relates at great length how King Puṣpabhūti, at the request of Bhairavāchārya, takes part in *Vetāla-sādhanā.*[106] The consequent spirit that emerges announces himself subsequently as the Nāga Śrīkaṇṭha, after whom this region, 'whereof I am Lord, is named.' From our point of view it is important to note that the country Śrīkaṇṭha was named after Nāga Śrīkaṇṭha who was guardian spirit of that country. About the pathetic tale of Jīmūtavāhana, the fairy prince, who sacrifices himself to save an unfortunate Nāga from being devoured by the giant bird Garuḍa, it may be mentioned that numerous versions of this legend exist in Sanskrit literature and this testifies to its great popularity. In *Kathāsaritsāgara,* the story is twice narrated in great detail. *Bṛhatkathā-mañjarī, Avadāna-Kalpalatā, Vetāla-pañchaviṁśatī* and *Nāgānanda* also contain different versions of the same legend. Garuḍa seizing a Nāga is a popular decorative device in Indian sculptural art too. *Divyāvadāna*[107] contains a story of Prince Sudhana of Pāñchāla, a different version of which is found Kṣemendra's *Avadāna-Kalpalatā* (XIV), under the title *Kinnarī Avadāna. Divyāvadāna* has another legend of the young

Nāga contained in it.[108] It is interesting to note that different versions of some of these fables are found in Western literary works like *Aesopus* and *Gesta Romanorum* and these have been recognized as truly Indian in spirit.

The traditional history of the Nāgas will remain incomplete without reference to the principal Nāgarājas, varying lists of which occur in the epics, the *Purāṇas*, Buddhist, Jaina and other literary works. It is remarkable that several Nāgarājas bore royal or Kṣatriya names, some of them being actually borne by such personages of eminence of the epics, like Dhṛatarāṣṭra, Dhanañjaya, Āryaka, Kauravya, Janamejaya, Dilīpa, Pṛthuśravas, Ambarīṣa, Udayana, Rāghava, Baladeva, etc.

According to one account in the *Mahābhārata* told in the *Ādi-parvan*, after the rape of the nectar by Garuḍa, Śaunaka wishes to hear the names of the sons of Kadrū. Sauti then enumerates no less than seventy-eight Nāgas[109] and declares at the end that these are only the principal Nāgas, as owing to their enormous number it would be impossible to name them all. Again, after the conclusion of the serpent sacrifice, Sauti at the request of Śaunaka, sums up the chief Nāgas who have perished in the sacrifical fire of Janamejaya, and adds the same remark regarding the impossibility of giving a complete list of their names. Here the victims are divided into five groups as descendants of Vāsuki, Takṣaka, Airāvata, Kauravya, and Dhṛatarāṣṭra.[110] Another long 'Catalogue of the Nāgas' comprising sixty-eight names, is inserted in the episode of Mātali's visit to Bhogavatī.[111] It differs materially from the lists of *Ādi-parvan*, although both have certain number of names in common. Shorter rolls, containing twenty and nineteen names respectively, occur in the description of the court of Varuṇa in the *Sabhā-parvan* and in the account of Baladeva's apotheosis in the *Mausala-parvan*.[112]

The *Harivaṁśa* contains two lists, one consisting of twenty-six names and the other eighteen; the *Bhāgavata Purāṇa*, one list consisting of fifteen names; and the *Vāyu Purāṇa* one of forty-one names.[113] The *Nīlamata Purāṇa* contains the names of five hundred Nāgas.[114] Some Buddhist works mention the names of a few Nāgas. The *Saddharma Puṇḍarīka* mentions eight great Nāga chiefs, Nanda, Upananda, Sāgara, Vāsuki, Takṣaka, Manasvin, Anavatapta and Utpala,[115] while the *Mahāvyutpatti*, a Buddhist Sanskrit dictionary, mentions among others Nāgas like Śaṅkhapāla, Anavatapta, Elāpatra, Nandopananda, Kāla, Kālika, Girika, Vidyujjvala, Apalāla, Āmratīrtha, Chāmpeya, Paṇḍara and Maṇikaṇṭha. Varuṇa and Sāgara are included here as Nāgarājas.[116]

According to the Brahmanical lists the principal Nāgas were Śeṣa, the world-serpent, Vāsuki, Dhṛatarāṣṭra, Airāvata (Elāpatra), Kārkoṭaka, Śaṅkha or Śaṅkhapāla, Mahāpadma, Kuḷika and Maṇi. The *Aṁśumadbhedāgama* gives a description of the iconographic features of Nāgadeva, the chief of the Nāgas. According to it, the image is to have three eyes, four arms, a beautiful countenance and be of red colour. It should be adorned with a *karaṇḍa-mukuṭa* on its head and all other ornaments on its person and should be standing upon a *padma-pīṭha*. The hands of the front arms should be kept in the *varada* and *abhaya* poses, while the back hands should be having a snake in it. Over the head of Nāgarāja should be a hood of a five-headed cobra and he must be draped in white clothes. The *Śilparatna* adds a few more details. "The Nāgas should be half-human and half-serpentine in shape, the lower part below the navel being that of a snake and the upper part that of a human being. Their heads must be covered with hoods having one, three, five or seven hoods, and they should have split tongues and two hands, one holding a shield, and the other a sword."[117] The *Maya-Śilpa* gives a good description of each of the seven principal Nāgas, namely, Vāsuki, Takṣaka, Kārkoṭaka, Padma, Mahāpadma, Śaṅkhapāla and Kuḷika. The description is as follows: "The colour of Vāsuki is pearl-white; that of Takṣaka glistening red and he must have on his hood the mark of the *svastika*. The colour of Kārkoṭaka is black and on his hood there should be three white stripes; Padma is of the rosy hue of the lotus flower, with a white streak and adorned with coral ornaments. The colour of Mahāpadma is white with the mark of *triśūla* on his hood; whereas that of Śaṅkhapāla is yellow with a white streak on his hood; the colour of Kuḷika is also red and his hood bears the mark of the crescent moon. These seven great serpents should each have two tongues and two arms and a hood with seven heads held over their human heads bearing on them gems. They must all be clad in one or three coats and carry in their hands an *akṣamālā* and *kamaṇḍalu*.[118]

Among the Nāgarājas, Śeṣa or Ananta (the endless one) figures first, and is mentioned in the *Bhagavadgītā* as the chief of the Nāgas, though Vāsuki holds an equally important place among them. Like 'Midgarsorme' of Norse mythology he is considered to be the great world serpent lying in the sea and encircling the earth. It is conceived that in between periodical creations and recreations of the world Lord Viṣṇu is reposing on the coils of Śeṣa in mid-ocean. This *Śeṣaśāyin* or *Anantaśāyin* aspect of Viṣṇu is a favourite theme of sculpture and plastic art, an early example of which in South India is found in one of the cave temples of Māmallapuram. The head of Viṣṇu is covered by a conical mitre, a peculiar feature of Pallava art and around it is Ananta's hood consisting of five snake-heads. In the Gupta temple of Deogarh is a relief of the *Śeśaśayana* aspect of Viṣṇu. Here he is reclining with his usual four arms, and over his head is seen the hood of Śeṣa with seven heads, each with its legendary jewel. Viṣṇu is also depicted as sitting in the *lalitāsana* pose on the top of the coiled-up snake with the seven or five hoods spread over his head. A similar representation of Śeṣa, associated with Viṣṇu, is seen in the Śiva temple of Prambanan, where Viṣṇu is depicted as seated on a Nāga in mid-ocean full of aquatic animals, and surrounded by Garuḍa and many others. The whole scene probably is a sculptural representation of the well-known passage in Kālidāsa's *Raghuvaṁśa*[119] which describes how Viṣṇu, just awakened from his cosmic sleep, was approached by the gods.

Śeṣa or Ādiśeṣa is associated with the Varāha or Ādivarāha incarnation of Viṣṇu also. In the sculptural representations of this aspect we find Ādiśeṣa supporting one of the feet of the boar while rising from the waters.[120] Such a representation of this aspect of Viṣṇu is a very familiar one in Indian art. Among the more important places where we find this Varāha *avatāra* represented in plastic art are Udayagiri (Madhya Pradesh), Bādāmi and Māmallapuram.[121] The Varāha from Baragaon, now in the Calcutta Museum, is accompanied by a Nāgi, presumably his consort, as at Bādāmi.[122]

One of the popular beliefs is that Balarāma, the brother of Kṛṣṇa was an *aṁśa* of Nāga. It is said in the *Anuśāśanaparva* of the *Mahābhārata* that by worshipping the serpent Baladeva one acquires the strength of the Varāha (Boar) incarnation of Viṣṇu.[123] In the *Mahābhārata* again is an interesting account of the death of Balarāma. According to it while he was seated alone engaged in *yoga*: "from his mouth there issued forth a large white Nāga, thousand-headed, red-mouthed, in size unto the girth of a mountain, who leaving his body, sped towards the great ocean. There Sāgara received him and so did the divine Nāgas and the pure and holy rivers."[124] There is a description of Baladeva in the *Harivaṁśa* where the superman and the super-snake are blended together. He is said to be thousand-headed with two long hands holding a plough and a mace, wearing a dark-coloured garment, a single ear-ring and a gold-crested diadem.[125] With this may be compared the specification in the *Viṣṇudharmottara*, namely, the figure of Ādiśeṣa should have four hands, two in the *añjali* pose and the other two holding respectively the plough and the mace.[126] It may be of interest to note in this connection that many statues with snake-hood over them found near Mathurā have been identified with those of Balarāma.[127]

Vāsuki was next only to Śeṣa among the Nāgas and he was their leader; and as their leader he made a pact with Garuḍa that he would send him a Nāga everyday for his food. To save the Nāgas from annihilation in Janamejaya's serpent-sacrifice he gave his sister Jaratkāru in marriage to a sage of the same name. In the churning of the nectar with mount Mandara as the churning stick he was used as the rope that was pulled by the *Devas* on one side and the *Asuras* on the other, and when unable to bear the force of the churning, Vāsuki emitted fire-like poison (*hālā-hala*) from his mouth which threatened to burn up the whole world, and when the gods sought the protection of Śiva against the danger he swallowed the terrible poison as if it was nectar.[128] This subject is a favourite one in Indian art, as may be seen from the representations of it at Udayagiri (M.P.), Garhwa (Allahabad district) and a number of other places. But as Havell says the subject "was never treated on so magnificient a scale or with so splendid an effect as in the bas-reliefs which adorn the colonnades of the great temple of Ankor Vat in Cambodia built about the twelfth century by Sūryavarman II, one of the last of the Hindu kings who ruled over the Indian colony in the Further East."[129] In the same way as Śeṣa is associated with Viṣṇu, Vāsuki is associated with Śiva and is represented as hanging freely round his neck. In regions like Gujarat, the Delhi area and in the valleys of the Western Himalayas this cult is very popular. The Iron Pillar near Delhi is believed to rest on the head of Vāsuki. It is said that when a king tried to dig the pillar, its base was found wet with the blood of Vāsuki. The pillar could not be fixed again properly. The result was that the Hindu kingdom of Delhi fell into the hands of the Muslims.[130] The cult of Vāsuki is popular in the Far Eastern countries also. In Java and Bali he is considered to be one of the attendants of Varuṇa, the Sea God.

Takṣaka is mentioned in the *Atharvaveda* as also in the epic and puranic literature. He is the chief hero in Janamejaya's sacrifice. According to the *Pauṣya-parvan* his places were Kuruksetra and the Khāṇḍava forest; and it was during his absence at Kuruksetra that the Khāṇḍva forest was burnt down by the Fire God. Though the idea of connecting Taxila with Takṣaka is tempting, the excavations at Taxila conducted by Sir John Marshall do not throw out any evidence of the existence of snake-worship in the area. It is surprising that this most terrible one among the snakes has a shrine dedicated to him under the name of Takṣakeśvara or Tākhā-jī near Naoli in Madhya Pradesh and he is worshipped along with Dhanvantari, the tutelary deity of Hindu medicine.

Another Nāgarāja was Dhṛtarāṣṭra Airāvata who was called Elāpatra in Buddhist literature. Probably Airāvata his matronymic is derived from the Irāvatī, the modern Rāvi. He was possibly the best and wisest among the Nāgas, whose advice was listened to at times of great danger to the Nāgas themselves, as for instance, when Janamejaya performed the serpent-sacrifice. He was also aged, and many Nāgas and Nāginis like Ulūpī traced their descent from him.

Kārkoṭaka, who is referred to along with the others mentioned above, and was the head of a group of Nāgas is closely associated with Baladeva-Śeṣa. It may be noted that a dynasty of kings who ruled over Kashmir for about two centuries (7th to 9th) and among whom was the great Lalitāditya Muktāpīḍa, the founder of the Martand temple, traced its descent from Nāga Kārkoṭaka. The worship of Kārkoṭaka is popular in Nepal, Kashmir and parts of Uttar Pradesh.

Śaṅkha bore many other names like Mahāśaṅkha, Śaṅkhamukha, Śaṅkhapiṇḍa, Śaṅkaśīrṣa, Śaṅkhaśirasa, Śaṅkharoman, Śaṅkhapāla, Śaṅkhachūḍa, etc. It was to his race that Śaṅkhachūḍa of the melancholy tale of Jīmūtavāhana belonged. His worship is popular in Benaras.

Maṇi, also called Maṇi-Nāga, Maṇimant, Maṇikaṇṭha, Maṇichūḍa, Maṇibhadraka and Maṇiakkhika, appears to have had his abode near Rājagṛha, the capital of Magadha. The *Mahābhārata* refers to the temples of two *Pannagas* or Nāgas, namely, Maṇināga and Svastika in Girivṛaja. In the early years of the last century the Maṇiarmaṭha or the temple of Maṇināga mentioned in the epic was exposed to view by archaeological excavations. The temple which is circular in shape contains the figures of a Liṅga, Bāṇāsura, six Nāgas, Gaṇeśa and Śiva, besides a stone sculpture presenting on one side standing figures of eignt Vāsukis, each with a cobra hood, and on the other side two standing human figures with an early Brāhmī inscription. Bloch says: "the temple was some kind of pantheon of Rājagṛaha, and the various figures of Nāgas and Nāgis represent certain serpent deities whom popular religion worshipped at distinct places on the surrounding hills".[131]

The above account shows that whatever we might think of the historical value of traditional history of the Nāgas, one thing is clear that they formed a part and parcel of Indian history and culture to which their contribution was not insignificant. This is amply clear from the history of the succeeding periods.

REFERENCES

1. Wilson, *Viṣṇu Purāṇa*, p. 204; also *Pātālakhaṇḍa* in the *Padma Purāṇa.*
2. *Ādiparvan,* III.
3. *op cit., XXIII,* pp. 107-112; Tawny's translation, Vol. II, p. 197; also *Rājataraṅgiṇī,* (Stein's translation) Vol. II, p. 446. The work says: "There are on this earth many openings leading to the lower regions, but there is a great and famous one in Kashmir made by Maya by which Uṣā, the daughter of Bāṇa, introduced her lover Aniruddha into the secret pleasure grounds of the Dānavas and made him happy there. And Pradyumna in order to deliver his son, laid it open

making a door in one place with the peak of a mountain and he placed Durgā there, under the name of Śārikā to guard that door, after propitiating her with hundreds of praises. Consequently, even now the place is called by the two names of Peak of Pradyumna and Hill of Śārikā. It may be noted that the Hill of Śārikā is the Hari Parbat near Srinagar in Kashmir."

4. Mc.Crindile, *Ancient India as described by Magasthenes and Arrian*; also K.A. Nilakanta Sastri, *Age of the Nandas and Mauryas*, pp. 75-76.
5. *Mahābhārata, Ādiparvan.*
6. *Ibid.*, Some scholars think that the Nāga country of Ulūpī was Assam. But the identification does not seem easy of acceptance for Ulūpī is said to have appeared before Arjuna in the river Ganges only and that does not pass through Assam. Further, Assam was really too far away from Arjuna's route and it could not have been reached by him in the course of his pilgrimage.
7. *Rāmāyaṇa, Bālakāṇḍa*, 43.8.
8. See Cunningham's *Ancient Geography of India*, App. I; Alberuni, however, thinks that it was in the south-western portion of the country.
9. See *Kathāsaritsāgara*, XXII, 16-53, 168-256; Tawny's translation Vol. I, pp. 174-86.
10. *Āraṇyakāṇḍa*, XXXII, 13-14; *Yuddhakāṇḍa*, VII, 3-9; *Uttarakāṇḍa*, XXIII, 4, 5.
11. *Kiṣkindhākāṇḍa*, XI, 34-8.
12. *Udyogaparva*, CIX, 19. Hiralal identifies Bhogavatī with Ramtill in the Nagpur district, and says with great cocksureness that "with this location, the legend of the city being situated in Pātāla quite fits in as this tract of country lies just below the high table of the Satpuras." (*Maharaja's College Magazine*, Vizianagaram, V, pp. 5-6). But the problem is too difficult and complicated to be so sure as Hiralal.
13. See Vogel, *Indian Serpent Lore*, p. 201.
14. *Ādiparvan*, XVI.
15. *Ibid.*, XX-XXIII.
16. *Ibid.*, XXV-XXXIV.
17. *Ibid.*, XXXVI.
18. *Ibid.*, XXXVII-XXXIX.
19. *Ibid.*, XLV-XLVII.
20. *Ibid.*, III. Also *Aśvamedhikā-parvan*, LIII-LVIII.
21. *Ibid.*, XL-XLIII.
22. *Ibid.*, XLIX-LVIII.
23. *Ibid.*, CXXVIII-14, CXXIX.
24. *Ibid.*, CCXIV.
25. *Ibid.*, CCXXIII-CCXXVII.
26. *Vana-parvan*, LXVI (= *Nalopākhyāna*, XIV).
27. *Udyoga-parvan*, XCVII-CV.
28. *Śānti-parvan*, CCCLII-CCCLXV.
29. *Harivaṁśa*, 3592-3702. Also *Bhāgavata Purāṇa*, canto X, last half XVI.

30. *Ibid.*, 4388-4460 (LXXXVIII. In the *Bhāgavata*, X. 39).
31 See Cunningham, *Ancient Geography of India*, p. 360; Mc.Crindle, *Ancient India as described by Ptolemy*, p. 133; B.C. Law, *Tribes in Ancient India*, p. 34.
32. See V. Rangacharya, *Pre-Musalman India*, Vol. II, p. 238.
33. Beal, *Buddhist Records of the Western World*, I, p. 200.
34. *Mahābhārata, Ādiparvan*, LXXXVII, 42-43; *Udyoga*, XVII, 17, 23.
35. *Ibid., Ādi*, LXXXVIII, 34-35.
36. *Ibid., Ādi*, CXXXVIII, 34-35; see also Banerjee Sastri, *Asura India*, p. 95.
37. *Mahābhārata, Ādi*, LXVIII, 152.
38. *Ibid., Sabhā*, XIV, 31-32, 49.
39. See Vogel, *op cit.*, pp. 27, 40, 93 ff, 98-99, 102 ff, and 285.
40. *Ibid.*, p. 107 ff.
41. Beal, *op cit.*, II, p. 167.
42. Pargiter: *Ancient Indian Historical Trdition*, 262, 266, 268, 269. According to the *Harivaṁśa*, Yadu had four sons by Nāga wives and they founded respectively the four kingdoms of Māhiṣmatī (Narmadā region), Sahyādrī table (in the middle of the Western Ghats), Banavāsi and Ratnapura (in Madhya Pradesh).
43. *Rāmāyana, Kiṣkindhā*, XI, 51-53.
44. Vogel, *op cit.*, pp. 115-116.
45. *Jātaka*, III, 124; IV, 150.
46. Tod, J., *Annals and Antiquities of Rajasthan*, I, p. 702.
47. Pargiter, *Ancient Indian Historical Tradition*, p. 73.
48. *JRAS*, 1905, p. 233.
49. *Lalitavistara* (ed. Lanman) Vol. I, p. 83, 11, 21-22. cf. also p. 93, 11, 3-4.
50. *Si-yu-ki* (tr. Beal), Vol. II, pp. 24 f.
51. *Mahāvastu* (ed. Senart), Vol. II, p. 23, 24.
52. *Lalitavistara*, pp. 269f; cf. *Mahāvastu*, Vol. II, p. 302; *Nidānakathā*, p. 70.
53. *Buddhacharita* (Cowell's translation), XII, 113-16; SBE, Vol. XLIX, pp. 135ff.
54. *Lalitavistara*, Vol. I, pp. 281-85.
55. *Mahāvastu*, Vol. II, pp. 265, 302, 304, 308, 398, 400.
56. *Jātaka* (ed. Fousball), Vol. I, p. 80. Rhys David's *Buddhist Birth Stories*, p. 109.
57. *Lalitavistara*, Vol. I, pp. 379ff.
58. *Mahāvastu* (ed. Senart), Vol. III, pp. 300ff. cf. *Buddhacharita*, XV, 49-53.
59. *Mahāvastu*, Vol. III, pp. 383ff. Also *Buddhacharita*, XVII, 3.
60. *Record of the Buddhist Kingdoms* (tr. Legge), p. 56.
61. *Mahāvagga*, I, 15; *Vinaya Piṭaka*, Vol. I, pp. 24ff; SBE, Vol. XIII, pp. 118ff.
62. Fergusson, *Tree and Serpent-Worship*, pp. 143ff.
63. *Mahāvagga*, I, 63.
64. *Vinaya Piṭakam* (ed. Oldenberg), Vol. I, pp. 86ff. SBE, XIII, pp. 217ff.
65. *Suttavibhaṅga, Pāchittiya*, LI. *Vinaya Piṭakam*, Vol. IV, pp. 108ff.
66. *Divyāvadāna*, XII, *Prātihāryasūtra*, pp. 143ff.
67. *Divyāvadāna* (ed. Cowell and Neil), pp. 50ff. Burnouf, *Introduction*, pp. 269ff.

68. *Ibid.*, pp. 55 ff.
69. Schiefner, *Lebensbeschreibung Çakyamuni's*, p. 272.
70. *Mahāvaṁsa*, I, 44-70; Geiger's tr., pp. 5ff; *Dīpavaṁsa*, II, 1-51; Oldenberg's tr., pp. 124 ff.
71. Hiuen Tsiang, *Si-yu-ki* (tr. Beal), Vol. I, pp. 93ff.
72. *Ibid.*, pp. 122ff.
73. *Ibid.*, pp. 128ff.
74. *Mahāparinibbāna-Sutta* (ed. Childers, pp. 68ff, SBE, XI, pp. 31ff.
75. *Si-yu-ki* (tr. Beal), Vol. II, p. 41.
76. *Ibid.*, pp. 26ff.
77. *Ibid.*, Vol. I, pp. 158ff.
78. *Ghatāsana Jātaka* (No. 133), Jātaka, Vol. I, pp. 471ff.; Cambridge translation, Vol. I, pp. 290ff.
79. *Bakabrahma-Jātaka* (No. 405), commentary, *Jātaka*, Vol. III, p. 362. Cambridge translation, Vol. III, p. 220.
80. *Daddara-Jātaka* (N0. 304), *Jātaka*, Vol. III, pp. 16ff. Cambridge translation Vol. III, pp. 10ff.
81. *Kharaputta-Jātaka* (No. 386), *Jātaka*, Vol. III, pp. 275ff. Cambridge translation Vol. III, pp. 174ff.
82. *Mahāvanija-Jātaka* (No. 493), *Jātaka*, Vol. IV, pp. 350ff. Cambridge translation, Vol. IV, pp. 221ff.
83. *Jarudapāna-Jātaka* (No. 256), *Jātaka*, Vol. II, pp. 294ff. Cambridge translation, Vol. II, pp. 205ff.
84. *Paṇḍura-Jātaka* (No. 518), *Jātaka*, Vol. V, pp. 75ff. Cambridge translation, Vol. V, pp. 42ff.
85. *Uraga-Jātaka* (No. 154), *Jātaka*, Vol. II, pp. 12ff. Cambridge translation, Vol. II, p. 9 ff.
86. *Vidhura-Jātaka* (No. 545), *Jātaka*, Vol. VI, pp. 255ff. Cambridge translation, Vol. VI, pp. 126 ff.
87. *Mahāpaduma-Jātaka* (No. 472), *Jātaka*, Vol. IV, pp. 187ff. Cambridge translation, Vol. IV, pp. 116ff.
88. *Sīlānisaṁsa-Jātaka* (No. 190), *Jātaka*, Vol. II, pp. 111ff. Cambridge translation, Vol. II, pp. 77ff.
89. *Maṇikaṇṭha-Jātaka* (No. 253), *Jātaka*, Vol. II, pp. 282ff. Cambridge translation, Vol. II, pp. 197ff.
90. *Śaṅkhapāla-Jātaka* (No. 524), *Jātaka*, Vol. V, pp. 161ff. Cambridge translation, Vol. V, pp. 84ff.
91. *Champeyya-Jātaka* (No. 506), *Jātaka*, Vol. IV, pp. 454ff. Cambridge translation, Vol. IV, pp. 281ff.
92. *Bhūridatta-Jātaka* (No. 543), *Jātaka*, Vol. VI, pp. 157ff. Cambridge translation, Vol. VI, pp. 80ff.
93. Mrs. Stevenson, *Heart of Jainism*, pp. 268-9.
94. IA, II, p.122.

95. See T.N. Ramachandran, *Tirupparuttikunram and its Temples*, pp. 194-5.
96. *Mysore Gazetteer*, Vol. II (New Edn.), pp. 257-59.
97. *MER*, 1926-7, pt. II, para, 8.
98. *Pañchatantra* (ed. Kosegarten), lib. III, fab. 5.
99. Pūrṇabhadra's *Panchatantra*, lib. I, fab. 3, cf. Benfey, *Pañchatantra*, Vol. II, pp. 144ff.
100. *Kathāsaritsāgara*, Tawney's translation, Vol. I, pp. 32ff.
101. *Ibid.*, Vol. I, pp. 55ff.
102. *Ibid.*, Vol. II, pp. 98ff.
103. *Ibid.*, pp. 54ff.
104. *Ibid.*, pp. 149ff.
105. *Ibid.*, Vol. I, pp. 174-86ff.
106. *The Harṣacharita of Bāṇa*, translation by E.B. Cowell and F.W. Thomas, London, 1897, pp. 90ff.
107. *Divyāvadāna*, XXX, pp. 435ff.
108. *Ibid.*, XXIV, pp. 344ff.
109. *Mbh, Ādi-parvan*, XXXV, 5-16.
110. *Ibid.*, *Ādi-parvan*, LVII.
111. *Ibid.*, *Udyoga-parvan*, CIII, 9-16.
112. *Ibid.*, *Sabhā-parvan*, IX, 8-10; *Mausala-parvan*, IV, 15-16.
113. Hari, 227-30; 9501-04;12821, *Bhāgavata Purāṇa*, V, XXIV, 29-31; *Vāyu Purāṇa*, II, VIII, 67-71.
114. Vogel, *op cit.*, p. 190.
115. *Saddharma Puṇḍarīka* (ed. Kern and Bunyiu Nanjio), p. 4.
116. *Mahāvyutpatti* (ed. Minayeff), pp. 48ff.
117. Ch. XXV, v, 130 and 131.
118. See Gopinatha Rao, *Elements of Hindu Iconography*, II, ii, pp. 556-7.
119. *op cit.*, XIII, 6.
120. See Gopinatha Rao, *Elements of Hindu Iconography*, I, i, pp. 128ff.
121. *ASR*, X, pp. 48ff; pl. XVIII; 1910-11, p. 57, pl. XXIX-C.
122. See Vogel, *op cit.*, pl. XXI.
123. XIII, 132, 8-11 (Poona Edn., 1933).
124. *Mausala*, p. IV, 13-17.
125. Hari, LXXXIII, 4388-4460.
126. Gopinatha Rao, *op cit.*, I, p. 134.
127. *ASIAR*, 1908-9, pp. 161ff.
128. *Rāmāyaṇa, Bālakāṇḍa*, XIV, v, 18-26.
129. *The Ideals of Indian Art*, pp. 64ff.
130. *ASR*, I, pp. 177ff; XX, pp. 171ff.
131. *ASR*, 1905-06, pp. 103-4; B.C. Law, *Memoirs of the Archaeological Survey of India*, No. 58, *Rajagriha in Ancient Literature*, pp. 33-4.

3

THE NĀGAS OF MAGADHA

Magadha was a seat of Nāga power from very early times. The earliest reference to the Nāgas of Magadha is found in two passages of the *Mahābhārata*, which enlighten us regarding the locality of this cult. In the *Sabhā-parvan*[1] there is a famous episode called 'The Death of Jarāsandha', in which it is related how Kṛṣṇa accompanied by Arjuna and Bhīma travels to Magadha and how Jarāsandha, the wicked king of that country, is finally killed by Bhīma. When the three heroes approach Rājagriha, the capital of Magadha, Kṛṣṇa describes the town with its fragrant *lodhra* groves, which is engirded and sheltered by five mountains (whence its name Girivraja). In the course of his description, Kṛṣṇa says: "Here are Arbuda and Śakravāpin, the two serpents who are tormenters of their foes, and here is the excellent abode of Svastika and of Maṇi-nāga. Manu (Maṇi?) hath made Magadha such that the clouds cannot keep aloof from it; Kauśika and Maṇimant, too, have shown it their favour."

The other reference to Maṇi is found in the extensive account of places of pilgrimage which belongs to the *Vana-parvan.* Immediately after the mention of Rājagriha we read the following: "Going thence to Maṇi-nāga, one will reap a benefit equal to a gift of a thousand kine. Whosoever partakes of the water of the *tīrtha* of Maṇi-nāga, had he been bitten even by a venomous snake, the poison will have no effect on him. By sojourning there during one night, he will reap a benefit equal to a gift of a thousand kine." It must be noticed that both the passages quoted agree in locating the abode of the

Nāga Maṇi at Rājagriha, the ancient capital of Magadha. The water of the *tīrtha* was believed to be an antidote against snake-bite, a circumstance which accounts for its popularity.

Though the most ancient Nāgas of Magadha find a place in the *Mahābhārata*, the Buddhist literary works give much more information about them at a later period. Frequent references are found no doubt, in the *Jātakas* like the *Bakabrahma*[2] and the *Maṇikaṇṭha*,[3] about the Nāgas inhabiting the provinces round about the Ganges;[4] but we also find references to the Nāgas staying in Magadha proper. The *Śaṁkhapāla Jātaka* relates the story of a king Duryodhana of Magadha as born a Nāga.[5] The *Champeyya Jātaka* again tells us that there was in the Champā River (the boundary between Aṅga and Magadha) a Nāga king, who, during a war between the kings of Aṅga and Magadha, helped the latter in the restoration of his lost kingdom. And for this splendid service of his, the Nāga king received a due tribute from the king of Magadha.[6] Buddhaghoṣa, in his commentary on the *Saṁyutta Nikāya*, speaks of the existence of a beautiful and extensive Nāga world under the Vebhāra (Vaibhāra) mountain.[7] The famous Muchalinda episode, again, finds a place in several literary works. Muchalinda was a Nāga king residing at Uruvelā in Gaya. The *Vinaya Piṭaka* relates that as the Lord Buddha, after his enlightenment at Uruvelā, was enjoying the bliss of emancipation, under a tree, there started, all of a sudden, an unexpected hailstorm with heavy rains and strong winds. And it was the Nāga king Muchalinda who protected the Buddha for seven days, from the storm.[8] Together with the *Mahāvagga*[9] as seen above, the *Dāthavaṁsa*,[10] the *Lalitavistara*,[11] and the *Mahāvastu*[12] also speak of this greatness of the Nāga Muchalinda of Uruvelā (Uruvilvā). The Nairañjana (modern Nilājan or Lilājan) River of Uruvelā, again, has been, according to the *Mahāvastu*,[13] frequented by Nāga maidens. The *Divyāvadāna*, while describing the Buddha's journey from Śrāvasti to Rājagriha, says that the Buddha crossed the Ganges on the hoods of the Nāgas,[14] meaning protected by the Nāgas. On his way from Uruvelā to Benares, the Buddha is said to have been hospitably received by the Nāgarāja Sudarśana, at Gayā.[15] The *Saddharmapuṇḍarīka* informs about the Buddha having been seated in all his glory, on the top of the Vulture peak, in the midst of an incredible multitude of Nāgas.[16]

The *Nīlamata Purāṇa*, while speaking about the different *Vāhanas* of the different rivers, ascribes to the river Śoṇa (Son), the Nāga as its *vāhana*.[17] This indicates, very probably, the presence of the Nāgas by the side of the river. Even the mythology of *Pañchatantra* hints at the existence of the Nāgas in Rājagriha,[18] the ancient capital of Magadha.

The presence of the Nāgas in ancient Magadha, as described above by the Sanskrit and Pali literary works, is further corroborated by the accounts of the Chinese travellers. According to Hiuen Tsang, there was an old tradition, during the time of his visit to Magadha, which said that the monastery of Nālandā took its name from a Nāga called Nālanda who resided in a pool close by.[19] I-tsing also refers to this tradition, but says that the Nāga was called Nanda.[20]

The above literary evidences about the Nāgas in Magadha is further corroborated by the archaeological finds from the same place. The Maṇiyar Maṭh of Rājgir, first exposed to view in 1905, is really the temple of the Mani-nāga the son of Kadrū, as mentioned in the *Mahābhārata*.[21] The many finds, here, of several Nāga images, with a bas-relief containing an inscription mentioning Maṇi-nāga, confirms the identification.[22] When in the cold season of 1905-06 Sir John Marshall and Dr. Bloch undertook excavations on the site of Rājagriha,[23] they noticed in the centre of the site of the ancient capital a modern dilapidated shrine which had been raised upon a mound of *debris*. This mound proved to contain the remains of a curious circular structure built of brick and decorated with ten well-preserved stucco figures. Out of these ten figures, which measured about two feet in height, five represented Nāgas and one a Nāgī, all shown standing and provided with the usual snake-hood. From their style these images could be attributed to the Gupta epoch. According to Dr. Bloch's conjecture, the building, "was some kind of Pantheon of Rājagriha, and the various figures of Nāgas and Nāgis represent certain serpent-deities whom popular religion worshipped at distinct places on the surrounding hills." Dr. Bloch informs us that the name 'Maṇiār Maṭh', by which the shrine was known is associated by popular tradition with a certain Nāga Maṇikāra ('jeweller'). This may be so, but a Nāga of this name is unknown to ancient literature. It is probable that the mysterious Nāga sanctuary and the name of the locality have something to do with the serpent demon Maṇi whose cult at the ancient town of Rājagriha is vouched for by the two passages quoted from the *Mahābhārata*.

In demolishing the modern structure which occupied the top of the mound, Dr. Bloch found concealed inside the masonry of its roof, small image of a seated Nāga with an inscription dated *Saṁvat* 1547, along with a basalt slab carved with two human feet. This slab had an inscription recording that it was put up in *Saṁvat* 1837 (AD 1781) by a lady, Sītābāi, the wife of Moti Lāl, the son of Keso Dās, and that it represented the footprints of the Nāga Śālibhadra.

At Gayā and Buddhagayā are found images of a female with a crown of coiled snake, canopied by a seven-hooded snake, and of Kulika Nāgarāja, respectively.[24] At Pāṭaliputra (Patna) is found another head of a Nāgiṇi, in terracotta, belonging probably to the Mauryan Period.[25] There is also another image of a Nāga goddess of the seventh century AD found at Nālandā.[26] An image depicting the story of the Buddha being protected by the Nāgarāja Muchalinda is also found at Buddhagayā at the Mahant's Maṭh.[27] The images of Balarāma, protected by a Nāga hood, proceeding from Kurkihār and Gayā,[28] the image of the Buddha with the Nāga hood found at Nālandā,[29] and the image of the Nāga goddess Manasā of Bīrbhūm[30] are further proofs of the inhabitance of the Nāgas in ancient Magadha and round about it. According to Mr. Paul there are many images of Nāgas and Nāginis, in the Indian Museum acquired from Bihar.[31]

We have seen in the preceding chapter that Bārhadratha dynasty ruled in Magadha at the time of the war of the Mahābhārata and the rulers of this dynasty were of Nāga lineage. Jarāsandha, the first great emperor of Magadha before that war, was succeeded by his son Sahadeva, who become an ally of the Pāṇḍavas, and was killed in the war. After Sahadeva, his son Somādhi became the king at Girivraja, at the foot of which Rājagriha, the ancient capital of Magadha, grew up. Ripuñjaya, the twenty-first in descent from Somādhi, is stated to have been the last king of the Bārhadratha dynasty. He is said to have been killed by his minister Pulika (Puṇika, Pulaka) who then installed his son Pradyota on the throne of Magadha. According to the *Purāṇas*, the Pradyota dynasty lasted for five generations covering a period of 138 years, and was supplemented by Śiśunāga who, after placing his son to rule over Kāśī, fixed his capital at Girivraja (or Rājagriha).[32] Bimbisāra and Ajātaśatru appear in the Pauranic lists as fifth and sixth in the descent from Śiśunāga, who founded a new royal dynasty, called the Śiśunāga.

The story of the *Purāṇas* is regarded as untrustworthy.[33] The Pradyotas were rulers of Avanti and not of Magadha,[34] and from the Buddhist sources we learn that Pasenadi of Kosala, Chaṇḍa Pradyota of Avanti, Udena of Kosambi, and Buddha were contemporaries of Bimbisāra and Ajātaśatru,[35] the fifth and sixth in the Puranic list of the Śaiśunāgas.[36] It is therefore patent that the *Purāṇas* have mixed up the dynastic list of Magadha by wrongly intruding the Pradyotas between the Bārhadrathas and Śaiśunāgas. The *Purāṇas* also are wrong in making Śiśunāga the founder of the family to which Bimbisāra belonged. Bimbisāra was a contemporary of Chaṇḍa Pradyota of Avanti, who was a very powerful king. How could Śiśunāga be the destroyer of the Pradyotas, evidently after Chaṇḍa Pradyota, when the fifth in descent to him, Bimbisāra was the contemporary of the latter. Therefore, Bimbisāra cannot be regarded as belonging to a period later than Śiśunāga. Geiger[37] pointed out long ago that "the greater probability seems to be in favour of placing Kākavarṇa and with him naturally his father Śiśunāga in the second half of the series of kings, not in the first."

The *Purāṇas* themselves in a way indicate the posteriority of Śiśunāga to Bimbisāra as they include Vārāṇasī in Śiśunāga's dominions, because Bimbisāra and Ajātaśatru were the first to establish Magadha domination in Kāśī. The hostility between Avanti and Magadha, again, is to be met with for the first time in Ajātaśatru's reign. There is no trace of it during the period of Bimbisāra, and hence Śiśunaga who supplanted the Pradyotas must come after Bimbisāra and Ajātaśatru. The probable reason for placing Śiśunāga before the Bimbisāra-Ajātaśatru group appears to be that Śiśunāga had his capital at Rājagriha, and as Udāyin was credited in the Puranic accounts with the removal of the capital to Pataliputra, it was thought by the ill-informed Pauraṇic chroniclers of a late date that Śiśunāga came before Udāyin. But the statement in the *Mālālaṅkārvatthu* that Rājagriha lost its rank as a royal city from the time of Śiśunāga indicates that Śiśunāga flourished after the palmy days of Rājagriha, i.e., the period of Bimbisāra and Ajātaśatru. Śiśunāga probably chose the old capital Rājagriha as his headquarters in order to meet the attacks from Avanti on that part of Magadha. It may thus hold that the Bārhadratha dynasty in Magadha ended with Ripuñjaya who was probably killed by his minister, and was succeeded by Bimbisāra.

In view of the above, most of the scholars today depend upon the *Mahāvaṁsa* list rather than the list supplied by the *Purāṇas*.

The *Mahāvaṁsa* list gives the names of the following kings before the Nandas:

1. Bimbisāra, 2. Ajātaśatru, 3. Udayabhadra, 4. Anuruddha, 5. Muṇḍa, 6. Nāgadāsaka, 7. Susunāga, 8. Kālāśoka (Kākavarṇin according to *Aśokavadana*), 9. Ten sons of kālāśoka.

On the other hand, the *Purāṇas* give the following list:

1. Śiśunāga, 2. Kākavarṇa, 3. Kṣemadharman, 4. Kṣatraujas, 5. Bimbisāra, 6. Ajātaśatru, 7. Darśaka, 8. Udāyin, 9. Nandivardhana, 10. Mahānandin.

Our description follows the *Mahāvaṁsa* list.

It is interesting to note that two dynasties ruled over Magadha during the period covered by the commencements of rule by Bimbisāra and the fall of the ten sons of Kālāśoka and both of these dynasties were of Nāga origin – one a major Nāga dynasty the other minor one. To quote Bhandarkar; "The name of the family to which Bimbisāra belonged is not definitely known, but it seems that it was Nāga. The last prince of Bimbisāra's dynasty is called Nāga-Dāsaka by *Mahāvaṁsa*. The second component of the name viz. Dāsaka, doubtless correspond Darśaka of *Purāṇas*. And the name of the Nāga has been prefixed to Dāsaka to distinguish him from his successor who belonged to a somewhat different family and who has therefore been called Śuśu-nāga, or little Nāga. Darśaka, and thus Bimbisāra, belong to the Great Nāga dynasty."[38] Aśvaghoṣa's statement that Bimbisāra belonged to Haryaṅkakula[39] simply meant that he belonged to "the dynasty whose insignia is a lion." It is not surprising for a Nāga ruler to use lion insignia or as matter of fact any other insignia. There are number of such instances in Indian history. Moreover, if Nāga-Dāsaka belonged to the line of Bimbisāra, Nāga origin of the line is undisputed. The use of the term 'Nāga' as prefix or suffix to a particular name has never been compulsory for a person to prove his Nāga origin and this has been a very common practise in Indian history during the ancient, medieval and even modern times. Bimbisāra, thus seems to be the founder of the Great Nāga dynasty of Magadha which was followed by the Junior Nāga dynasty of Śiśunāga.

Though we have undoubted positive evidence about the historicity of Bimbisāra and some event of his reign, his father cannot be identified. He was probably a high official, minister or commander-in-chief of Ripuñjaya, the last of the Bārhadrathas, who staged a coup d'etat and installed his son Bimbisāra on the throne.[40] Being an upstart, Bimbisāra for a long time was content with the humble title of Śreṇīya as his father was Bhaṭṭīya.

The accession of Bimbisāra on the throne of Magadha heralded a new era of territorial conquests and administrative consolidation. Aṅga, which lay to the east of Magadha in south-east Bihar along the southern bank of the Gaṅgā, was a rich country with luxurious overseas trade.[41] Just before Bimbisāra, the king of Aṅga, Brahmadatta had defeated the ruler of Magadha, probably Bimbisāra's father.[42] Provoked by a spirit of legitimate vengeance and inspired by the ambition to become universal overlord (*samrāṭ*) for which, the *Aitareya Brāhmaṇa* says, the kings of the east were desirous, Bimbisāra invaded Aṅga and annexed it to his capital. According to Jaina sources, Ajātaśatru became a viceroy at Champā.[43] Thus Bimbisāra ushered in an epoch of military conquests and territorial expansion for Magadha which ended only with the conquest of Kaliṅga by Aśoka. Bimbisāra realised the importance of stabilising his position and strengthening his kingdom by establishing friendly relations with powers nearby and far off. He married a Kosalan princess, to whom were assigned the revenues of Kāśī villages as her toilet money by the Kosalan king.[44] This paved the way for the eventual absorption of Kāśī into Magadhan empire. He also married a daughter of the Lichchhavi chief.[45] This matrimonial alliance, besides ensuring for the time being the friendship of the powerful republic across the Gaṅgā in the north, proved of great significance in the later years of the history of Magadha. Ajātaśatru was born of the Vaiśālian princess.[46] Bimbisāra also showed skilful diplomacy in his relations with Pradyota, king of Avanti, and the king of Gāndhāra.[47] Pradyota and Pukkusāti were enemies. Bimbisāra welcomed the embassy and a letter from the king of Gāndhāra but at the same time took care to be friendly to Pradyota to whom he sent Jīvaka to treat him for jaundice. He also had married a Madra princess named Khemā (Kṣemā).[48] He is rightly regarded by Charpentier as the 'mightiest ruler of Eastern India.'[49] Magadha and Avanti, one extending its sphere towards the west and the other to the east towards Vatsa, were bound to come into clash, and it appears that Chaṇḍa Pradyota even in the life-time of Bimbasāra had threatened Magadha.[50]

According to the *Mahāvaṁsa* Bimbisāra ruled the kingdom for 52 years. Bimbisāra was an elder contemporary of the Buddha who died in the eighth year of Ajātaśatru's reign. According to most scholars the Buddha died in 486 BC, so Bimbisāra came to the throne in 486+7+52 = 545 BC. He ruled till 493 BC.[51] According to Buddhaghoṣa the United Kingdom of Magadah and Aṅga was 300 leagues in extent.[52]

Bimbisāra was succeeded by his son Ajātaśatru. It is generally believed that Bimbisāra was imprisoned by Ajātaśatru who put him to death.[53] The Jaina sources exonerate him of intentional parricide.[54] In the opinion of Rhys Davids, "the main fact that Bimbisāra was put to death by his son Ajātaśatru may be accepted as historical."[55]

Ajātaśatru continued the aggressive policy of his father. The king of Kosala gave him the necessary provocation. On the death of Kosaladevī, the Kosalan wife of Bimbisāra, Prasenajit, the king of Kosala, withdrew the revenues of Kāśī villages which were granted to his sister.[56] Ajātaśatru waged a war against Kosala. It is difficult to trace the vicissitudes of the long war, but it ultimately ended in the merger of Kāśī villages in Magadha and the marriage of Ajātaśatru with the daughter of Prasenajit.[57] According to Buddhaghoṣa the area of Ajātaśatru's kingdom at the beginning of the conquest was 500 leagues. Thus the kingdom of Bimbisāra was almost doubled before Ajātaśatru embarked on his conquering campaign.

Ajātaśatru's invasion of the Lichchhavi republic with its capital at Vaiśālī marked another important step in the march of the Magadhan imperialism. The Lichchhavis were a powerful republican community across the Gaṅgā, which divided the kingdom of Magadha and the Vṛjji republic. A head-on clash between aggressive militant Magadhan monarchy and powerful independence-loving Vṛjji republic lay in the logic of history. Immediate causes are said to be (i) the escape of step-brothers of Ajātaśatru and Lichchhavi's grandson to Vaiśālī with a costly necklace and famous elephants, and (ii) the dispute between the two states over the distribution of mineral wealth, probably precious gems, near a port on the Gaṅgā.[58]

Ajātaśatru had built a fort on the southern bank of the Gaṅgā opposite Vaiśālī in orders to repel the Vṛjjis.[59] This fort later developed into the imperial city of Pāṭaliputra. Buddha had spoken to Vassakāra (Varṣakāra), a minister of Ajātaśatru in charge of the construction of the fort, that the Lichchhavis, as long a they were united and loyal to their leaders, were invincible.[60] Varṣakāra who had gone to the Buddha for advice at Ajātaśatru's orders reported the conversation to him. Ajātaśatru took the hint, and made it known to the Lichchhavis that Varṣakāra was dismissed and humiliated. Varṣakāra went to Vaiśālī and there he cleverly took advantage of freedom of discussion in the republic and secretly began to poison the relations between leaders, and to undermine the confidence of the people in the judicial system. After sometime the leaders began to quarrel among themselves and question each other's authority and patriotism. After creating the atmosphere of unrest, lack of confidence and mutual bickerings, Varṣakāra stepped across the Gaṅgā and advised Ajātaśatru about this being the opportune time to stike.[61] The Magadhan army was equipped with new war-machines like Rathamūsala and Mahāśilā-kaṇṭaka.[62] The Vṛjjians were helped by a confederacy of nine-Mallas and Kāśī-Kosala.[63] The war is said to have lasted for more than sixteen years, but ultimately Magadha triumphed, and the Vṛjji state became a part of the Magadhan empire.[64] The poem *Pārāyaṇa*, included in the *Sutta Nipāta*, mentions Vaiśālī as a Magadhan city, meaning now a city under Magadha and thereby proves the conquest of Vaiśālī by Magadh after the death of the Buddha, as in the *Mahāparinibbāna-Sutta* Vaiśālī is an independent republic.[65] It appears from Kauṭilya's *Arthaśāstra* that the Vṛjjis maintained some autonomy and continued to live under a republican constitution.[66] According to the *Ārya-Mañju-Śrī-Mūla-Kalpa*, besides Magadha, Aṅga, Vārāṇasī and Vaiśālī formed part of Ajātaśatru's dominion.[67]

Ajātaśatru had thus extended the territorial boundary of his empire both westward and northward. Chaṇḍa Pradyota appears to have brought Vatsa under his sphere of influence, and was jealous of the growth of the Magadhan empire. It appears that Pradyota's attack on Rājagriha shortly after the death of the Buddha was imminent and Ajātaśatru strengthened its fortifications. It is not known if the attack was really came made.[68] The policy of friendship initiated by Bimbisāra was thrown overboard to the two states having come face to face.

Ajātaśatru ruled for 32 years; in the eighth year of his reign, the Buddha died.[69] The *Purāṇas* assign to him a reign of 25 years.[70] According to the Buddhist sources Ajātaśatru's reign might have come to an end in 486-25 = 461 BC. But Smith[71] thinks that the figure 32 includes the seven years of viceroyalty at Champā and his reign came to an end in 493-25 = 468 BC.

Ajātaśatru was succeeded by his son Udāyibhadda (Bhadra) according to both the Buddhist and Jaina traditions,[72] but the *Purāṇas* mention Darśaka as Ajātaśatru's successor.[73] Geiger considers the Pauranic version as "certainly an error."[74] Darśaka as a ruler of Magadha and a contemporary of Udayana of Vatsa is mentioned in the *Svapna-Vāsavadattam* attributed to Bhāsa. Udayana, king of Vatsa, was under the influence of Avanti because of his queen Vāsavadattā. So Udayana's ministers to counteract this, arranged a marriage between Udayana and Padmāvatī, sister of Darśaka. Pradyota, the king of Avanti, was also seeking her (Padmāvatī's) hand for his own son.[75] This enmity with Avanti went on and continued in the time of Udāyī also.[76] According to Bhandarkar, Darśaka of the *Purāṇas* is to be identified with Nāga-dāsaka, last member of Bimbisāra's dynasty. But R.M. Smith thinks that the *Purāṇas* are right and Darśaka was the king, who followed his father Ajātaśatru, because the former was born when the latter had become king, 25 years given to Darśaka is his life figure. He remained king for a short time and was followed by Udāyī (Udāyibhadda) who was not his son but his brother.[77]

Raychaudhury takes Darśaka to be a *Māṇḍalika rājā* and not king of Magadh.[78] Udāyī may have advanced better claims for the throne not only because he was elder to Darśaka but also because like his father Ajātaśatru, he was also a viceroy at Champā.[79] According to *Mahāvaṁsa*, Udāyī became king after killing his parents.[80] The Jaina tradition knows of the violent death of Kuṇika Ajātaśatru.[81] Udāyibhadda or Udāyin in the fourth year of his reign is credited with the transfer of the capital from Rājagriha to Pāṭaliputra (Kusumapura), on the confluence of the Gaṅgā and the Son.[82] This gave the city great commercial advantage and it also lay in a more central position than Rājagriha in view of the then territorial limits of the Magadhan empire. Moreover, Rājagriha was under constant threat of the Pradyotas.[83] That Udāyī made Pāṭaliputra his new capital is confirmed both by the Jaina and Puranic traditions.[84] According to the Buddhist sources, Udāyibhadda ruled for 16 years.[85] The *Purāṇas* give him 33 years of reign.[86] Jainas gave him 60 years.[87] Jayaswal identified one of the Yakṣa statues of Patna with Udāyī. But this view is not acceptable to many scholars.[88] According to the *Purāṇas*,[89] he was succeeded by Nandivardhana followed by Mahānandin. Jainas attribute no direct heir to Udāyī.[90] Ceylonese chronicles[91] mention Aniruddha, his son

Muṇḍa and the latter's son Nāgadāsaka in that order as successors of Udāyī. All are parricides. The *Aṅguttara-Nikāya* knows of King Muṇḍa of Pāṭaliputra[92] who may be one of the successors of Udāyī. Of the three, Muṇḍa appears to be of some importance, as the *Divyāvadāna* also mentions him, and omits Aniruddha and Nāga-dāsaka. The rule of Aniruddha and Muṇḍa taken together lasted for 8 years, and Nāga-dāsaka ruled for 24 years.[93] R.M. Smith has tried to reconcile the Purāṇic and the Buddhist versions. In his opinion Nandivardhana, successor of Udāyī according to the *Purāṇas*, had two other nick names, Aniruddha and Muṇḍa. He identified Mahānandin of the *Purāṇas* with Nāga-dāsaka of the Ceylonese chronicles.[94] The Great Nāga dynasty of Magadha came to an end with the death of Nāga-dāsaka.

All these kings might or might not have been parricides. But their rule was not popular and the people in disgust selected Śiśunāga, the wise minister, to be the king of Magadha. He was at that time acting as a viceroy at Vārāṇasī.[95] According to the *Mahāvaṁsaṭīkā*, when the populace became infuriated against the rājā Nāga-daśaka, they deposed him, and Śiśunāga was augmented monarch with the title of Śiśunāga rājā.[96] He was the founder of the Junior Nāga dynasty of Magadh. A large number of scholars have accepted his Nāga origin.[97]

Origins of Śiśunāga are shrouded in mystery. According to the *Mahāvaṁsaṭīkā*, he was the son of a Lichchhavi rājā and the *nagara-śobhinī* (city queen of beauty, chief courtesan of Vaiśālī) and was abandoned and protected by a serpent ('nāga'), later brought up by an official.[98] Śiśunāga's dominion included Vārāṇasī and Vaiśālī. According to the *Malankaravatthu*, a late Pali work, Śiśunāga had a royal residence in Vaiśālī, which he made his capital,[99] probably because of its being his mother's birth-place. But according to the *Purāṇas*, Rājagriha was the capital of Śiśunāga.[100] It appears that because of Pradyota's open hostility, Śiśunāga might have strengthened fortification of Rājagriha and stayed there for some time; or he transferred the capital to Vaiśālī for some time, as we find Pāṭaliputra again as the residence of his son Kālāśoka. Rājagriha since then "lost her rank of royal city which she never afterwards recovered".[101] It is probably because Śiśunāga's capital, for some time at least, was at Rājagriha that the *Purāṇas* made the confusion of placing him and his dynasty earlier than Bimbisāra and his family whose grandson Udāyī had transferred the capital from Rājagriha to Pāṭaliputra for the first time.

Śiśunāga's main achievement is the destruction of the power of the Pradyotas. The *Purāṇas* make specific mention of this.[102] The Pradyota king who suffered this disaster was Avantivardhana. In the progress towards realisation of political integration of northern India, this success of the Magadhan imperialism against the Pradyotas of Avanti registered a great leap forward. Now there was left hardly any great power to resist Magadhan imperialism successfully. Śiśunāga facilitated the success of Mahapadma Nanda as the *Ekarāṭ* and *Chakravartin*. According to the *Dīpavaṁsa*, Śiśunāga reigned for 18 years. According to the *Purāṇas*, his reign lasted for 40 years.

According to the *Purāṇas*, Śiśunāga was succeeded by his son Kākavarṇa.[103] He was first appointed by his father at Vārāṇasī as viceroy.[104] The Buddhist sources name him as Kālāśoka.[105] The *Dīpavaṁsa* refers to him as Aśoka, son of Śiśunāga and to the former's rule in the towns of Pāṭaliputra.[106] He brought back the capital to Pāṭaliputra permanently[107] and in the 10th year of his reign the second Buddhist council after 100 years of the death of the Buddha was held at Vaiśālī.[108] According to a Jaina source quoted by Smith,[109] Kālāśoka had besieged Ujjayinī and captured it after killing its king who was Ajaka. Kālāśoka-Kākavarṇī died soon after. Kākavarṇī had a tragic end. According to Bāṇa, he had a dagger thrust into his chest in the vicinity of his city.[110] He appears to have been murdered by Mahāpadma Nanda.[111] According to Buddhist sources, Kālāśoka ruled for 28 years,[112] according to the *Purāṇas*,[113] 36 years or 26 years (*Matsya*).

According to the *Mahāvaṁsa*, his ten sons ruled after him simultaneously,[114] the ninth and the tenth being Nandivardhana and Pañchamaka.[115] Bhandarkar[116] sought to identify him with Nandivardhana who is mentioned in the *Purāṇas*. R.D. Banerji and Jayaswal[117] tried to identify him with Nandarāja of Khāravela's Hathigumpha inscription. This identification is unacceptable. The attempt by Jayaswal and Banerji to identify one of the Patna statues with Nandivardhana and their readings of the inscription have been seriously challenged by eminent scholars.[118] Nandivardhana of the *Purāṇas* was a scion of the Śiśunāga dynasty, and not one of the *Nava* (nine) Nandas.[119] The last of the Śaiśunāgas was done away with by Mahāpadma Nanda,[120] the founder of the Nanda dynasty. This event may be placed in c. 345 BC. The Minor Nāga Dynasty of Magadh founded by Śiśunāga thus came to an ignorable end.

Some scholars, like Fergusson, believe that the Nandas were also of Nāga origin. To quote him: "The second convocation was held 100 years after the death of Buddha, during the reign of Kālāśoka, and we gather, though somewhat indistinctly, that his successors, including the nine Nandas, till the accession of the celebrated Chandragputa (BC 325) were Nāgas or serpent worshippers pure and simple".[121] "Mahāpadma and Nanda, the only two of their names we know with certainty, are both names of serpents. Their coins I believe to be those depicted, in JASB, Vol. VII, pl. LX, No. 1-9.

On all these the serpent is the principal symbol."[122] In view of the absence of any other reasonable corroborative evidence, the theory of Fergusson is difficult to accept.

On the throne of Magadh, the Nandas were followed by the Mauryas. There is mention of the Nandas and Mauryas in the Sangam literature. At one place it is stated that "the Moriyar were the Chakravāla emperors or Vidyādharas and Nāgas."[123] As the interpretation of this passage itself is controversial and it has been argued that the composers of Sangam literature had vague notions about the Mauryas and their achievements, it is difficult to subscribe to the theory of the Nāga origin of the Mauryas. Arguments advanced by Hewit[124] and Oldham[125] to prove that Chandragupta Maurya was possibly of Nāga origin is difficult to accept in view of their theory of foreign origin of the Nāga race to which we do not subscribe, vide Chapter I.

It appears that the Nāga power went into oblivion till we again find them ruling in the region of Vidishā-Padmāvatī-Kāntipurī-Mathurā during the period c. first century BC to AD 350.

REFERENCES

1. *Mahābhārata, Sabhā-parvan*, XXI, 9-10; *Vana-parva*, LXXXIV, 106-7.
2. Fausboll, *The Jātaka*, III, p. 361.
3. *Ibid.*, II, p. 283.
4. cf. *Mahāvastu*, III, p. 383; *Lalitavistara*, I, pp. 379ff.
5. Fausboll, *op cit.*, V, p. 161.
6. *Ibid.*, IV, pp. 454-55.
7. *Saratthappakāsini*, I, p. 38.
8. *Vinaya Piṭakam*, I, p. 3; cf. Beal, *Buddhist Records of the Western World*, II, p. 128.
9. *Mahāvagga*, I, 3, 2.
10. *Dāthavaṁsa*, 1st Canto, v. 56.
11. *Lalitavistara*, I, pp. 379ff.
12. *Mahāvastu*, III, pp. 330ff.
13. *Ibid.*, II, p. 264.
14. *Divyāvadāna*, pp. 55-56 (Ed. Cowell and Neil).
15. *Mahavastu*, III, pp. 324ff.
16. p. 5, (SBE, XXI).
17. ".... ज्ञोण: सर्पगतस्तथा I", V, 211.
18. cf. Vogel, *Indian Serpent Lore*, p. 174.
19. Beal, *op cit.*, II, p. 167.
20. *JRAS* (N.S.), XIII, p. 571.

21. *Mahābhārata, Ādi Parva*, XXXV, 6.
22. *Memoirs of the Archaeological Survey of India*, No. 58, p. 34.
23. *ASIAR*, 1905-6, pp. 103ff. pl. XXXIX-XL.
24. *Vide*, Sarkar, *Kurkihar, Gaya and Bodhgaya*, pp. 50-56.
25. *Archaeological Survey of India Report*, 1926-27, p. 139 (pl. XXXI, d).
26. *Ibid.*, 1930-34, pl. LXVIII.
27. *Vide*, Sarkar, *op cit.*, p. 55.
28. *Ibid.*, pp. 20, 44.
29. *Archaeological Survey of India Report*, 1919-20, p. 28, pl. XX, XXI; 1923-24, pl. XXXVI.
30. *Ibid.*, 1921-22, pl. XXVIII.
31. *Early History of Bengal*, II, p. 107.
32. Pargiter, *Dynasties of the Kali Age*, pp. 18-22.
33. *PHAI*, pp. 115-116.
34. *Ibid.*, p. 68, 114.
35. Rhys Davids, *Buddhist India*, pp. 2-9; Ch. I, pp. 310-11.
36. *DKA*, p. 21.
37. *MV* (Geiger), p. XLVI. Also, Bhandarkar, CL, I, 67ff.
38. Bhandarkar, D.R., CL, I, p. 71.
39 *Buddhacharita*, XI, 2.
40. According to the *MV*, Bimbisāra was installed by his father Bhaṭṭīya in his 15th year (MV, pt. I, ch. II p. 8; N.L. Dey, *JASB*, 1914, p. 321). Other names given for his father by later writers are Bodhīśa, Mahāpadma, Hemajit and Kṣemajit. According to the *Purāṇas*, his father was Kṣatrauja who reigned for 40 years (*DKA*, p. 21).
41. *Jāt*. 539, p. 20; *Ind. Ant.*, VI, 229.
42. *The Vidhura Paṇḍita Jātaka* (Cowell, VI, 133) describes Rājagriha as a city of Aṅga; *PHAI*, p. 110.
43. *JASB*, 1914, p. 321; *PHAI*, p. 207, Note-3. It is not clear whether Aṅga was annexed by Bimbisāra as a crown prince and he became a viceroy at Champā (*PHAI*, p. 110) or it was annexed by Bimbisāra when he was already the king of Magadha (*PHAI*, p. 267).
44. *PHAI*, p. 206.
45. *Ibid.*, p. 206.
46. *CHI*, I, p. 156; *PHAI*, p. 206-7ff. According to the *Jātakas* (239, 283, 492), Ajātaśatru was born of Kosalan princess.
47. *Ibid.*, pp. 205-6. Gāndhāra's ruler sent an embassy with a view to secure Magadha's goodwill against aggressive Pradyota of Avanti. Bimbisāra sent Jivaka to cure Pradyota of jaundice.
48. *CHI*, I, p. 183.
49. *CHI*, I, p. 157.
50. *PHAI*, p. 205, note I.
51. *MV*, pt. I, p. 8; The *Purāṇas* assign him a reign of 28 years (*DKA*, p. 21); the

Brahmāṇḍa makes it 38 (note 21). According to the *Matsya Purāṇa* his father Kṣatrauja ruled for 24 years (*Matsya, DKA*, p. 21, note 17), though other *Purāṇas* give him 40 years (*DKA*, 21). The *Mahāvaṁsa's* 52 years may mean the combined rule of Bimbisāra and his father (Bhaṭṭīya) and of Bimbisāra alone after his father's death. Smith thinks that 52 years was the life year of Bimbisāra, who was born in 544 BC and came to throne in 521 BC, and if his rule for 38 years is accepted then he comes to throne in 531 BC. He was contemporary of the Buddha, who got enlightment in the same year. Bimbisāra was not *Yuvarāja* but a co-king with his father even if the Buddhist sources are to be believed (*JAOS*, Vol. 77, No. 4, p. 271). According to Smith, the figure 40 for Kṣatrauja given in the *Purāṇas* is his life-figure, and the *Matsya* gives his regnal period. So he must have revolted at the age of 16, and we are to believe that he had just then a son born to him (*Ibid.*). It is not impossible but very unlikely.

52. Yojanas, *Sum*, I, 148, qu. in CHI, I, p. 182, note 8.
53. *MV*, pt. I, ch. II, pg. 10; *Vinaya*, II, 190; *Digha*, I, 86; *Sum*, I, 133-136; *PHAI*, p. 209.
54. Jacobi referring to the *Niryāvalī Sutra* in his *Kalpasūtras* of Bhadravāhu, 1879, p. 5; V.A. Smith who first believed that Ajātaśatru slew his father (*EHI*, p. 35), in the 4th edition of the work held that it was difficult to accept the story of the parricide as historically true.
55. *CHI*, I, p. 184.
56. *Ibid.*
57. *Ibid.* According to *Samyutta Nikāya* at first Pasenadi was forced to retreat to Sāvaṭṭhi (Śrāvastī), but he rallied back and captured Ajātaśatru. R.M. Smith thinks that Ajātaśatru hurriedly reconciled with Pasenadi because of the threat to Rājagriha by Pradyota (*JAOS*, 77, No. 4, p. 267). According to the *Ārya-Mañju-Śrī-Mūla-Kalpa* (*AMMK*, 23, 332), Kāśī was a part of Ajātaśatru's dominion.
58. *PHAI*, pp. 211-12.
59. *Mahāvagga*, *SBE*, XI, pp. 1. 5.
60. *Mahāparinibbāna Suttanta* – Dialogues of the Buddha by Rhys Davids, II, p. 78; R.M. Smith thinks that Ajātaśatru's first attack on the Vṛjji republic was repulsed in 488 BC. "A repulse is far better explanation of his building a fort at Pāṭaliputra. An unexpected check is a more likely explanation for the defensive." *JAOS*, 77, No. 4, p. 268.
61. *JRAS*, 1931; *DPPN*, II, 846.
62. *PHAI*, p. 213; *Uvāsaga-dasao*, Vol. II, App. p. 60.
63. *Niryāvali Sūtra*, qu. *PHAI*, p. 212.
64. *CHI*, I, pp. 185; *PHAI*, p. 214.
65. *CHI*, I, pp. 188-189.
66. *KA*, XI, 1.5. The Lichchhivikas and the Vṛjikas are referred to separately.
67. *AMMK*, III.

68. *Majjhima Nikāya,* III; *PHAI,* p. 215. According to Rapson, Pradyota had established temporary sovereignty over Magadh as a result of the attack on Rājagriha in the time of Ajātaśatru (*CHI,* I, p. 311). Udena or Udayana of Vatsa (Prayāga region) was a junior contemporary of Chaṇḍa Pradyota whose daughter Vāsavadattā fell in love with Udayana, who remained under the influence of his father-in- law. Smith suggests that Pradyota in fact conquered the kingdom of Vatsa (*JAOS,* 77, No. 4, p. 267). This must have brought Magadh and Avanti quite close to each other. This might have happened quite early in the reign of Ajātaśatru, who fortified Rājagriha in apprehension of Pradyota's attack at about the same time when the war with Kosala was on. Both Kosala and Magadha were afraid of Chaṇḍa Pradyota's aggressive intentions (*Ibid.,* pp. 267-68). This event may have taken place in circa 489 BC. It appears that Prasenajit had to flee to Rājagriha for shelter with his son-in-law against revolt in Kosala engendered by Avanti. Prasenajit died at the city gate of Rājagriha; however, this might have provoked Chaṇḍa to besiege Rājagriha. But nothing came out, as the defence under Prince Abhaya, son of Bimbisāra and brother of Ajātaśatru, proved successful. It is not necessary to believe that the attack came in the time of Bimbisāra himself (*ABORI,* 1920-21, p. 3; *DPPN,* I, 128). Ajātaśatru might have employed his brother to lead the defence of the capital city. The tension appears to have continued in the time of Udāyī also (Jacobi, *Pariśiṣṭaparvan,* pp. 45-46).
69. *MV,* pt. I, ch. II, p. 8.
70. *DKA,* p. 21. In some *Matsya mss.,* reign of 27 years is attributed to Ajātaśatru.
71. *JAOS,* Vol. 77, No. 4, pp. 271-2.
72. *Dīghanikāya,* I, 50; *Dialogues of the Buddha,* I. 68; *DV,* IV, 38; V. 97, 11.8; *MV,* pt. 1, ch. III, p. 11; *Pariśiṣṭaparvan,* p. 42. Udāyibhadda is a parricide according to the *Mahāvaṁsa* (IV, p. 11).
73. *DKA,* p. 21.
74. Geiger, *Mahāvaṁsa,* p. XLV.
75. *EHI,* p. 39, note I.
76. Udāyin had dethroned a king whose son entered into the service of Udāyin's rival, the king of Avanti and promised to kill Udāyin if the former made him his ally and equal. This son of the king later in the guise of a Jaina ascetic went to Pāṭaliputra and killed Uddāyin) *Pariśiṣṭaparvan,* Intro. Jacobi, p. 45).
77. *JAOS,* Vol. 77, No. 4, p. 270 (table, p. 272).
78. *PHAI,* p. 216.
79. Jacobi, *Pariśiṣṭaparvan,* p. 42.
80. *Mahāvamsa,* pt. I (Turnour), ch. IV, p. 11.
81. Jacobi, *Pariśiṣṭaparvan,* 2nd edn, p. XII.
82. *DKA,* p. 22. *Pariśiṣṭaparvan,* VI, 34; 175-80; Jacobi's view that Udāyī and Kākavarṇa are identical has been rightly rejected by Geiger (MV, p. XLIII).
83. *Pariśiṣṭaparvan,* pp. 45-46, refers to the enmity between Udāyī and the king of Avanti. Vatsa had already become a part of Avanti's king Pālaka's dominion

(Tawney's trans. of the *KSS*, II, p. 484), and so the struggle begun in the time of Ajātaśatru continued. Magadha had Avanti as its only important rival to deal with.

84. *Pariśiṣṭaparvan; DKA*, p. 21.
85. *DV*, IV, 38; *MV*, IV, p. 11.
86. *DKA*, p 22.
87. *JAOS*, Vol. 77, No. 4, p. 270. The 60 years may be his life figure.
88. *PHAI*, p. 218, footnote I.
89. *DKA*, p. 22.
90. *Pariśiṣṭaparvan* (Text) VI. p. 236. *udāyyaputrogotrīhiparalokamagāditi.*
91. *MV*, ch. IV, p. 11. All the three are regarded as parricides.
92. *Aṅguttara Nikāya*, III, 57-63.
93. *MV*, ch. IV, p. 11.
94. *JAOS*, Vol. 77, No. 4, p. 270.
95. *MV*, pt. I (Turnour), ch. IV, p. 11. Wise minister = viceroy at Vārāṇasī, *PHAI*, 219.
96. *Ibid.*, p. XXXVIII. The author of the *Pariśiṣṭaparvan is* certainly confused when he speaks of selection of Nanda as king after Udāyī (*Pariśiṣṭaparvan*, Intro, p. 46).
97. Fergusson, *Tree and Serpent Worship*, p. 60; Banerji Shastri, *ABORI*, XVIII, p. 347; Hewitt, *JRAS*, 1888, pp. 354, 362; Hewitt, *History and Chronology of the Mythmaking Age*, p. 590; Mehta, *Pre-Buddhist India*, p. 66; Wake, *Serpent Worship*, p. 141.
98. *MV* (Turnour), pt. I, p. XXXVII. The story is said to have been taken from the *Atthakatha.* It is relevant to note that Tārānātha mentions that the Second Buddhist Council was held under King Nandin of the Lichchhavi race in Kusumapurī Vihāra. We know that in Kālāśoka's time the Second Buddhist Council was held at Vaiśālī. Filliozat had reconciled the contradiction. Nandin has been identified with Kālāśoka (Nandin means happiness and Aśoka means free from chargin). Kusumapurī Vihāra may have been in Vaiśālī (*Studies in Asokan Inscriptions*). Being son of Śiśunāga born of a Lichchhavi chief and city courtezan, Kālāśoka (Nandin) could well be taken to belong to the Lichchhavi race. Filliozat identified Kālāśoka with Nadivardhana of the *Purāṇas* (*Ibid.*, p. 8; JA, 1948, p. 194).
99. qu. in *PHAI*, pp. 116, 219.
100. *DKA*, p. 21.
101. *SBE*, XI, p. XVI.
102. *DKA*, p. 21.
103. *DKA*, p. 21. Filliozat (*Studies in Asokan Inscriptions*, p. 8) identified Kālāśoka with the Nandin of Tārānatha in whose reign the Second Buddhist Council was held and with Nandivardhana of the Pauranic list.
104. *DKA*, p. 21.

105. *MV*, IV, p.11. *DV* refers to him as Aśoka, son of Śiśunāga (V. 25). Kālāśoka and Kākavarṇin are identical (*PHAI*, revised 5th edn., 221-222). Aśokavardhana refers to Kākavarṇī, not Kālāśoka.
106. *DV*. V. 25.
107. *DV*. *Susunāgassa putto Aśoko tadā āsi mahīpato, Pāṭapiputta nagaramhi rājjam Kāresi Khattiya* (V. 25).
108. *DV*, V. 23-29; *MV* (Geiger), IV, 8.
109. *JAOS*, VA. 77, No. 4, p. 269.
110. *Harṣacharita* (ed. by Kasinath Pandurang Parab, p. 233). It has been suggested on the authority of Jaina sources that Kākavarṇin had attacked Avanti and temporarily occupied it; and later, on return was murdered in the vicinity of his city (*JAOS*, Vol. 77, No. 4, p. 269). The Jaina reference may actually suggest the victory over Pradyotas of Avanti in the time of Śiśunāga when Kālāśoka-Kākavarnin might have been in charge of the invasion.
111. See infra.
112. *MV* (Turnour), pt. I. ch. IV, p. 11ff. 5.
113. *DKA*, p. 21, note 11.
114. *MV* (Turnour), pt. I, ch. V, p. 21.
115. *PHAI*, (6th edn.), p. 222. *Mahabodhivaṁsa* (Strong) p. 98 has them as sons of Kālāśoka, Bhadrasena, Koraṇḍavarṇa, Mangura, Sarvañjaka, Jālika, Ubhāka, Sanjaya, Kosavya, Nandivardhana and Pañchamana.
116. Bhandarkar, D.R., Carm. Lect., 1918, p. 83.
117. *PHAI*, 6th edn. 222-24 & *JBORS*, 1918, p. 91.
118. *Ibid.*, p. 222-23, footnote 5.
119. *DKA*, p. 22. According to the *Purāṇas* Kṣemadharman was Kālāśoka's successor.
120. According to a Jaina tradition Nanda became king after the assassination of Udāyī and 60 years after the death of Mahāvīra (*Pariśiṣṭaparvan*, VI, 243). Was this Nanda, Nandivardhana, who followed Udāyī according to the *Purāṇas*?
121. Fergusson, J., *Tree and Serpent Worship*, pp. 83-84.
122. *Ibid.*, p. 84, fn.1.
123. Sastri, KAN., *Age of the Nandas and Mauryas*, Delhi, 1967, pp. 253-54.
124. Hewitt, *JRAS*, 1890, p. 432.
125. Oldham, *The Sun and the Serpent*, p. 113.

4

THE NĀGAS OF VIDISHĀ, PADMĀVATĪ, KĀNTIPURĪ, MATHURĀ AND OTHER NĀGA DYNASTIES

The origin and the account of the rule of the Nāgas with their capitals at Vidishā, Padmāvatī (modern Pawāyā in Gwalior district), Kāntipurī (Kutwār in Gwalior district) and Mathurā are still shrouded by considerable obscurity. Whatever little we know about this dynasty is that it began its political career sometime towards the close of the first century BC and gradually emerged into prominence when the foreign Kuṣāṇa power was disintegrating, succeeded in driving it out from the Gangetic Valley. This was the time when a number of indigenous powers, like the Yaudheyas, the Arjunāyanas and the Mālavas were gaining strength. None of the rulers belonging to the Nāga dynasty ruling at the above-mentioned places have left any epigraphic record. No doubt some of them issued coins, on the basis of which attempts have been made by scholars to reconstruct their history. An additional source of information is the evidence supplied by the *Purāṇas*.

The evidence of the *Purāṇas* about the rulers of this dynasty is vague and carries little practical value and it has given rise to sharp differences of opinions amongst scholars. The *Viṣṇu Purāṇa*, for example, discloses the existence of nine (*nava*) Nāga kings who ruled at Padmāvatī, Kāntipurī and Mathurā[1] and this account is corroborated by the *Vāyu Purāṇa* which mentions only two houses of the Nāgas – one at Padmāvatī and the other at Mathurā, the number of kings at each of the places being stated to be nine and seven, respectively.[2] The rulers of the Nāga dynasty at Vidishā have also been referred to by the *Purāṇas*.[3]

K.P. Jayaswal in his important work entitled *The History of India (AD 150-350)*, has made a serious attempt to reconstruct the history of the Nāgas ruling at the above-mentioned places. Not only the Pauranic and the numismatic evidences have been harnessed by him to draw conclusions, he has taken into account the statements contained in the inscriptions of the Vākāṭakas and the Guptas.

While discussing the history of the Nāgas and their relationship with the Vākāṭakas, he has discussed exhaustively the question of their coinage which deserves careful consideration, as they have an important bearing on the contemporary history. The coinage of the Vākāṭakas were quite unknown till recent times. The coins of a number of Nāga rulers like Bhīmanāga, Skandanāga, Bṛahaspatināga, Vyāghranāga, Vasunāga, Devanāga, and Gaṇapatināga were published by Cunningham as early as AD 1865 but all these rulers belonged to the period AD c. 250 to 350.[4] Dr. Jayaswal, however, refers in his history to an earlier Nāga coinage extending from c. 100 BC to AD 50, and maintains that the coins usually attributed to kings Śeśadatta, Rāmadatta, Śiśuchandradatta of Mathurā are really the issues of the Nāga rulers of Vidishā mentioned in several *Purāṇas*, bearing the names of Śeṣa, Rāmachandra and Śiśunandi, respectively. The coins of Puruṣadatta, Uttamadatta, Kāmadatta, Bhavadatta, and Śivanandi, which also occur in the Mathurā series, are also attributed by him to the early Nāga rulers of Vidishā. The discovery of these coins in this territory around Mathurā is attributed by him to the circumstance that Mathurā has been a mart for ancient coins from adjoining territories like Ahichchhatra, Padamāvatī and Vidishā; he has no doubt that these kings were ruling with their capital in Vidishā in eastern Mālwā. When his reading *Bhavanāga* was challenged by Sir Richard Burn, Dr. Jayaswal published a new coin of the Kauśāmbī series from the cabinet of Babu Sri Nath Sah of Benares, which he averred, clearly bears the legend Bhavanāga.[5] A.S. Altekar has critically examined this theory of Jayaswal with interesting conclusions.[6]

The Pauranic evidence undoubtedly makes it appear that there was a Nāga dynasty ruling at Vidishā, some members of which belonged to the pre-Śuṅga and some to the post-Śuṅga Period. The question at issue, as Altekar points out, is whether we can identify any or some of the Nāga rulers of Vidishā with any or some rulers of the Datta dynasty, which is usually taken to have ruled at Mathurā.

The *Purāṇas* mention the following Nāga kings as ruling at Vidishā before the overthrow of the Śuṅga power in c. 31 BC:

Bhogi
Sadāchandra, Rāmachandra or Vāmachandra,
Dhanadharmā or Dhanavarmā
Vaṅgāra (who is expressly described as the fourth in the dynasty), and
Bhūtinanda.

It is also stated that Śeṣarāja was the father of Bhogi, but according to Altekar, it is likely that he was more a mythical than a real ruler. If he had ruled before Bhogi, Vaṅgāra would become the fifth ruler of the dynasty and the *Purāṇas* could not have described him as the fourth king of the house. If Śeṣa-Nāgarāja was at all a historical ruler, his importance relative to his son must have been like that Ghatoṭkachagupta to Chandragupta I.

After the overthrow of the Śuṅgas, the *Purāṇas* mention the following Nāga rulers as ruling at Vidishā:

Śiśunandi,
His younger brother, Nandiyaśas,
In his line Śiśuka, the daughter's son.

Jayaswal argues that out of these Nāga rulers of Vidishā, we should identify Śeṣa Nāgarāja, Rāmachandra, Śiśunandi and Śivanandi with kings Śeṣadatta, Rāmadatta, Śiśuchandradatta and Śivadatta of the Mathurā series, which in his opinion is really a series of Nāga coins issued from Vidishā. He further maintains that kings Puruṣadatta, Uttamadatta, Rāmadatta, Bhavadatta, and Śivanandi, occuring in the same series, are also Nāga rulers of Vidishā, whose names are not given in the Pauranic lists.

According to Altekar this theory is not tenable. At the outset he points out that there is no evidence to justify the conclusion that Śeṣadatta, Rāmadatta, Śiśuchandradatta and the rulers of the Mathurā series were ruling at Vidishā. Their copper coins have been usually found only in the territory round about Mathurā and, therefore they are rightly regarded as being the rulers of that city. The contention that the discovery of the coins of these rulers at Mathurā is due purely to the circumstance of the city being a well-known mart for ancient coins would have had some force if they had been found also at Vidishā and some other ancient sites in and near Mālwā. Such however is not the case at all. The coins of the above Mathurā rulers are conspicuous by their absence in Mālwā. Cunningham found hundreds of ancient coins of this period in Mālwā, but he could not get a single coin of the Mathurā series, alleged to be issued from Vidishā. Thousands of coins of the Mālwas were found at Nagarī, but this site yielded only one coin of Rāmadatta.[7] When Dr. D.R. Bhandarkar carried out his excavations at Besnagar or ancient Vidishā, he found 56 copper coins, 49 of which were *kārṣāpaṇas*, two were the issues of the Kṣatrapas, and five of the Nāga rulers Bhīmanāga and Gaṇapatināga. No coins of any rulers of the Mathurā series like Rāmadatta, Śeṣadatta, or Śiśuchandradatta were found. There is therefore no shred of evidence to show that the above rulers were ruling with Vidishā as their capital. If such was the case, why should their coins be totally absent in and round about Vidishā. We cannot therefore *prima facie* identify them with the members of the Nāga dynasty, which was ruling at Vidishā before the rise of the later Nāgas in the 3rd century AD.

According to Altekar another important thing to note is this: while the names of the rulers of the later Nāga dynasty like Bhīmanāga, Skandanāga, etc. all end in *nāga*, the names of none of the rulers of the Mathurā series has a *nāga*-ending. It may be pointed out that the coins of the later Nāga rulers are very small in size; and yet their engravers never failed to add the epithet *nāga* after their names. The coins of the Mathurā rulers, Rāmadatta, Śeṣadatta, etc are much bigger in size; why then should the epithet *nāga* not have appeared on them after the proper names? If these rulers were really Nāgas like the later rulers of Padmāvatī, why should they have omitted the genetic term *nāga*? Not only do they do this, but most of them add the ephthet *datta* after their names.

In order to forestall the argument that these Mathurā ruler belonged to a 'Datta' and not to a 'Nāga' dynasty, Jayaswal avers that the last two letters on the Mathurā coins are to be read as *dāta* and not as *datta* or *data. Dāta,* says Jayaswal, stands for *dātā* or *dātṛi,* meaning donor or liberal sacrificer. The legend, therefore, are to be read not as Śeṣa-data, Rāma-data, etc meaning King Śeṣa the celebrated donor, King Rāma, the celebrated donor, etc.

In reply Altekar points out that suffix *dāta* or *dātṛi* at the end of the names of the rulers of a dynasty is not known to be occurring anywhere either in inscriptions or in the *Purāṇas*. The coins in question further make it clear that the last two letters are *data* and not *dāta*, the horizontal stroke of medial *ā* can nowhere be detected on the letter *da*.

Altekar further pointed out that if, agreeing with Jayaswal, we identify Rāmadatta, Śiśuchandradatta, and Śivadatta with Rāmchandra, Śiśunandi and Śivanandi of the *Purāṇas*, we shall have to suppose that the coin engravers were permitted to take all kinds of liberties with the names of their employers. In the case of King Rāmachandra, they supplant the suffix *chandra* with *dāta.* Perhaps it may be said that in the interest of abbreviation, the uninteresting suffix *chandra* is dropped and the more siginficant suffix *dāta*, i.e., *dātā* is added. But abbreviation is not the governing principle; in the case of Śiśunandi,

nandi has been dropped, but two new suffixes, *chandra* and *dāta* are added. It is very doubtful if the coin engraver would ever have been permitted to change and supplant important suffixes in royal names in this way. We cannot, therefore, subscribe to the view that Śivadatta and Śiśuchandradatta of the coins are identical with Śiśunandi and Śivanandi of the *Purāṇas*. In the case of Rāmachandra, Jayaswal's counterpart of Rāmadatta of the coins, it has to be further observed that only the *Viṣṇupurāṇa* spells his name as Rāmachandra; others read it as Sadāchandra or Vāmachandra. Śeṣa Nāgarāja, Jayaswal's counterpart of Śeṣadatta of coins, was most probably a mythical person, as the *Purāṇas* do not include him in counting of the Nāga kings of Vidishā. No king of the earlier Nāga dynasty of Vidishā can thus be identified with any ruler belonging to the Mathurā coin series.

Altekar then examines the other arguments advanced by Jayaswal to assign the Mathurā rulers to the Nāga dynasty ruling in Vidishā. He points out that the Vidishā Nāga rulers, are described as *vṛṣas*, 'bulls' by the *Purāṇas*, and so on their coins, Śiva's *Nandi* or bull and *triśūla* are to be seen figuring prominently. The figure of the Nāga or serpent also makes its appearance, often completing the name of the king in a symbolic manner.

He points out at the outset it is only some Mss. of the *Vāyupurāṇa*, which describe the Vidishā Nāga rulers as *vṛsas*; other Mss. of this *Purāṇa* as well as all the Mss. of the *Brahmāṇḍapurāṇa* describe them as *nṛpas*, kings, and not as *vṛṣas* or bulls. *Vṛṣa* in fact is the scribe's mistake for *nṛpa* and it was quite a natural one in early palaeography. But granting for the sake of argument that these Nāga rulers of Vidishā are really described as *vṛṣas*, do we find the bull and *triśūla* of Śiva prominently figuring on their coins, as averred by Dr. Jayaswal? An examination of the Mathurā coins shows that such is not the case at all. Out of the coins of the five Mathurā rulers who have been ascribed to the Vidishā Nāga dynasty, the bull appears only on one variety of the coins of Rāmadatta; it does not at all appear on the coins of any of the remaining four rulers. On the coins of Rāmadatta too, Lakṣmī standing (obv.) and three elephants facing (rev.) are the usual and prominent symbols; the bull appears as an unimportant element on the obverse of only the variety.[8]

As per Altekar, the symbol of the *triśūla* does not at all appear on the coins of any of the five Nāga rulers of Jayaswal. On the coins of Rāmadatta, Kāmadatta and Puruṣadatta we have a symbol partially resembling *triśūla*. But it cannot be described as a *triśūla* at all. It has only three prongs but no handle. We have undoubted instances of *triśūlas* on the coins of Dhanadeva of Kauśāmbī[9] and Śivadāsa, Mahādeva and Rudravarmā of the Audumbaras,[10] where we see the three prongs and a long handle, which later is absent in the case of the symbol on the Mathurā coins. The symbol, which Dr. Jayaswal mistakes for a *triśūla*, is in fact exactly identical with the second of the three *Pañchāla* symbols.

To see whether the serpent symbol appears on any of the Mathurā coins under discussion, rendering their attribution to a Nāga dynasty probable, Altekar points out at the outset that on the coins of the rulers of Padmāvatī, who invariably attach the suffix *Nāga* to their names, the serpent symbol does not appear at all. Curiously enough on some of their coins the symbol of peacock, the traditional enemy of the serpent, makes its appearance. Wheel, dagger, bull and *triśūla* are other symbols appearing on their coins, but the serpent is conspicuous by its absence. This would be quite clear from a glance at Pl. II of Cunningham's *Coins of Medieval India*, where the coins of Bhīmanāga, Skandanāga, Bṛahaspatināga, Gaṇapatināga, Vyāghranāga and Devanāga have been illustrated.

But even if we grant for the sake of argument that the serpent symbol may connect a coinage with the Nāga dynasty, Altekar points out that it does not occur on the coins of the five Mathurā rulers who are taken to be the members of the Nāga dynasty by Jayaswal. There is no serpent symbol on the coins of Śeṣadatta, unless we suppose that the tree in the field on the left on the reverse is a serpent standing on its tail. The serpent is usually represented in this way when its hood is to be shown. But there is nothing like a hood at the top of this symbol; it is clearly a tree. On the coins of Śivadatta also there is a short wavy perpendicular line, which can hardly be mistaken for a serpent.[11] On only one out of the four varieties of the coins of Rāmadatta, there is a horizontal wavy line, looking like a serpent.[12] But such a line occurs also on the reverse of the Western Kṣatrapa coins. It is not serpent but a kind of decorative platform for the symbols shown above it. But granting even that this wavy line stands for a serpent, Altekar points out that it occurs only on one variety of the coins of Rāmadatta. As far as the coin of the other Mathurā rulers like Kāmadatta, Uttamadatta, etc are concerned, there is nothing on them like a wavy or a perpendicular line which by any stretch of imagination can be supposed to be serpent symbol.

In Altekar's opinion, the argument, therefore, that the rulers of the Mathurā series are Nāga rulers of Vidishā because of the occurrence of the serpent symbol on their coins, completely fails. If the occurrence of a wavy line were to be regarded as proving the Nāga origin of the rulers issuing the coins concerned, we shall have to conclude that King Dhanadeva of Ayodhyā, Bṛahaspatimitra of Kauśāmbī, and the Kuninda, Yaudheya and Western Kṣatrapa rulers were all Nāgas because a wavy line in some form or other occurs on their coins.[13]

Altekar thus makes it clear that the arguments advanced to prove that the Datta rulers of the Mathurā series were the Nāga rulers of Vidishā are all untenable. There are some other cogent reasons also which go against such a theory. These coins are not to be found in Vidishā and Narwar, which have yielded hundreds of contemporary coins of their types. If the Datta rulers of the Mathurā series were the rulers of Vidishā in Mālwā, the 'Ujjayinī' symbol should have appeared on their coins, as it does on almost all the coins hailing from Mālwā. It is conspicuous by its absence. It is worth noting that many of the non-Datta rulers of Mathurā, who have not been assigned to Vidishā by Jayaswal, like Gomitra, Dṛḍhamitra, Sūryamitra and Brahmamitra, put the 'Ujjayinī' symbol on their coins; it is only on the coins of the so-called Vidishā rulers of Jayaswal that it has been replaced by a symbol resembling the Brāhmī letter *śa*. This deliberate supplanting of the Ujjayinī symbol on the coins of the Datta group will show that they had no connection with Mālwā or Vidishā.

The symbols on the coins of the Datta group of kings show that they were closely connected with one another. There is 'therefore' no sufficient reason to explain why the names of only some of them should have been mentioned in the *Purāṇas*, and why kings like Puruṣadatta, Uttamadatta, Kāmadatta, and Bhavadatta should have been omitted. Jayaswal can suggest the identification of five of the rulers with the Nāga kings of Vidishā only after taking considerable liberty with their names. Their coins are not found in Vidishā and bear no 'Ujjayinī' or Nāga symbols. Altekar therefore concludes that the theory that the Mathurā series of coins was issued by the Nāga rulers of Vidishā belonging to the Śuṅga times has to be abandoned as untenable.

According to Altekar, really there are no coins of the Nāga rulers, who according to the *Purāṇas*, ruled contemporaneously with the Śuṅgas and the Kaṇvas. He next examines whether there are any coins of the Nāga rulers of the post-Kaṇva Period, who according to Jayaswal, belonged to the different branches of the Bhāraśiva Nāga family, ruling at Mathurā, Padmāvatī and Kāntipurī.

Jayaswal's theory is that the Bhāraśiva Nāga dynasty was founded by a Nāga ruler named Navanāga, who ruled from c. 140 to AD 170. Coins, the legends on which have been wrongly read as *Devasa* or *Nevasa*, are to be attributed to this Nāga ruler, the correct reading being *Nevasa*. Some of these coins are dated in his regnal year 27. Navanāga was succeeded by Vīrasenanāga, who was a powerful ruler and succeeded in ousting the Kuṣānas from the upper U.P., Mathurā and the eastern Punjab. Coins bearing the legend Vīrasena were issued by this ruler, his tribal name Nāga being suggested by the serpent symbol occurring on the reverse of his coins. Some of them bear his regnal year 34. After Vīrasenanāga, the Nāga kingdom was divided into three branches which ruled at Mathurā, Padmāvatī and Kāntipurī. Mathurā rulers have left no coins. The coins of Nāga rulers of Padmāvatī have been already published by Cunningham in *CMI*, pl. II. The Nāga rulers of Kāntipurī have left us their coinage, but it was so far not recognized by scholars. Hayanāga, Trayanāga, Barhiṇanāga, Chharajanāga, Bhavanāga, and Rudrasena belonged to this branch. Some of their coins can be seen in the section on "Unassigned miscellaneous coins of Northern India" published in the *Indian Museum Catalogue of Coins*, Vol. I, pp. 205-207. Many of these coins are also dated.[14]

Jayaswal has raised various problems connected with the Bhāraśivas in his *History* without going into them. Altekar examines whether the coins referred to by Jayaswal were issued by Nāga rulers and whether they belonged to Bhāraśiva stock.

According to Altekar the Pauranic passage referring to the Nāga rulers ruling on the eve of the rise of the Gupta power reads as follows:

Nava nāgāstu bhokshyanti Purīm Padmāvatīm[15] *nṛipāḥ*
Mathurām cha purīm ramyām Nāgā bhokshyanti sapta vai.

Altekar opines that the mention of the *seven* Nāga rulers of Mathurā mentioned in the second-half of the above verse makes it almost certain that first half refers to *nine* (*nava*) Nāga rulers of Padmāvatī and not to *new* (*nava*) Nāga rulers of that city. It may, however, be assumed for the sake of argument that the expression *Nava nāgāh* refers to new Nāga rulers of Padmāvatī founded by King Navanāga and proceed to examine whether the coins concerned can be attributed to him.

Altekar observes at the outset that the legend on the coins under discussion does not read as *Devasa* as supposed by Smith; Jayaswal's reading *Navasa* seems to be the correct one and has been accepted by Allan also, though it cannot be denied that on some coins the first letter appears to be *ne* and not *na*. The medial *e* stroke may be due to the carelessness of the engraver and we may tentatively accept the reading *Navasa* as the correct one.

To describe the coins of Nava, on the reverse there is the bull which appears almost invariably on Kauśāmbī coins. On the obverse, in the upper half, there is a tree within railing in the centre with a symbol on either side. On the coin illustrated in the *IMC*, Pl. XXIII. 15, the symbol to left no doubt appears like the one for 20 and that on right as the one for 7, and both Smith and Jayaswal naturally take them to stand for the number 27. But in the case of a large number of coins illustrated in the *B.M. Catalogue of Coins of Ancient India*, Pl. XXXI, 4-8, as well as those examined by Altekar in the valuable collections of Babu Srinath Sah of Benaras and Rai Bahadur B.M. Vyas of Allahabad, one of these symbols appears to be a spear and the other is indistinct and is taken as a *chauri* by Allan.[16] It would therefore be hazardous to conclude from the solitary specimen in Indian Museum that the coins of Nava are dated in his regnal years. It is, however, immaterial for the present purpose to decide as to whether these coins are dated; it has to be found out whether King Nava or Neva, who issued these coins, is identical with Jayaswal's Navanāga, the founder of the Nāga dynasty.

Altekar confesses that the various arguments adduced by Jayaswal to support his view do not carry any conviction. Jayaswal ascribes this type to King Navanāga because there is the figure of a Nāga or serpent with raised hood above the legend (p. 18). It is interesting to point out that Jayaswal takes this symbol to right of the tree on the obverse once for numeral 7, when he wants to argue that the coins bear the date of issue, 27, and then again for the hood of a serpent when he wants to prove that King Nava, who issued them, was a Nāga ruler.[17] The symbol in question cannot obviously stand both for the numeral 7 and for the hood of a snake. Altekar has examined a large number of these coins and have found that the symbol in question is too indistinct to interpret with confidence. It is only on the solitary specimen published in the *IMC* that it appears as the hood of a serpent.

But even if it is assumed that the serpent's hood appears on all the coins of Nava its occurrences will not prove that he was a Nāga ruler. On none of the coins issued by the Nāga rulers of Padmāvatī, the serpent or its hood makes its appearance. On the other hand, as already shown before, the symbol which looks like a serpent or its hood makes its appearance on the coins of Dhanadeva of Ayodhyā,[18] Bṛhaspatimitra II of Kauśāmbī,[19] and the rulers of the Western Kṣatrapa dynasty and the Yaudheya republic,[20] none of whom belonged to a Nāga family, even according to Jayaswal.

It must be further remembered that according to Jayaswal, Navanāga was the founder of a new Nāga house, which emerged into prominence by ousting the Kuṣāṇas from eastern U.P. Navanāga, therefore, would have taken effective and unmistakable measures to proclaim his Nāga origin on his coins; he would not have left it to be inferred by serpent's hood on his coins but would have announced it by adding the unmistakable suffix *nāga* to his name, as has been done by the Nāga rulers of Padmāvatī.

The next argument advanced by Jayaswal to ascribe these coins to a Nāga dynasty is their close affinity to the coinage of the Nāga dynasties of Mathurā, Vidishā and Padmāvatī (p. 19). It has been shown already how the so-called Mathurā-Vidishā series of Jayaswal was not issued by any Nāga ruler at all. But even supposing that the Datta coins are the issues of Nāga rulers, it has to be pointed out that they bear no resemblance whatsoever with the coins of King Nava. On the Datta series of coins of Mathurā, the legend is either circular or in a straight line at the top; on the coins of King Nava it is always at the bottom. On the Datta coins, there is usually standing Lakṣmī on the obverse and three elephants on the reverse; on none of the coins of Nava does either of these objects make its appearance. They have on the other hand tree within railing on one side and bull on the other, which do not figure on Datta coins at all. The average weight of the coins of Nava is about 65 grains, that of the coins of the Datta series is about 110 grains. There is, therefore, no affinity at all between Datta coins of Jayaswal's so, called Mathurā-Vidishā series and the coins of Nava.

Regarding any kind of affinity existing between the coins of King Nava and the rulers of Padmāvatī, who undoubtedly belonged to a Nāga family, the only point of similarity, according to Altekar, is the occasional appearance of the bull on the reverse of the coins of the Nāga rulers of Padmāvatī. Bull, however, is an invariable element of the coins of Nava, whereas it is often replaced by peacock, wheel or trident which often figure on the latter, are never to be seen on the coins of Nava. The legend on this ruler's coins is always at the bottom and in a straight line, that on the coins of the Nāga rulers of Padmāvatī is generally circular, and covering the entire surface of the coin. The Padmāvatī rulers prefix the title Mahārāja to their names; Nava never takes up this or any other royal title. The suffix *Nāga,* which invariably occurs on the coins of Padmāvatī rulers, is always absent on the coins of Nava. The Padmāvatī coins are usually tiny in size and weight. They were apparently issued in three denominations weighing 9, 18 and 36 grains; only Skandanāga has issued a few coins weighing about 50 grains. The coins of Nava on the other hand are never so tiny; they usually weigh about 65 grains. There is, therefore, no affinity at all between the coins of the Nāga rulers of Padmāvatī and those of King Nava in order to justify the latter's attribution to a Nāga family.

The *Purāṇas* place their Nava-Nāgas at Padmāvatī and their statement can be well accepted, for coins of ten Nāga rulers have been found at that place. If we agree with Jayaswal and hold that Navanāga was the founder of this house, we should find some of this coins at Padmāvatī. This place has yielded a large number of Nāga coins, but not a single coin of Nava has been found there. This would be indeed strange if King Nava was a Nāga ruler and the ultimate founder of the Padmāvatī dynasty.

The coins of Nava have been found only in the eastern U.P., and mostly at Kauśāmbī. The tree within railing on one side and the bull on the other side of the coins of this ruler also show that he hailed from Kauśāmbī, for both these symbols occur on most of the coins issued from that city. King Nava was therefore most probably a Kauśāmbī ruler and had no connection with the Nāga family of Padmāvatī. Nor was he himself of Nāga extraction. He does not care to add to his name the ephithet Nāga, as was done by other Nāga rulers. There is no Nāga symbol on his coins. Kauśāmbī, which was his capital, is not mentioned in the *Purāṇas* as the seat of any Nāga family of rulers, though they mention Mathurā, Padmāvatī, Kāntipurī and Champā as the seats of Nāga families. His coins are not found at Mathurā and Padmāvatī and there is no evidence at all to show that he was the founder of the Nāga families ruling at these places. If the Bhāraśiva dynasty was a Nāga one, there is no evidence to show that King Nava was its founder.

According to Jayaswal, King Navanāga was succeeded in c. 170 AD by King Vīrasena, who was also a Nāga ruler. King Nava had ousted the Kuṣāṇas from eastern U.P.; King Vīrasena drove them from the western U.P. also and regained independence for the Madhyadeśa. He was the immediate founder of the Nāga families which according to the *Purāṇas*, were ruling at Mathurā, Padmāvatī and Kāntipurī.[21] His coins are common at Mathurā and also found in Eta, Farukkabad and Bulandshahar districts of U.P.; sometimes they are to be met with even in the eastern Punjab. It is therefore clear that he had wrested these areas from the Kuṣāṇas. This Vīrasena, who was a Nāga ruler, is however to be distinguished from another ruler, whose coins are illustrated in *IMC*, Pl. XXII, No. 19, and who was a later ruler. Smith is quite wrong in reading the legend on this coin as Vīrasena; the correct reading of the legend is Pravarasena, and the issuer is to identified with Pravarasena I, the Vākāṭaka emperor.[22]

Altekar is of opinion that Jayaswal is right in maintaining that Vīrasena was a ruler of Mathurā. But we have no evidence to show that he was himself a Nāga ruler and was the founder of the Nāga dynasties of Mathurā, Kāntipurī and Padmāvatī. Though the size of the coins of the Padmāvatī Nāga rulers is very small, every ruler of that house takes care to see that the epithet Nāga was engraved after his name on his coins. Though the size of the coins of Vīrasena is much larger, the legend does not contain the epithet Nāga after the king's name; it is simply *Vīrasenasa*. This would be rather inexpicable if Vīrasena was the founder of the Nāga greatness and the establisher of three Nāga houses. Jayaswal contends that the Nāga figure on the reverse of the coins of Vīrasena symbolically suggest his Nāga extraction. Even when their

Nāga origin hecame quite well-known in later items, the rulers of Padmāvati never thought of indicating their family name in this symbolical fashion; could then Vīrasena, the founder of the house, have remained content by suggesting his descent or family name in this dubious manner, when it was practically unknown to his contemporaries? He would have naturally adopted the last unequivocal and the most obvious method proclaiming his Nāga descent by adding the epithet Nāga after his name, as has been done by the Nāga rulers of Padmāvatī.

Altekar notes that what Jayaswal takes to be the Nāga symbol occurs not on the obverse of these coins, where the names of the King Vīrasena has been engraved, but on their reverse. If the Nāga symbol was intended to complete the legend Vīrasena into Vīrasenanāga, it should have occurred at least on the same side as the legend. But this is not the case on a single coin of Vīrasena.

Altekar points out that it is extremely doubtful whether there is Nāga symbol on these coins. On their reverse we have no doubt a vertical wavy line by the side of the deity, which can no doubt be taken to be the representation of a serpent. But it can as well be regarded as the long stalk of a flower held by the standing goddess Lakṣmī in her hand. On many Gupta coins we have the representation of a Lakṣmī holding a lotus with a long stalk in the same manner as is done on the coins of Vīrasena. See *Allan, Catalogue of Gupta Coins*, Pl. VII, No. 6 and 15; Pl. VIII, No. 6, 7 etc. In order to exclude the obvious view that on the reverse we have Lakṣmī with a lotus of long stalk, Jayaswal maintains that this goddess is the Ganges. There is, however, no evidence to support this theory. Makara, the *vāhana* of the Ganges, is nowhere represented on the reverse by the side of the deity. And Hindu mythology is unaware of the symbolism of serpent holding its hood as a canopy on the Ganges, as Jayaswal wants to interpret the reverse of the coins of Vīrasena.

According to Altekar, Jayaswal held that Vīrasena was the immediate founder of the three Nāga families of Mathurā, Kāntipurī and Padmāvatī, it was necessary for him to show that his coins are found at Padmāvatī also, as they are found at Mathurā. In order, therefore, to show that Vīrasena is also represented in the Padmāvatī Nāga coinage, Jayaswal attributes the coins illustrated in Pl. II, 13 and 14 of Cunningham's *Coins of Medieval India* to King Vīrasena. There is however no sufficient evidence to do so. Only the first letter of the legend can be read on each of these coins. On the coins in Pl. II, 13, it is distinctly *kha* and so it cannot be attributed to Vīrasena. On the coin in Pl. II 14, the letter is probably *va* and the name of the issuer may have begun with that letter. But though there is ample space over the head of this letter, it does not show any trace of the mark for medial *i*. On the other Nāga coins of Padmāvatī, medial vowels are invariably indicated and there is no reason why this should not have been done on the present coin, if it was really issued by Vīrasena, especially when there was ample space to accommodate the medial mark for *i*.

Perhaps in order to render his theory plausible that Vīrasena was a great ruler who ruled gloriously for a long time, Jayaswal observes[23] that he had issued coins of four different varieties, illustrated in *IMC*, Vol. I, Pl. XXII, 15; Cunningham, *CAI*, VIII, 18; *JRAS*, 1900, fig. 15 facing p. 97; and Cunningham, *CMI*, Pl. II, 13,14, respectively. Altekar points out in this connection that the first three of the coins referred to above are practically identical in type. All of them are rectangular in size and have on the reverse a female figure standing or sitting under a canopy with a flower of long stalk to the left. On the obverse of all of them there is the inscription at the top in a straight line and a palm tree below. Only in the case of the coin illustrated by Rapson in *JRAS*, 1900, there does not appear any palm tree on the obverse. The coin in question is however considerably worn out and it is quite possible that the palm tree symbol may have been obliterated. Vīrasena has therefore issued coins of only one variety and not of four, as mentioned by Dr. Jayaswal.

To conclude, Altekar observes that Vīrasena had issued coins of one variety only which are found usually in the upper Doab, rarely in the eastern Punjab and not at all at Padmāvatī. There is no evidence to show that he was a Nāga ruler. What is taken to be serpent raising its hood (on the reverse of his coins) is more likely to be a lotus flower with a long stalk held by Lakṣmī in her hand. He is not represented among the numerous Nāga coins found at Padmāvatī and Vidishā. Nor do his coins show any resemblance to the coinage of the Nāga rulers of Padmāvatī. The coins of Vīrasena are rectangular in size, those of the Nāga rulers are circular. The coin legend on one is at the top and in a straight line, that on the other is circular and covering the entire face. Palm tree of Vīrasena's coins never occurs on the Nāga coins, as also Lakṣmī standing under a canopy with a flower of a long stalk in her hand. Bull, peacock, wheel and trident which appear on the different Nāga coins never figure on the coins of Vīrasena.

The coins of Vīrasena thus bear no resemblance whatsoever to any known Nāga coinage. There is no evidence, epigraphical, numismatic, or literary, to show that he was a Nāga ruler, and the founder of the Nāga families of Padmāvatī, Kāntipurī, and Mathurā. The view therefore that he was a Nāga ruler and the founder of the Bhāraśiva Nāga family cannot be upheld.[24]

According to Jayaswal, the Nāga family of Vīrasena was divided into three branches after his death, the first ruling at Padmāvatī, the second at Kāntipurī and the third at Mathurā. The Mathurā rulers, he says, have left no coins. The coins of the rulers of the Padmāvatī house are well known and have been published by Cunningham in *JASB*, 1865 and require no comments. Jayaswal, however, maintains that the Kāntipurī Nāga family, ruling at Kantit in Mirzapur district, was the Bhāraśiva family and Hayanāga, Trayanāga, Barhiṇanāga, Chharajanāga and Bhavanāga were its members. Jayaswal maintains that these rulers have left their coins behind; only we failed to notice and identify them. The coins of the first four of the above rulers have been discussed and illustrated by Jayaswal in his *History*, pp. 24-28. Later on when Sir Richard Burn challenged some of Jayaswal's readings, he published two new coins in *JBORS*, Vol. XXII, pp. 70-76 and Pl. I, which he claimed were the coins of Bhavanāga and Bhīmanāga, respectively. Altekar proceeds to see whether the above coins relied upon by Dr. Jayaswal as Nāga coins really be attributed to any Nāga dynasty.

Jayaswal claims that among the unassigned, miscellaneous coins of northern India, published in the *Indian Museum Catalogue*, Vol. I. on pp. 205-6 and illustrated in Pl. XXIII, have the coins of Hayanāga, Trayanāga, Barhiṇanāga and Chharajanāga. Numismatists failed to read properly the legends on these coins and so the fact of their being issued by a Nāga dynasty remained undetected so long.

Altekar points out that as far as the coins from the Indian Museum relied upon by Dr. Jayaswal are concerned, it may be observed that their facsimilies published both by Smith in the *IMC* and Jayaswal in his *History* are very indistinct and no confident readings can be proposed with their help. Altekar took an opportunity to study the original coins in the Indian Museum in 1935 and found that only one of them, Serial No. 10, could probably be attributed to a Nāga ruler. Among the letters of the legend can be read Trayanāga or Eyanāga on the original coin but not in its photograph. There are however some letters preceding this legend. It may however be agreed with Jayaswal and tentatively assign this coin to a Nāga ruler named Trayanāga. It has however to be pointed out that legend cannot be read in the photoprint of these coins reproduced by Jayaswal in Pl. I of his *History*.

As far as the coins attributed to Chharajanāga and Barhiṇanāga are concerned, Altekar points out that the facsimiles reproduced by Dr. Jayaswal in his Pl. I, are too indistinct to permit any confident reading of their legends. When Altekar examined the original coins in 1935, he was unable to read the legends as proposed by Jayaswal. As a matter of fact the coins are in a very

Pl. 1. Midholi (Mathura Dist.): Door-jamb carved with Nāga deity (c. 9th cent. AD).

Pl. 2. Patna Museum: Nāgarāja (c. 7th cent. AD).

Pl. 3. Patna Museum: Nāga and Nāgī under snake-hood (c. 9th cent. AD)

Pl. 4. Patna Museum: Nāga (c. 10th cent. AD)

Pl. 48. Indore Museum: Ambikā.

Pl. 50. Papet (Sagar M.P.): Nāgī standing in Varada-Mudrā (c. 13th cent. AD).

Pl. 49. Sagar (M.P.): Nāga couple (c. 11th cent. AD).

poor state of preservation and no confident reading of their legends is possible, unless better preserved specimens are forthcoming.

Pl. VIII, 10-11 published in *JNSI*, V are attributed to Chharajanāga by Jayaswal. The second line on the obverse of No. 10 reads Nāgasa, and above the lion on the reverse, it is contended, there are figure symbols for 20 and 8. "It is a coin of Chharaja Nāga, dated in his 28th year." On coin No. 11 one can read Chharaja, but the reading on No. 10 seems to be Śrīchhaja. But the point at issue is not whether Chharaja or Chhaja is the correct reading, but whether this name is followed by the epithet Nāgasa in a second line. Jayaswal does not state where exactly is this second line to be looked for. Smith did not suspect its existence nor could Altekar succeed in detecting it when he examined the coin in 1935. To the left of the tree on the obverse there is most probably the figure of a man or a woman coming to worship it, vide Pl. VIII, 10. It is to the right hand side of the legend Chharaja and has been mistaken by Jayaswal for the letters *Nāgasa*, very roughly executed. But it is certain that there is no legend here, but the figure of a devotee coming to worship the tree. The coin affords no evidence to prove that Chharaja was a Nāga ruler. Jayaswal's numerical symbol for 20 on the reverse is obviously the railing of a tree.

Coins published in *IMC*, Vol. I, Plate XXIII, Nos. 9 and 12 (Pl. VIII. 9, 12 of *JNSI*, V) are taken by Jayaswal, to be the issues of Hayanāga. Altekar has examined these coins; they are in a very poor state of preservation and a confident reading of their legends is impossible. The facsimiles given both in the *IMC* and Jayaswal's *History* are useless to control and verify the reading. The legend on Pl. VIII, 12 of *JNSI* V has been read by Smith as *ratha yanagicham* (i) ta (*sa*) (?). Jayaswal reads the same legend as *[Śrī] Haya-Nāgasa*, 20, 10 and observes, "What Smith read as *ra* is probably a part of *Śrī.*" What he read as *tha* is really a *ha* and his *nāgi* is *nāga*. What he read as *chha* Altekar reads as the figure for 20. His *ma* stands for 10. Jayaswal contends that this is a coin of Hayanāga issued in his 30th regnal year. Altekar points out that the coin and its photos are too indistinct to permit a confident reading but it may be observed that Jayaswal's reading is rendered extremely suspicious, by his assumption of their being the two numerical symbols, 20 and 10. As is well known, there was one symbol for 30, and in the whole range of Indian epigraphy and numismatics there is not a single instance of 30 being denoted by two separate symbols for 20 and 10. The symbols concerned are obviously letters *tha* and *ma*; this would render the reading of the whole legend as proposed by Jayaswal extremely dubious.

In *IMC*, Vol. I, Pl. XXIII (Pl. VIII, 9 of *JNSI*, V), Jayaswal can read the legend *Hayasa* only by supposing that the legend is reversed; he reads it *sayaha*. Reversed legends on ancient Indian coins are not quite unknown; but they are very rare. The facsimile in the *IMC* however shows that the letters *sayaha* also cannot be read. What is taken to be a *sa* (at X) is most probably a cross of the Ujjayinī symbol joined to a depression at the top of the coin. Hayanāga flourished according to Jayaswal in c. 250 AD, the second letter (at VIII) looks like *ya* of the 3rd century BC and not of the 3rd century AD. It is most probably a *na* as was supposed by Smith. What is taken to be a *ha* (at VI) is clearly a railing. The reading *sayaha* is therefore impossible and it cannot be attributed to Haya even by supposing that the legend is reversed. It is further to be noted that the epithet *nāga* does not appear after the name of the ruler.

IMC, Vol. I, Pl. XXIII, No. 13 (Pl. VIII, 13 of *JNSI*, V) is taken by Jayaswal to be a coin of Barhiṇanāga. Here again it has to be noted that the facsimile is poor and the legend not free from doubt. Smith doubtfully read the legend on the obverse as (?) *gabhemanapa,* adding that only *bha* and *na* were certain. Jayaswal reads it as *Śrī Ba (r) hinasa.* A glance at Pl. VIII, 13 of *JNSI*, V or at the plate either of Smith or of Jayaswal shows that we cannot hope to check either of these readings from the facsimiles. The coin itself is too blurred to permit any confident reading. There is a peacock on the reverse of this coin, which perhaps may be supposed to lend support to the view that the coin is of Barhiṇanāga. But we have peacocks on the coins of rulers who did not bear this name, as is shown by the coins of Bhīmanāga and Skandanāga of the Padmāvatī series. On the reverse of this coin Jayaswal reads the legend (*nā*) *ga* (*sa*). He is sure only of the letter *ga*. On the facsimile we can however read the letter *pa* at II. The reading Nāgasa is therefore very problematical even on Jayaswal's admission. It is therefore extremely doubtful whether this coin was issued by Barhiṇa, and if so, whether this ruler was a Nāga prince.

Out of the four Nāga successors of Vīrasena postulated by Jayaswal, it is thus seen that Trayanāga alone is perhaps probable. The legend on the coins attributed to Hayanāga, Barhiṇanāga and Chharajanāga are extremely blurred and cannot be read with any reasonable certainty or probability. Nor are the find spots of these coins known; there is therefore no evidence to show that these kings were ruling at Kantit or Kāntipurī and belonged to the Bhāraśiva house.

The last ruler of the Bhāraśiva dynasty, according to Jayaswal, was Bhavanāga. At the time of the publication of his *History* Jayaswal could rely only on the references to this ruler in the Vākāṭaka records; later on, however, he published a coin of this ruler also in *JBORS*, Vol. XXII, pp. 72-73, belonging to the collection of Babu Sri Nath Sah of Benares. As the facsimile published by Jayaswal along with this paper could not prima facie support his reading of the legend, Altekar requested Babu Sri Nath Sah to lend him this coin for study and permit him to publish it afresh with a better facsimile. He was kind enough to accede to his request, and the coin is illustrated in Pl. VIII, 17 of *JNSI*, V.

On the reverse of this coin Jayaswal reads the legend (*Śrī*) *Bhavanāgo* in front of the bull. He observes, 'The head of the first syllable *Śrī* is worn off leaving only traces. The box on the heads of *bha, va* and *na* exists in outlines, and the syllable *go* has become faint: all the other letters still stand out in bold relief. The hanging line of *bha* was cut thinner in the original mould.'

Altekar points out that there is no doubt that this coin bears an inscription. It is one of those rare Lankey Bull types of Kauśāmbī coins which are inscribed. Allan has published another inscribed coin of this type with the legend *Kosa [m] bi (Catalogue*, Introduction, pp. xcviii-xcix). The point at issue is not whether Lankey Bull types of coins are inscribed, but whether the inscription on the present coin can be read as *Śrībhavanāgo*, as contended by Jayaswal. He admits that the first letter (at II), taken as *Śrī* by him, is worn off. Altekar has examined the original coin carefully and to him it appears more like a *ma* than *Śrī*. The facsimile published by Jayaswal, as also the new one published in Pl. VIII, 17 of *JNSI*, V, show that this letter is most probably a *ma*. One cannot be, however, certain about it. In the facsimile published by Jayaswal, as well as on the original coin, the second letter certainly appears as a *ka* and not as a *bha*. The right hand horizontal limb of *ka* is slightly shorter than the left hand one. But it can be clearly seen in Jayaswal's facsimile also. There it appears slightly detached from the vertical of *ka;* but such is not the case on the original coin, as can be seen from its fresh facsimile (Pl. VIII, 17 of *JNSI*, V). Jayaswal pleads that the hanging line of *bha* was cut thinner; it can hardly be detected in his facsimile and does not exist at all on the original coin. The third letter is taken by Jayaswal as *va*; but his own facsimile as well as the one published in *JNSI*, V, show that it can be *vi* and nothing else. The fourth letter is no doubt *na* or *nā*, but there is no letter after it.

Nor has any of these letters a box-head as contended by Jayaswal. The right hand limb of *ka* and the medial *i* mark of *vi* are taken by Jayaswal as parts of the box-heads over these letters. A glance at the Vākāṭaka plates in box-headed characters will however show that the 'boxes' were always engraved to the left side of each letter and not to its right side, as assumed here by Jayaswal. Prima facie therefore what Jayaswal has taken to be box- heads cannot be so regarded at all. An examination of the enlarged facsimile of this coin published by Jayaswal will show that the second and third letters of the legend are ordinary form of *ka* and *vi* and not box-headed forms of *bha* and *va.* This will be absolutely clear from the facsimile of the coin published in *JNSI*, V.

Altekar points out that the legend on this so-called coin of Bhavanāga is partly obliterated and no definite reading can be proposed of the whole of it. But it is absolutely certain that the letters taken to be *bha* and *va* are *ka* and *vi*, respectively. The name Bhavanāga cannot be read on the coin and it cannot be attributed to him. He has read the legend as *ma (?) kavina nā(?).*

Along with the so-called coin of Bhavanāga, Jayaswal has published another coin, which he attributes to Bhīmanāga. This coin also belongs to the valuable collection of Babu Sri Nath Sah of Benares, who was good enough to lend it to Altekar for study and publication in *JNSI*, V, Pl. VIII, 18.

As per Altekar, Jayaswal reads the legend Bhīmasa on the elephant side of this coin, but does not state where exactly we can find it. Altekar saw no traces of any of the letters *bhī, ma* or *sa,* either in Jayaswal's facsimile or on the original coin. On the head of the elephant there are probably traces of *triratna* symbol, which is quite common on the Kauśāmbī coins of this type. It is probably traces of this symbol which may have been regarded as parts of a legend by Jayaswal. Altekar examined both the obverse and reverse of this coin carefully and found no traces of any legend anywhere.

To conclude, Altekar is of the opinion that the coins of the rulers of Mathurā with *datta*-ending names cannot be attributed to any Nāga family ruling before the Christian Era. Kings Nava and Vīrasena have issued coins and were ruling in the Gangetic Doab, but there is no evidence whatsoever to show that they were Nāga rulers, or were the founders of the Bhāraśiva dynasty. Coins attributed to Hayanāga, Barhiṇanāga and Chharajanāga are so blurred that no definite readings can be proposed of the legends partially legible on them. Most probably they are not Nāga coins; even if they are supposed to be Nāga issues, there is no evidence to connect the issuers with the Kāntipurī Bhāraśiva family of Jayaswal. The coin attributed to Bhīmanāga bears no inscription and the one attributed to Bhavanāga bears the legend *ma* (?) *kavina*, and so cannot have been an issued of Bhavanāga, the maternal grandfather of the Vākāṭaka ruler Rudrasena. If Nāgas were powerful rulers who had ousted the Kuṣāṇas and performed ten horse sacrifices, they have left no coins which can lend any support to such a claim.

According to Altekar so far no coins of any Nāga families ruling either at Mathurā or at Kāntipurī have been found. The only Nāga coins known so far are the Nāga coins of the rulers of Padmāvatī. When Cunningham published them in 1865, seven rulers of the series were known – Bhīmanāga, Skandanāga,

Bṛhaspatināga, Vyāghranāga, Vasunāga, Devanāga and Gaṇapatināga. Subsequently, coins of Prabhākaranāga were discovered and published by Rapson in *JRAS*, 1901, p. 116 and accompanying Pl. In number IV of *JNSI*, Altekar has published the coins of two new Nāga rulers, Vibhunāga and Bhavanāga, and shown that Bhāraśiva Bhavanāga most probably belonged to the Nāga family of Padmāvatī. In *JNSI*, V, V.S. Agrawal has published a coin of another new Nāga ruler named Puṁnāga.

Many of the above-mentioned arguments advanced by Altekar against the Nāga attribution of the Datta rulers of Mathurā are now outdated in the light of the two coins of Nāgarāja Śeṣadatta discovered at Gwalior. As per Dr. Santlal Katare who has edited them in *JNSI*, XXXIV, pt. II (1972) and has written a detailed note on the subject in the *Journal of Indian History*, Vol. LIV, pt. I-II, 1977,[25] Nāgarāja Śeṣadatta was the founder of the earlier Vidishā branch of the Nāgas which reigned during the later half of 1st century BC.

Of the earlier coins of Śeṣadatta, three come from the White King collection,[26] three from Sir Richard Burn,[27] one from the British Museum,[28] and of the two from Hastinapur,[29] only one[30] may be confidently attributed to Śeṣadatta.

As per Dr. Katare one of the coins has a horizontal legend in the Brāhmī characters above the figure of Lakṣmī and it reads *Rājño Śeśadatasa*, and the symbol 'A' that looks like the Brahmi *śa*, on the *obverse*, and the symbol formed of two *Nāgas* (serpents), facing each other with what looks like a post in between them and coiled up over a rectangular but hollow basement, a *pīṭhikā* perhaps, on the reverse. The second coin follows the same patterns of the obverse and the reverse designs, although it is of a different metal, size and weight. Although it is worn out, the figure of Lakṣmī and the *Śeṣadatasa* part of the legend can be easily identified. Other symbols, if any, are all effaced. The reverse design is the same as on the first coin, with the only difference that on this coin the Nāgas coil up on what looks like a straight line and that it has some traces of what may or may not have been a symbol. That Brāhmī *śa*-like symbol A had occurred on this coin also, may be presumed.

Dr. Katare is of opinion that the symbol A, like the Brāhmī *śa*, on the above coins of Śeṣadatta occurs on his all other coins.[31] It also occurs on those of kings Puruṣadatta, [32] Uttamadatta,[33] Rāmadatta I, Kāmadatta,[34] Bhavadatta[35] and Rāmadatta II[36] all associated with Mathurā,[37] but not on the coins of any other king associated with Mathurā[38] or any other place. This leads to the inference that Śeṣadatta of the two coins from Gwalior is no other than Śeṣadatta of the other coins, and that he and the other kings with *datta*-ending names associated with Mathurā belonged to the same ruling house. The reverse design of the Nāga symbol on the two Gwalior coins distinguished them not only from the other coins of Śeṣadatta which have wheel on *chaitya*[39] as their reverse design, but also from those of his and of the other kings associated with Mathurā which have three, sometimes one, elephant as their reverse design.[40] The symbol has been identified as the *Śrīvatsa* symbol.[41] In almost an exactly similar form as on the present two coins, the symbol occurs on an image of Viṣṇu from Vidishā[42] and on another, of Viṣṇu again, in the Udayagiri Cave No. 6 near Vidishā.[43] On an image of Narasiṁha, which also comes from Vidishā[44] although the symbol is damaged and not quite distinct, its form appears to be similar. The only difference that may be noted between its form on the present coins and the one of the above images is that while on the coins the two Nāgas coil up on a *pīṭhikā* or what looks like a straight line, on the images they do not have such basement.[45] In another from, evolved from the above, it occurs on another image of Viṣṇu from Vidishā[46] yet again and on a railing from Barhut.[47]

In an exactly form as on the three images, two from Vidishā and one from the Udayagiri Cave No. 6, noted above, the symbol occurs on some punch-marked coins from Vidishā,[48] on some others, punch-marked again, whose provenance is not known,[49] on some Yaudheya coins[50] and on those of the Kulūta king Virayaśa[51] while on the coins of Viśākhadeva of Ayodhyā,[52] two Kuninda kings, Amoghabuti[53] and Bhagavata Chatreśvara Mahātmanaḥ[54] it is found with the minor modification that the post in between the two Nāgas is replaced by a triangular dot at their lower ends.

Katare records that on all the coins noted above, the symbol occurs as one of the many, either on the obverse or on the reverse, and not, as on the present coins of Śeṣadatta, exclusively as the reverse design. This makes all the difference in the significance of its association with the coins of Śeṣadatta from the one with all the other coins. Its association with the coins of Śeṣadatta as their exclusively reverse design and with the two images from Vidishā and the one from Udayagiri noted above, leads to the conclusion that it was characteristic of coins and images of the Vidishā region, rather associated with the Vidishā region. The origin of the two coins may then be traced to Vidishā, and if they are found at Gwalior, it is because they were in circulation in this region also. What follows is that the reverse design of one or three elephants on the coins of Śeṣadatta from Hastināpur and Mathurā and on those of the other kings with *mitra-* and *datta*-ending names, from Mathurā and its vicinity, was characteristic of coins which had their origin at Mathurā. Under the circumstances the origin of coins of Śeṣadatta which have wheel on *chaitya* as their reverse design may have to be traced to a different place than to Vidishā or to Mathurā. Since the symbol is not noticed on any other coin, punch-marked or otherwise, it is not possible to identify the place.

Katare opines: "The mintage of coins of Śeṣadatta at Vidishā and Mathurā and their find from excavation at Hastināpur would suggest that he ruled over a vast territory in Middle India which extended from Hastināpur down to Vidishā and included Mathurā, and Kāntipurī (modern Kotwar)[55] in the Morena district, and Padmāvatī (modern Padam Pawāyā)[56] in the Gwalior district, of M.P. The find of coins of Puruṣadatta at Bhuila near Kapilavastu in the Basti district of U.P.,[57] of Uttamadatta at Sunet some four miles west of Ludhiana in the Punjab,[58] and of Rāmadatta at Indore Khera[59] eight miles SSW of Anupshahar in U.P., and Chitor[60] in Rajasthan, might suggest that the kings with *datta* ending names had their dominion extended to the borders of Rajasthan and it included some portions of western U.P."

"The Nāga symbol as the reverse design of the coins of Śeṣadatta and its association with Vidishā also suggests that he was no other than the *Nāgarāja* Śeṣa of the *Purāṇas*.[61] He had a son, who is called Bhogin, and as stated before, he is spoken of in such glorious terms as *para-purañjayaḥ* and *Nāgakulodvahaḥ*.[62] But, what relationship Sadāchandra, Chandrāmśa who is praised as the second *'Nakhavanta'*, Dhanadharmman, Vaṅgāra and Bhūtinanda, included in the Purāṇic list of Vidishā kings had between themselves or with Śeṣadatta, is not indicated. None of them is known from coins or any other source. Whether they were connected with Mathurā, is also not known. But, when the *Purāṇas* say that these kings preceded the Śuṅgas at Vidishā,[63] the authenticity of their list of the Vidishā kings becomes at once questionable. It appears that names of some kings who ruled from Vidishā or elsewhere sometime between the first and the third centuries AD were collected together by some annalist of the ilk of Tārānatha into a list of kings of Vidishā in the most arbitrary fashion. Of these king Bhūtinanda, a corruption from Bhūtinandi evidently, appears to have belonged to the family to which Śivanandi of the Padam Pawāyā Maṇibhadra image inscription[64] belonged. So were it seems Śiśunandi and Nāndiyaśas (Yaśonandi), both of whom (and some others also) according to the *Purāṇas* ruled from Vidishā after the Śuṅgas.[65] The epigraphy of Śivanandi's inscription would suggest that he ruled about a couple of centuries later than the Śuṅgas. Vaṅgāra appears to be more of a sphinx or the mere ghost of some copyist's imagination.[66] Dhanadharmman is an equally mysterious name. Whether Sadāchandra and Chandrāmśa were of Nāga origin and ruled from Vidishā or in some neighbouring region, remain uncertain; it appears that they were Nāga kings."

To quote Dr. Katare, again, "If Śeṣadatta was a Nāga king, the other kings of Mathurā whose names end in *datta* were also Nāgas. Whether all of them ruled from Vidishā also, may be speculated upon the evidence of the *Purāṇas*, which in their present corrupt forms associated seven Nāga kings with Mathurā and the *Nava-Nāgas* with Champāvatī (Padmāvatī in some texts) or Padmāvatī, Kāntipurī and Mathurā.[67] Even if it is reprehensible to amend a text for its reconstruction, with the help of the evidence discussed above the Padam Pawāyā Maṇibhadra image inscription of Śivanandi,[68] the Allahabad inscription of Samudragupta[69] in so far as it relates to the mention of some Nāga kings, the Seoni copperplate inscription of the Vākāṭaka Pravarasena II[70] in so far a it relates to Bhavanāga, and the *Harṣacarita* in so far as it relates to the mention of Nāgasena,[71] and the coins it may be suggested that the *Purāṇas*, before they had corrupted into the present form, read as:

Nava-Nāgāstu bhokshyanti purīṁ Padmāvatīṁ tathā
Kāntipurīṁ purīm Mathurām Nāgā bhokshyanti sapta vai.

This makes some sense if not all: That seven Nāga kings ruled from Mathurā and Vidishā, therefore from Padmāvatī and Kāntipurī also, the evidence discussed above bears out and the *Nava-Nāgas* only from Padmāvatī and Kāntipurī the one discussed below. Besides these, there were other Nāga kings also, of another branch of the family, who ruled from Kāntipurī and Padmāvatī, and if we trust the *Purāṇas*[72] from Vidishā also."

The Nāga kings appear to have lost Mathurā to the Śakas sometime when Śeṣadatta was king or soon after when his son Bhogin, who is said to have ruled from Vidishā according to the *Purāṇas*, came to the throne. Their loss of Mathurā to the Śakas is evidenced by the coins of Śivadatta who holds the title Kṣatrapa. Possibly he joined hands with the Śakas against his own kinsmen and was rewarded with the office of the Kṣatrapa of Mathurā for his treachery. He does not appear to have held the office long and was replaced by Hagāmaṣa, a Śaka himself perhaps. It is not unlikely that the Śakas had wanted one of their kinsmen to hold charge of the office of the Kṣatrapa of Mathurā because of the great strategic importance of the city.

What happened to the Nāgas after they had lost Mathurā to the Śakas, is too obscure to be connected into a story. It appears that Bhogin, son of Śeṣadatta, was required to do some hard fighting with the Śakas to retain his hold over regions south of Mathurā. That the Śakas carried war into the heart of the Nāga dominion, even beyond, finds ample support from a Bheraghat image inscription of the time of Mahārāja Bhūvaka,[73] the Baghora inscription of Śivaghoṣa,[74] the Eran inscription of a Śaka chieftain whose name is lost,[75] and the Kanakhera (Sanchi)[76] and Eran[77] inscription of the śaka

Śrīdharavarmman. Bhogin's claims of victory over his enemies and as the exalter of the Nāga family, would then stand substantiated, although in a conventional way only. From the evidence it is certain that he had not been able to recover Mathurā from the Śakas; but his success in beating them back from Padmāvatī-Kāntipurī region was in itself quite adequate to justify the claims. His success was, however, short lived, for clouds of misfortune came crashing down upon the Nāgas from another direction and not long after they lost Vidishā to the Sātavāhanas who had failed to conquer it before when their king Sātakarṇī I conquered Tripuri[78] and Ujjain[79] sometime about the middle of the second century BC. The evidence of Sātavāhana occupation of Vidishā begins to appear from the close of the first century BC or the first century AD, that is about the same time as the Śaka conquest of Mathurā, when coins of Sātakarṇī II begin to appear in the region. The Sanchi railing inscription of Sātakarṇī II is an indisputable evidence of the Sātavāhana occupation of Vidishā.[80] The Sātavāhanas were finally driven away from Vidishā by the Śakas[81] and the Śakas by Samudragupta.[82]

Dr. Katare says that the Nāgas appear to have retained their hold over Padmāvatī and Kāntipurī somehow, if Śivanandi of the Maṇibhadra inscription, Śiśunandi, Yaśonandi, and Bhūtinandi of the *Purāṇas* belonged to the Nāga family; if they did, they were of a different branch, and unlike the Nāgas of Mathurā who were the followers of Viṣṇu, they were Śaivites. How long kings with *nandi*-ending names ruled and how they disappeared from the scene is not known. The ambition of the Kuṣāṇas who had supplanted the Śaka rule in Mathurā in meantime and who sought expansion of their dominion southward, added to their misfortune. Even if the Sanchi image inscription of Vāsaṣka dated in the year 28[83] of the Era used by the Kuṣāṇas is a slender evidence of a Kuṣāṇa occupation of the Padmāvatī-Kāntipurī region, for the image, of Mathurā red sandstone as it is, might easily have been carved and inscribed at Mathurā, and carried to Sanchi to be installed there, there is no denying the fact that under the stress of a long struggle with the Śakas, the Sātavahanas and the Kuṣāṇas, the Nāgas were overwhelmed temporarily, until a new line of the family with *nāga*-ending names retrieved their fortune and restored their dominion in the Padmāvatī-Kāntipurī region, as would the enormous quantity of coins of these kings from the above region indicate.[84] The epigraphy of the coins suggests that the kings with *nāga*-ending names ruled for about two centuries before they were wiped out by Samudragupta.[85]

It is these kings who are evidently referred to as the *Nava-Nāgas* in the *Purāṇas*.[86] and in view of the fact that the number of these kings is more than nine and of the evidence discussed above, '*Nava*' should be interpreted to mean 'New' and not 'Nine'. All this evidence would further lead to the conclusion that while Nāga kings with *datta*-ending names ruled over a dominion which included Hastināpur, Mathurā, Kāntipurī, Padmāvatī and Vidishā, those with *nandi*-ending names and the *Nava-Nāgas* ruled over the one which included only Kāntipurī and Padmāvatī.

The credit of conducting a detailed examination of thousands of coins of later Nāga dynasty preserved in the Gwalior Museum goes to Dr. H.V. Trivedi who has published a *Catalogue of the Coins of the Nāga Kings of Padmāvatī*,[87] bringing to light the names of twelve Nāga rulers. Also, he has framed a tentative chronology of these rulers.

According to Dr. Trivedi[88] the originator of the house appears to be Vṛṣa, whose coins he has published in the *JNSI*, XV, p. 121. Referring to the Pauranic statement '*Vaideśikāstu Vṛṣabhāḥ*,' he has concluded that he began to rule at Bhilsā and the palaeography of the legend on his coin shows his time to be the latter part of the second century AD. About his Nāga lineage he was not then certain, but this became more definite in view of more coins of this ruler discovered at Padmāvatī. Bhilsā appears to have been a stronghold of the house; a number of Nāga coins were found in excavations at that place by D.R. Bhandarkar,[89] and even today a very large number of this series of coins, obtained from the ancient site of Vidishā, can be seen in the local market.

Vṛṣa or Vṛṣabhava seems to have been followed by Bhīma, whose coins bear the legend in two horizontal lines, and not in a circle around the edge, as we find on those of the other members of the house. His legend is in Prakrit, ending in *sa*, and the palaeography is earlier. The epithet of Mahārāja and the way of engraving the legend in two horizontal lines reminds of the coins which were found at Pawāyā and were published by Dr. Trivedi in *JNSI*.[90] Thus it is possible to hold that Bhīma, who was probably the earliest of the rulers to shift to that place, may have imitated this design.

Dr. K.P. Jayaswal tentatively placed Bhīma from c. 210 to c. 230 AD; and Dr. Trivedi's examination of the palaeography of the legend on his coins goes to support the same.

Bhīma's immediate successor, according to Jayaswal, was Skanda. The learned scholar gave no reasons for holding this view, but on the evidence of the peacock emblem and the study of the palaeography of the letters in his legend, Dr. Trivedi tempted to agree with him. It is true that identity of types and palaeography of letters are not sure grounds for fixing the order of succession among rulers; but in the absence of any other evidence, this alone is the guide.

The 'dagger and the peacock emblem' was adopted by three ruling members belonging to this house, viz., by Bhīma, Skanda and Vasu. Thus Skanda and Vasu do not appear to have been far removed in time from Bhīma who may have adopted it originally. They were his successors, as they give the legend ending in *sya*, unlike Bhīma, on whose coins it ends in Prakrit, in *sa*, as seen above.

The coins of Skanda and Vasu are marked by another peculiarity; a number of them appear to be re-struck or counter-struck, their original device being obliterated beyond recognition, leaving only traces to be detected. This may go to indicate some political disturbance, the nature of which is unknown.

Dr. Trivedi assigns the next member of the house to be Bṛhaspati, whose coins show a slight advancement in palaeography. He also issued coins with the symbol of a couchant bull, as we find on those issued by Skanda, whose peacock-type connects with Bhīma on the one hand, and the bull type, with Bṛhaspati, on the other.

Dr. Trivedi presumes that if the order of succession among these fives rulers, viz., Vṛṣa, Bhīma, Skanda, Vasu and Bṛhaspati, is correct, the last of these kings appears to have closed his reign sometime about the end of the third century AD, calculating each of the reigns to be of about 20 years.

Dr. Trivedi notes that excepting Vṛṣa no other ruler from among those mentioned above uses the honorific *Śrī* with his name. Another peculiarity is that each of the rulers beginning from Bhīma issued coins with the emblem used by his predecessor and added at least one device of his own. Thus on the coins of Bhīma and Vasu the peacock always faces the left, whereas Skanda, who also issued coins with the emblem of a bull, always to right, depicts on his coins the figure of a peacock facing right also; and Bṛhaspati, who follows the bull type, introduces the trident type. All these points go to show that these five rulers belonged to the earlier stock of the Nāga house of Padmāvatī.

From about the close of the third to that of the fourth century AD, towards which the house was exterminated by Samudragputa, Dr. Trivedi places the following rulers: Vibhu, Ravi, Prabhākara, Bhava, Deva and Gaṇapati. Of these, Ravi, only three of whose coins were made available to Dr. Trivedi, appears to have had a very short reign. Bhava has been known to be ruling from c. 310 to c. 345 AD and Deva, who uses *'Indra'* with his name, like Gaṇapati, may be placed just before him. About the relative priority between Vibhu and Prabhākara, nothing can be definitely stated; the former of these may perhaps be placed before the latter, in view of the fact that the animal on his coins is exactly similar to that on those of the latter, who also uses the new device of a lion. After Bhava, Trivedi places Deva between him and Gaṇapati. Prabhākara seems to have seen a successor of Bhava in view of the study of palaeography of the letters of their legends. In the light of the above discussion, the order of succession among these rulers may, as proposed by Trivedi, be as follows: Vibhu, Ravi, Bhava, Prabhākara, Deva and Gaṇapati.

On the basis of numismatic evidence, Dr. Trivedi presumes[91] that of the later Nāgas, there was only one single Nāga kingdom with its capital at Padmāvatī and that Mathurā and Kāntipurī were subsidiary capitals or important places in the Nāga territory. The statement of the *Viṣṇu Purāṇa* mentioning the Nāgas as ruling at the three places does not make any distinction in this respect; and the seven Nāga rulers who are mentioned in the *Vāyu Purāṇa* as holding sway over Mathurā may have been out of the same nine who flourished at Padmāvatī. Coins of the same house are found at all the three places. In this connection it may be pointed out that Dr. Trivedi's suggestions are only tentative and nothing final may be said at this stage till strong evidences are found.

The Nāgas of Padmāvatī with their subsidiary branches at Kāntipurī and Mathurā made unique contribution in different spheres of cultural activities.

In the matter of administration, scholars have suggested that the different capitals of the Nāgas within and outside of Madhya Pradesh had formed one confederation amongst themselves and they were governed by the republican form of government with their chief capital at Padmāvatī.[92] The precise nature of administration cannot be determined in the existing stock of knowledge. It was the united effort of the Nāgas of Padmāvatī and their contemporaries, viz., the Yaudheyas, the Arjunāyanas, the Kunindas and the Mālavas who worked in their individual way and with resources that they could command, but almost simultaneously, that was responsible for the overthrow of Kuṣāṇa power in Northern India.

In the matter of religion, the Nāgas of Padmāvatī and other allied branches were not followers of snake-worship. The *Purāṇas* have designated them as 'Vṛṣa', i.e., 'Nandi' of Śiva. That the Nāgas were devout followers of Śiva is evidenced by their names, their coins, the art and other archaeological remains that they have left as well as numerous epigraphic and literary references. The Bhāraśiva Nāgas were so much devoted to Śaivism that they always used to carry Śiva 'Liṅga' with them. On their coins and sculptures were carved Śaiva symbols of Triśūla, Nandi, Siṁha, Mayūra, along with Nāga and Nāga-Chhatra.

They were devout worshippers of the river goddess Gaṅgā, whose sculptures have been found from Vidishā and Jankhat. The Bhāraśiva Nāgas performed ten Aśvamedha *Yajñas* on the bank of the Gaṅgā and, as per K.P. Jayaswal, the Daśāśvamedha Ghāṭa of Varanasi was possibly originally constructed and named by them in commemoration of their victory over the Kuṣāṇas and performance of the *Daśāśvamedha Yajña.* They also possibly worshipped Viṣṇu and Sūrya and this is evidenced by archaeological remains at Padmāvatī. They were worshippers of palm tree and palm leaf motif formed a part of their national flag. The palm leaf motif is found on their coins as well as in the form of sculptural representation.

The sculptural and architectural remains from Pawāyā (60 km to the south-west of Gwalior and situated on the confluence of the river Sindhu and Parvati) which is the original site of Padmāvatī gives a peep into the cultural life of the people. The site of the original town is studded with numerous antiquities and carved fragments ranging in date from 1st to 8th centuries AD. Of the sculptural remains, the life-size free-standing statue of Yakṣa Maṇibhadra with Brāhmī inscription of about the 1st century AD,[93] datable to Nāga rule, is the most ancient. The importance of the statue lies in the fact that it is one of those Yakṣa statues which are peculiarly Indian in their outlook. In their dress and ornamentations these Yakṣa figures reflect primitiveness in Indian art, but they represent the earliest phase of the indigenous art of India.

Other important specimen are the pieces of two fan-palm capitals.[94] These are of white sandstone and fairly well-polished on the surface. The capital is shaped like a cylinder tapering towards the top covered with three courses of palm leaves, with a closed bud at the top and branches of fruit in the intervals between the leaves. The top-bud and the uppermost course of leaves are pointed upwards, while the two courses point downwards. A lion rampant is seated on a leaf in the lowermost course.

Some statues of Nāga and Nāgī, both in human and serpent form, have been found from Vidishā[95] and Sanchi[96] which originally formed the territory of the Nāgas. The Nāga of Sanchi is six feet and seven inches in height and is of grey-white sandstone. The Nāga possesses seven hoods, holds an uncertain object (lotus) in the right hand, and a flask in the left. The style proclaims it to be a clumsy work of the first or second century AD. Nearby is a smaller figure of a Nāgī of the same age and style. Similar Nāga and Nāgī sculptures datable to about second century AD have also been found at Gulgaon in Raisen district.[97]

At Padmāvatī, other important archaeological finds comprise an image of four-armed Viṣṇu, a double-faced sun capital, the statue of a Nāga king, a large carved fragment of a huge gateway lintel containing in relief scenes from Hindu mythology and the sculpture of a Nandi having body of a man with bull's face.[98] A stone slab containing the scene of a dance accompanied by music, reflecting an important aspect of the social life of common man is a masterpiece of Nāga sculptural art.

In the archaeological excavations conducted at Pawāyā, one of the mounds standing near the northern bank of the river has revealed an interesting terraced brick structure consisting of three platforms, placed one upon the other, receding in suitable proportion.[99] It seems that the top platform once occupied a superstructure, which should have been the shrine proper, the remains of which are not traceable now. The two other platforms below probably served the purpose of a path of circumambulation or *pradakṣiṇāpatha*, all around the structure. The shrine was sacred to Viṣṇu as is evidenced by the discovery of an image of that god as well as other terracotta figurines depicting Brahmanical subjects. The site has also yielded a number of beautifully modelled terracotta figures and figurines which, probably once, adorned the side-walls of the temple. They consist of numerous human busts and heads with beautiful expressions and fine arrangements of hair. All these antiquities, along with coins are now preserved in the State Archaeological Museum at Gwalior.

The coins issued by the Nāgas of Padmāvatī are the main source of information for this dynasty. Coins of this series are uniform in type, almost from the beginning to the end of the dynasty. They are of copper, and none of the rulers of this ruling house is known to have issued gold or silver coins as in case of other contemporary dynasties. The coins are die-struck and round in shape, their diameter varying from about 0.3" to 0.55" and weight from about 5 to 60 grains. A few specimens, however, show the rectangular shape. Their size recalls that of the coins of the Mālwas, who were their contemporaries.

On one side of the coins of this series is found a symbol in a circle of pellets, and from this point of view they may be taken to fall into two main groups, one, bearing the figure of a peacock, and the other, of a humped bull, to right or to left, recumbent, standing or walking. Some of the Nāga rulers issued coins with an additional recurring symbol. These symbols are: a trident, a crescent, a lion and a wheel. Excepting the last one, all these are Śaivite emblems.

The other side of these coins recalls that of the silver coins of the Western Kṣatrapas of Malwa and Saurashtra, in showing the circular Brāhmī legend, around the edge, only with a few exceptions. The legend usually commences at VII, with the title of Mahārāja (in one case, Adhirāja), followed by the name of the king and dynastic name 'Nāga'. Often the honorific *Śrī* is placed before the name of the ruler.

The legend on most of these coins is fragmentary or imperfect, and very often the medial vowels are partially or wholly missing. This is because sometimes the die is not equal in size with the flan or is wrongly arranged on it. Recent researches have shown that there was great influence of the Nāga coins on the coinage of the Vākāṭakas who were matrimonially related to them.[100]

Important light on the geography and topography of the city of Padmāvatī is provided by Bhavabhūti in his *Mālatimādhava*. Act IX of the drama gives a vivid account of the rivers Sindhu and Pārā, on the confluence of which the city was habited. It provides details of the high ranking buildings, the palace, the temples, the city, its roads, entrance and the waterfall. The people, the trees of various kinds, the garden and flowers and fruits and the Śiva temple of 'Suvarṇabindu' have all been vividly described by Bhavabhūti who had come from Vidarbha to live in this city as a student to learn *Nyāyaśāstra*, implying thereby that Padmāvatī was, during his times, recognised as a celebrated centre of learning. Bhavabhūti's account of the city has been repeated in a Chandella inscription dated AD 1000 found from Khajuraho in the following words: "This most excellent town named Padmāvatī, built in an unprecedented manner, was crowded with lofty rows of streets of palaces, in which tall houses were curvetting. With its shining white topped walls, which gazed the clouds, it irradiated the sky; (and) it was full of bright palatial dwellings that resembled the peaks of the snowy mountain."[101]

Besides the Nāga houses mentioned above, there appears to have been others smaller Nāga principalities in different parts of North India immediately before the rise of the Guptas. Thus, a copper seal inscription of the fourth century AD speaks of a king name Maheśvaranāga, the son of Nāgabhaṭṭa.[102] Some coins found at Ahichchhatra, having close resemblence to that of the Nāgas, refer to a king named Achyuta, who thus may have been a Nāga king, and was ultimately couquered by Samudragupta. The Allahabad Pillar Inscription further refers to kings like Nāgadatta, Nandi and others who were also rulers of the Nāga stock. Dr. Raychaudhuri points out that in the *Purāṇas*, Śisunandi and Nandiyaśas are connected with the Nāga family of Central India. We also know the name of a Nāga prince named Śivanandi.[103] We come across another Nāga family settled at Eran.

The ancient city of Erikiṇa corresponding with modern Eran, about 9 km from Mandi-Bamora railway station on South-East Railway. in Sagar district of M.P. is a place of great antiquity, as it was capital of several ruling dynasties in ancient India. The abundant archaeological wealth of this site is a witness to the importance that it enjoyed during the ancient times. That a powerful Nāga family of warriors used to reside here during the middle of the 4th century AD has been evidenced by the discovery of a stone pillar inscription of Śaka Kṣatrapa ruler Śrīdharavarman who flourished from AD 339 to 368.

As per description given in the inscription (vide, Mirashi, V.V., CII, IV, pt. II, Ins. No. 119, pp. 605-11), the pillar was erected by Satyanāga who was the Senāpati of Śaka king Śrīdharavarman. The purpose of erecting the pillar was to commemorate some great battle fought at Erikiṇa in which several Nāga soldiers are said to have met their heroic death. This is indicated by the original sculptures carved on it. On each of the three faces of its middle octagonal part on the same side as the present inscription, there is a compartment showing a horseman holding the reins of his horse in the left hand and a sword or a javelin in the right. In the inscription Satyanāga expresses the hope that the *Yaṣṭi* (memorial pillar) raised by the Nāgas themselves would inspire future generations of war-like people to perform similar heroic deeds, for it was a place where friends and foes met in a spirit of service and reverence. The description fits well with Eran, as it was the battle-ground of hostile powers for many centuries, as shown by several *Sati* stones, and inscriptions with dates ranging from the fourth to the eighteenth century AD (vide, Cunningham, ASI Reports, X, pp. 89ff) found from this place. An interesting information given in the present inscription is that the family of Satyanāga is said to have migrated from Maharashtra. No further information about this Nāga family or its successors is available.

REFERENCES

1. Jivananda Bhattacharya (ed.), *Viṣṇu Purāṇa*, p. 585; Pargiter, *The Purana Text of the Dynasties of the Kali Age*, p. 53.
2. Pargiter, *op cit.*, p. 53.
3. *Ibid.*, p. 49.
4. *JASB*, 1865, pp. 115ff.
5. *JBORS*, XXII, pp. 70-76.
6. *JNSI*, V, pp. 111ff.
7. *CASIR*, VI, pp. 178-79.
8. Allan, *Catalogue of Coins*, p. 181.
9. *Ibid.*, pl. XX, 12.
10. *Ibid.*, pl. XV, 1-4; XIV, 16-18.
11. *Ibid.*, pl. XXV, 26.
12. *Ibid.*, pl. XXIV, 10.

13. *Ibid.*, pl. XVII, 1-2; XX, 2; XXII, 1-6; XXXIX, 21, etc. Also, Rapson, *Andhra Kshatrapa Catalogue*, pls. X to XVIII.
14. Jayaswal, *History of India*, AD 150-350, pp. 18-28.
15. Some texts read *Champāvatīm* for *Padmāvatīm*, but that reading is obviously incorrect. So is the reading *Nāka* for *Nāga.*
16. Allan, *op cit.*, p. 154.
17. Jayaswal, K.P., *op cit.*, p. 19, n. 1 and p. 18, 2nd para.
18. Allan, *op cit.*, p. 133.
19. *Ibid.*, p. 151.
20. *Ibid.*, p. 270.
21. Jayaswal, *op cit.*, pp. 19,35.
22. *Ibid.*, p. 22, n. 1 and pp. 37-38.
23. *Ibid.*, p. 20.
24. Vīrasena's coins have now been found from Padmāvatī. The coins are of Nāga affiliation. However, he may be a different ruler. See *JNSI*, XVII, pl. II, pp. 49-51.
25. Katare, Sant Lal, *JNSI*, XXXIV, pt. II (1972), pp. 189ff; *Journal of Indian History*, Vol. LV, pt. I-II, 1977, pp. 35-47.
26. *JRAS*, 1900, p. 110, No. 9-11; Allan, *BMC, AI*, p. cx.
27. Allan, *op cit.*, p. cxi.
28. *Ibid.*, pp. cx & 174.
29. *Ancient India*, No. 6, p. 103 C; *Coins of the Mathurā Kings*, No. 1 & 3.
30. *Ibid.*, No. 1.
31. Allan, *op cit.*, p. cx.
32. *Ibid.*, pp. 176-77, pl. XXIV, 1-4; Smith, *op cit.*, p. 192, pl. XXII. 10.
33. Allan, *op cit.*, p. 177, pl. XXIV, 15-16.
34. Allan, *op cit.*, p. 182, pl. XXIV, 18; XXIX, 24.
35. *Ibid.*, p. cx; *JRAS*, 1900, p. 113, fig. 13.
36. Even if Allan's arguments in favour of two kings of the names Rāmadatta (*op cit.*, p. cx) are based on a slender evidence, two kings of the name seem quite probable. That Viśākhadatta (?) of some coins (*JNSI*, XXX, pp. 179-81) from Padmāvatī (*Ibid.*, XVII, p. 53, XV, 1) and Vidishā (*Ibid.*, XXII, p. 133, pl. VI, 23) had anything to do with the Datta kings of Mathurā, is doubtful. There is no trace of the Brāhmī *śa*-like symbol (*Ibid.*, XVII, p. 53), which would have been a conclusive evidence to include him among these kings, on the poor illustrations of the coins published in the journal. The epigraphy of the two coins seems also later than the period of the Datta kings.
37. Allan, *op cit.*, pp. cx-cxi; Smith, *op cit.*, pp. 190-91.
38. Allan, *op cit.*, pp. cviii-cxi, 170-76.
39. *Ibid.*, p. cx; *JRAS*, 1900, p. 110, No. 11.
40. Allan, *op cit.*, pp. 170-182.
41. On the *Śrīvatsa* symbol reference may be made to C. Sivaramamurti, *Amaravati Sculptures in the Madras Government Museum, Bulletin of the Madras Government*

Museum , IV, pp. 58-59, 83-85; *JUPHRS*, 1941, pp. 21ff; *Ancient India*, No. 6, pp. 44-46.

42. This image is now in deposit in the Gujari Mahal Archaeological Museum, Gwalior. See also Thakore, *Catalogue of Sculptures in the Gujari Mahal Archaeological Museum*, p. 4, No. 10, where it is identified as a Viṣṇu image. Bhandarkar's view (*ARASI*, 1913-14, pt. ii, pp. 195-96) that it is an image of Garuḍa and that it had adorned one of the pillars as its capital, that the Gupta king Chandragupta II set up at Vidishā is not borne out by the features of the image itself. In one of its two left hands, the image holds a *Siṁhamukha gadā*, which Bhandarkar does not seem to have noticed. The art of the image seems to be earlier than the Guptas. The image is that of Viṣṇu and there is nothing in the image that would even distantly suggest that it was set up as the capital of a pillar.
43. *Annual Report of the Gwalior Archaeological Survey*, 1928-29, pl. III (b); *Ancient India*, pl. XVIII. (d), p. 44., fig. 1 (a). The date of the construction of this cave also requires to be re-examined in view of the fact that the panel with the inscription dated in Gupta Era 82 and which refers to Chandragupta II as king was counter-sunk in the wall and has only a two-line inscription when it appears to have been prepared to accomodate about eight lines. How was it that the inscription was not incised on the wall itself by the author of the record if he were responsible for its construction?
44. This image is also in deposit in the Gujari Mahal Archaeological Museum, Gwalior; see also Thakore, *op cit.*, p. 4, No. 14.
45. A similar symbol '212' occurs on a brick from Padam Pawāyā (Padmāvatī) in the Gwalior district of M.P.; *Annual Report of Gwalior Archaeological Survey*, 1942-46, pl. VII, figure on the right hand side.
46. This image is also in deposit in the above Museum at Gwalior; see Thakore, *op cit.*, p. 3, No. 2.
47. Barua, *Barhut*, III, pl. XXVII.
48. *ARASI*, 1913-14, pt. ii, pl. LXVI, fig. 19.
49. Allan, *op cit.*, 84. But there is neither the post nor the triangular dot between the two Nāgas on these coins.
50. *Ibid.*, p. cli.
51. *Ibid.*, p. 158, pl. VI, 4.
52. *Ibid.*, p. 131, pl. XVI, 14 & 15.
53. *Ibid.*, pp. cii, 159-67, pl. XXII, 1-16; pl. XXIII, 1, 4-10.
54. *Ibid.*, pp. ciii, 167-69, pl. XXII, 11-15, xliii, 12-14.
55. Trivedi, H.V., *op cit.*, p. xxxvi.
56. *ARASI*, 1915-16, pt. ii, pp. 101-03.
57. *ASR*, XII, p. 164 & 145.
58. *Ibid.*, XIV, p. 65.
59. *Ibid.*, XII, p. 47.
60. *Ibid.*

61. Pargiter, *op cit.*, p. 49.
62. *Ibid.*
63. *Ibid.*
64. *ARASI*, 1915-16, pt. ii, pp.101-03.
65. Pargiter, *op cit.*, p. 49.
66. The *Purāṇa* texts are hopelessly at variance where the name of Vaṅgāra occurs (*Ibid.*, p. 49, fn. 14), and this makes his historicity doubtful.
67. Pargiter, *op cit.*, p. 53 & fn. 2.
68. *ARASI*, 1915-16, pt. ii, pp. 101-03.
69. *CII*, III, pp. 5-6.
70. *Ibid.*, p. 190.
71. *Nāga-kula janmanaḥ sārikāsrāvita-mantrasya asita nāśo Nāgasenasya Padmāvatyāṁ.*
72. Pargiter, *op cit.*, p. 53.
73. This image is now in deposit in the Nagpur Museum. It belongs to about the first century AD.
74. *Journal of Oriental Institute,* Baroda, Vol. XX, pp. 442ff.
75. The inscription is in deposit in the Department of Ancient Indian History & Culture, Sagar University.
76. *CII*, IV, pt. i, pp. 13-16, pl. III-A; *EI*, XVI, pp. 230ff; Marshall & Foucher, *Monuments of Sanchi*, I, pp. 390ff; *JASB* (New Series), XIX, p. 342.
77. *CII*, IV, pt. II, No. 119, pp. 605-11.
78. For Śātakarṇi I's coins from, and conquest of Tripurī, see JNSI, XIII, pp. 35ff; *IHQ*, XXVIII, pp. 71ff; *JNSI*, XXXII, pp. 46ff, etc. His coins are now reported in large numbers from Tripurī.
79. Rapson, BMC, *Coins of Andhras and Kshatrapas,* pp. xcii-iii.
80. Luder's List, No. 346; *EI*, II, pp. 88-89; Marshall & Foucher, *Monuments of Sanchi,* I, pp. 5, 275-77.
81. The two inscriptions of Śaka Śrīdharavarmman cited above provide the evidence.
82. The Eran inscription of Samudragupta (*CII*, III, pp. 18ff); and the coins of Rāmagupta provide the evidence.
83. EI, II, pp. 369-70; IX, p. 244; Marshall & Foucher, *op cit.*, I. p. 386.
84. H.V. Trivedi, *op cit.*, pp. xxxviiiff. There are thousands of their coins in the Archaeological Museum, Gwalior and with the local collectors.
85. *CII*, III, pp. 6-7.
86. Pargiter, *op cit.*, p. 51.
87. *Catalogue of the Coins of the Nāga Kings of Padmāvatī*, Gwalior, 1957.
88. Trivedi, H.V., *op cit.*, p. IX.
89. *ASIAR*, 1914-15, p. 88.
90. *JNSI*, XVII, pt. I, pp. 53ff.
91. Trivedi, H.V., *op cit.*, pp. xxxvii-xxxviii.
92. Dwivedi, H.N., *Madhya Bhārat Kā Itihās*, Gwalior, 1956, pp. 478ff; Sharma, Mohanlal, *Padmāvatī*, Bhopal, 1971, pp. 33-38.

93. *ARASI*, 1915-16, p. 105.
94. Banerjee, J.N., *Development of Hindu Iconography*, p. 424.
95. *JMPIP*, No. 2, 1960, p. 19.
96. Marshall, *The Monuments of Sanchi*, Vol. I, p. 244.
97. *Ibid.*, p. 253.
98. *Catalogue of Sculptures in Archaeological Museum at Gwalior*, p. 6.
99. Patil, D.R., *The Cultural Heritage of Madhya Bharat*, Gwalior.
100. *Numismatic Digest*, Vol. 25-26, 2001-2002, pp. 65ff.
101. Khajuraho Inscription of Kokalla, year 1058, *EI*, Vol. I, pp. 151.
102. *CII*, III, p. 283.
103. *PHAI*, p. 473.

5

THE BHĀRAŚIVA NĀGAS

In the history of North India the Kuṣāṇa power declined shortly after the reign of Vāsudeva (AD 145-176). On the ruins of the Kuṣāṇas, in different parts of the Kuṣāṇa possessions, especially in Uttar Pradesh, Rajasthan and northern parts of Madhya Pradesh, subordinate ruling houses and tribes gradually raised their heads finally leading to the elimination of the Kuṣāṇa power. The credit of defeating the Kuṣāṇas is given to the Bhāraśiva Nāga family. According to Dr. Mirashi, Bhāraśivas may originally have been reigning in Vidarbha: for, an early stone inscription of a Bhāra king has been found at Pauni in Bhandra district of Vidarbha.[1] Subsequently, they appear to have raided North India where they established themselves. Copper coins of their *Adhirāja* (Emperor) Bhavanāga have been found at Padmāvatī, the capital of the Nāgas. From *Vākāṭaka* records we learn that the Bhāraśivas were staunch Śaivas. They carried on their shoulders the emblem of Śiva (perhaps *triśūla*) and believed that they owed their royal position to that god's grace.

The late Dr. Jayaswal has advocated the view that it was the Bhāraśiva Nāgas who drove out the Kuṣāṇas from the Gangetic Valley.[2] He mainly relied upon a passage in the *Vākāṭaka* plates which states that the Bhāraśivas, to whose line King Bhavanāga, the maternal grandfather of Rudrasena I belonged, had performed ten *Aśvamedhas* (horse-sacrifices) and been coronated with the Ganges water, which the Bhāraśivas had obtained by their valour.[3] Dr. Jayaswal has identified the Bhāraśivas with the dynasty of Nava-Nāgas mentioned by the *Purāṇas* as ruling before the Guptas. It is contended that the Nava-Nāgas of the *Purāṇas* did not constitute a dynasty of nine (*nava*) Nāga rulers but of new (*nava*) Nāga rulers; it was so called because its founder's proper name was Nava. This ruler, who is so far known to us from his coins only, ruled from c. 140 to c. 170 AD and drove out the Kuṣāṇas from Mirzapur and Benaras districts; he could thus get the Ganges water for his coronation by his valour. He made Kāntipurī, Kantit in Mirzapur district, his capital. Nava was succeeded by King Vīrasena, also known to us mainly from coins. He was the real founder of the Nāga greatness, for he drove out the Kuṣāṇas beyond Mathurā right up to Sirhind in the Punjab in c. 185 AD. Vīrasena, who ruled from c. 170 to 210 AD, was the founder of three Nāga families, which ruled at Mathurā, Padmāvatī and Kāntipurī. The main Nāga line, known as the Bhāraśiva line, ruled at the last mentioned place in Mirzapur district; Hayanāga, Trayanāga, Barhiṇanāga, Chharajanāga and Bhavanāga belonged to it and ruled in the stated order from c. 210 to 310 AD. During the reigns of Hayanāga and Trayanāga, the Kuṣāṇas were so hard pressed by the Bhāraśivas that they ultimately sought the protection of the Sassanian emperor Shahpur, sometime between AD 238 and 269. From c. 260 AD, however, the Bhāraśivas passed under the Vākāṭaka sovereignty. It was the emperor Pravarasena I of that house who ousted the Kuṣāṇas from the Punjab and compelled them to seek shelter in Afghanistan under the aegis of the Sassanians.

There are number of difficulties in accepting the views of Dr. Jayaswal so brilliantly put forth. It has naturally invited attention of different scholars like D.R. Bhandarkar,[4] A.K. Sur,[5] (Miss) Karuna Kana Gupta,[6] A. Banerji Sastri,[7] Sudhakar Chattopadhyaya[8] and others who have put forth their views in research journals and books. While taking into consideration all the views published till date, it was Dr. A.S. Altekar who handled different aspects of the numismatic evidences pertaining to the Nāgas in his long paper published in the *Journal of the Numismatic Society of India*, Vol. V and *Indian Culture*, Vol. XIII.[9] However, recent discoveries have added fresh dimensions to the subject.

Jayaswal thinks that the Bhāraśivas should be considered as a great imperial power for the reason that reference to them in the *Vākāṭaka* inscriptions state that they had performed ten *Aśvamedha* sacrifices. As D.R. Bhandarkar and Atul Sur have pointed out,[10] the *Aśvamedha* sacrifice had lost its true implication about this age, and it could be performed even without actual conquest. All the king had to do was to multiply ten or eleven times the usual *dakṣinā*, given to the Brāhmaṇas. Thus the Viṣṇukundin king Mādhvavarman is said to have performed eleven horse-sacrifices, while Mayūraśarman, the Kadamba king performed eighteen.[11] None, however, would regard them as Imperial suzerains or even ruling over a vast kingdom. In case of the Bhāraśivas, an additional difficulty is that the *Vākāṭaka* records which are the source of information were inscribed at least about a century later than Bhavanāga. There is every possibility that the actual fact was much exaggerated by them. The performance of the ten horse-sacrifices can prove the independence and power of the Bhāraśivas: it need not necessarily prove that the enemies defeated by them were the Kuṣāṇas. As Altekar rightly points out: "The claim put forth on behalf of the Bhāraśivas in the Vākāṭaka records is simply to the effect that they had acquired the holy Ganges water by means of their valour. This may be due to a successful raid into and not necessarily a conquest of the Gangetic valley. The Kuṣāṇas were so great an imperial power that if the Bhāraśivas had really driven them beyond the Sutlej, a phrase like *parākramavidhvasta-Kuṣāṇānām*, who had destroyed the Kuṣāṇas by their valour would certainly have been added to their achievements even in the Vākāṭaka records. The performance of the ten horse sacrifices can prove the independence and power of the Bhāraśivas; it need not necessarily prove that the enemies defeated by them were the Kuṣāṇas."

As per Altekar, there is no evidence to show that the Bhāraśivas were identical with the new (*nava*) Nāgas of Kāntipurī mentioned in the *Purāṇas*.[12] He believes that the Nava-Nāgas of the *Purāṇas* did not constitute a dynasty of new Nāgas, but were so called because there were nine rulers in the dynasty. Nor can it be maintained that the dynasty was so called because it was found by King Nava, known to us from coins. There is not the slightest evidence that King Nava of the coins was a Nāga ruler; he does not assume the epithet of Nāga on his coins nor do they bear any resemblance to the known coinage of any Nāga family. His coins are not found at Kantit, which is said to have been his capital, but at Kauśāmbī. Their findspot therefore does not support the view that he was ruling either at Kantit or at Mathurā or at Padmāvatī, all of which were the Nāga capitals at this time. His coin type suggests that he ruled in the third rather than in the second century AD; he, therefore, could not have been the founder of a Nāga family starting its career in c. 150 AD.

Altekar also asserts that "there is no evidence to show that Vīrasena, who is said to have been the successor of Nava, was a Nāga ruler and the founder of the Nāga families at Kāntipurī, Mathurā and Padmāvatī. The Nāga rulers of the last mentioned place invariably attach the epithet Nāga to their proper names in their coin legends even on their tiny pieces; Vīrasena, however, never does so on his coins, though they are much larger in size. His coins bear no resemblance to any known Nāga pieces nor are they found among the hoards of Nāga coins.[13] Since his coins are found in Mathurā there is no doubt that he was ruling there as an independent king, but there is no evidence to show that he had ousted the Kuṣāṇas from the eastern Punjab, for his coins are but rarely found beyond the Jamunā. The view that the successors of Vīrasena pressed the Kuṣāṇas so hard that they were eventually compelled to seek the protection of the Sassanian emperor Shahpur between AD 230 and 269 has no shred of evidence to support it. According to Dr. Jayaswal, Hayanāga and Trayanāga were on the Bhāraśiva throne during the period, but he has adduced absolutely no evidence to show that the Punjab was the scene of the military or diplomatic activities of either of them. The coins of these rulers are never found in the Punjab; nay, it is extremely doubtful if we have got their coins at all, for the coin legends on the coins attributed to them are hopelessly blurred and cannot be read with any certainty.[14] There is no evidence whatsoever to support the view that the Kuṣāṇas welcomed the Sassanian sovereignty in order to secure protection against any attack from the east; they were conquered by the Sassanians in the normal course of their imperial expansion."

The weakest point in Jayaswal's theory is his identification of the Bhāraśivas with the Nāga family at Kāntipurī which he identifies with Kantit in Mirzapur district. Only one *Purāṇa* the *Viṣṇupurāṇa* – refers to a Nāga family ruling at this place;[15] the rest of the *Purāṇas* enumerate the Nāga families ruling at Mathurā, Padmāvatī and even Champāvatī, but are unware of any branch at Kāntipurī. According to Altekar, "The coins of kings Nava and Vīrasena, who were the first two rulers of the dynasty, are found at Kauśāmbī and Mathurā, but never at Kāntipurī or in the adjoining districts of Mirzapur or Benaras. As for their alleged successors, Hayanāga, Trayanāga, Barhiṇanāga nothing whatsoever is known about the findspots of their coins; it is even doubtful whether we have their coins at all, for most of the readings of the legends are extremely doubtful. There are thus no traces of any powerful Nāga dynasty having flourished at Kāntipurī or in the districts of Benaras and Mirzapur; we cannot, therefore, identify it with the Bhāraśivas of the Vākāṭaka records. Nāga families no doubt ruled at Padmāvatī, and Mathurā; they did reassert their independence and secure the possession of the holy Ganges water by defeating and ousting the Kuṣāṇas from the United Provinces. The recent discovery of the coins of Bhavanāga in the Nāga series of Padmāvatī shows almost conclusively that this Nāga family was the Bhāraśiva family of the Vākāṭaka records. But there is absolutely no evidence to support the view that the Nāga rulers of Padmāvatī organized a powerful federation to oust the Kuṣāṇa power. Jayaswal has suggested that the Mālavas, the Yaudheyas and the Kuṇindas recognised the Nāga suzerainty and worked under their leadership, but this view is untenable. In the first place it must be remembered that no inscriptions have been found in the territories of these republics suggesting Nāga overlordship, nor is it hinted by the *Purāṇas* or literary traditions or any other evidence. Nāga coins are also never found in the homelands of the Yaudheyas or Kuṇindas. It is inconceivable that the Yaudheyas who had the reputation of being the Kṣattriyas *par excellence*, who were continuously proclaiming their victory even on their coin legends, and were so uniformly successful in their military ventures that they were believed to have a mystic formula ensuring victory against all odds, would ever have recognised the overlordship of the Nāgas, whose kingdom power and resources were much smaller than those of their own. The only evidence that Dr. Jayaswal has adduced to support his theory of the Nāga overlordship over the Yaudheyas is the alleged presence of Nāga symbols on their coins. There are no Nāga symbols on the Yaudheya coins nor do they bear the slightest or remotest resemblance to any recognised Nāga coinage.[16] The coinage of the Nāgas of Padmāvatī bears a striking resemblance to that of the Mālavas, who were their western neighbours. But the Mālava coin type is a continuation of the type in vogue in that republic since the second century BC. The Nāgas therefore were the borrowers, and if the theory of Dr. Jayaswal is to be accepted, the resemblance will show the overlordship of the Mālavas over the Nāgas and not *vice versa*. The fact, however, is that the resemblance of the coin type does not prove any overlordship in ancient India, it only points to a chronological or territorial connection. If we accept Jayaswal's theory, the close resemblance between the silver coinage of the Kṣatrapas and the Guptas will show that the latter were the feudatories of the former. It is well known that the Guptas had conquered the Kṣatrapas and were never their feudatories. To conclude, there is no evidence whatsoever of the Mālavas having ever recognised Nāga overlordship. The theory of the Nāga leadership in the movement against the Kushāna rule towards the beginning of the third century has therefore to be abandoned."[17]

Some of the above-mentioned observations of Dr. Altekar have now become obsolete in the light of fresh discoveries. On the basis of latest evidences discussed in the preceding chapter, it can now be safely said that the earlier Nāga dynasty of Vidishā founded by Nāgarāja Śeṣadatta was overwhelmed temporarily under the stress of a long struggle with the Śakas, the Sātavāhanas and the Kuṣāṇas, until a new (*nava*) line of the family with nāga-ending names retrieved their fortune and restored their dominion in the Padmāvatī-Kāntipurī region, as would the enormous quantity of coins of these kings from the above region indicate.[18] The epigraphy of the coins suggests that the kings with nāga-ending names ruled for about two centuries before they were wiped out by Samudragupta.[19] It is to this line that Bhavanāga the Bhāraśiva belonged. It is these kings who are evidently referred to as the Nava-Nāgas in the *Purāṇas*,[20] and in view of the fact that the number of these kings is more than nine, '*Nava*' should be interpreted to mean 'New' and not 'Nine'. On the basis of evidences discussed in the preceding chapter, we have already concluded that while the Nāga kings with datta-ending names ruled over a vast dominion which included Hastināpur, Mathurā, Kāntipurī, Padmāvatī and Vidishā, those with nandi-ending names and the Nava-Nāgas ruled over the one which included only Kāntipurī (Kutwār) and Padmāvatī. The Bhāraśivas belonged to this branch of the Nāgas.

With these evidences at our disposal, it is difficult to agree with the views of Dr. Jayaswal that the Bhāraśivas were great emperors, the only imperial power during the pre-Gupta Period who were the leaders of Indian National War of Independence against the Kuṣāṇas whom they drove out not only from the Gangetic Valley, but out of the country. Dr. Altekar seems to be right in stating that: "when considering the question of the disintegration of the Kuṣāṇa empire, we must therefore disabuse our mind of the notion that it was the Bhāraśivas of Kāntipurī who annihilated the Kuṣāṇa empire. The riddle of disappearance of the Kuṣāṇa power from the Gangetic can be solved only by carefully studying the coins and inscriptions of the contemporary powers. If we do so, we shall find that the Yaudheyas, the Kuṇindas, the Mālavas, the Nāgas and the Maghas, who began to strike coins as independent powers in the third century, all played their own part in driving out the Kuṣāṇas."[21]

The Bhāraśivas had close relations with the contemporary powers. We have already noted that Bhavanāga, the powerful ruler of the Nāgas of Padmāvatī, was contemporary of Pravarasena I, the Vākāṭaka ruler. He gave his daughter in marriage to Gautamīputra, who was most probably the eldest son of the Vākāṭaka emperor. This alliance with the powerful Nāga family of the North appears to have greatly strengthened the power and prestige of the Vākāṭakas; for, it is invariably mentioned in all grants of Gautamīputra's descendants. Bhavanāga must have been of considerable help to his young grandson Rudrasena I at the critical juncture of the premature demise of his father Gautamīputra, and also on some more occasions. What was the nature of the help cannot be determined in the existing state of knowledge. That is the reason why in the records of the *Vākāṭakas*, the name of Bhavanāga and the Bhāraśiva family is proudly mentioned. As a general rule, maternal grandfathers are mentioned in royal genealogies only when they happen to have rendered conspicuous help to their daughter's son.

Another power with whom the Bhāraśiva Nāgas came in contact were the Guptas. The Allahabad Pillar Inscription of Samudragupta[22] contains a very detailed account of the conquests of Samudragupta. The chronological scheme of his *digvijaya* may be arranged in the following order:

(a) First Campaign in Āryāvarta
(lines 13-14)

(b) Campaign in Dakṣiṇāpatha
(lines 19-20)

(c) Second campaign in Āryāvarta
(lines 21-23)

Available evidences seem to indicate that Samudragupta led really two campaigns in North India, though some scholars do not favour such a theory on the ground that while lines 13-14 of the Allahabad record state that Samudragupta violently uprooted (*unmūlya*) Achyuta, Nāgasena, a king of Kota family, etc Achyuta and Nāgasena are again referred to in line 21. Had they been uprooted in the first campaign how are they mentioned again in course of the supposed second one? In this connection the following points are noteworthy:-

(a) The king of Kota family is referred to in line 14, but not in line 21.

(b) Line 21 speaks of Nāgasena along with Gaṇapatināga whose coins have been found at Padmāvatī. Now, *Harṣacharita* refers to the death of Nāgasena, the king of Padmāvatī.[23] As both Gaṇapati and Nāgasena belonged to the Nāga house of Padmāvatī, and as Samudragupta killed both of them, the latter must have attacked them at two different times, after one had succeeded the other.

(c) Line 14 informs us that the prince of Kota family was captured while Samudragupta had been playing at the city of Puṣpa, i.e., Pāṭaliputra. This is evidently the poetic way of stating that Samudragupta was a young man at the time of the conquest. It also refers to his earlier conquests.

Thus in his first campaign in North India, Samudragupta defeated Achyuta, Nāgasena and a prince of the Kota family. In the Allahabad record, after the word Nāgasena, there occurs the letter '*ga*' and then a lacuna, which Dr. D.C. Sircar thinks, can be filled up by *Ganapatyādiṇ-nṛpāṇ Saṇgare*.[24] If the proposed reading is accepted, we have to assume that Samudragupta had to fight in the Padmāvatī region twice in course of the same campaign in as much as both Nāgasena and Gaṇapatināga belonged to the same house. Achyuta probably ruled in the Ahichchhatra region (modern Rāmnagar in Bareilly district) where copper coins bearing the legend Achyu have been found.[25] Altekar observes: "A king named Achyuta had risen to power in Ahichchhatra by the middle of the 4th century AD. His coin type bears a close resemblance to that of some Nāga coins and it is not improbable that he was himself a Nāga ruler, perhaps a scion of a collateral branch of the Mathurā family."[26]

About Nāgasena, *Harṣacharita* states: "At Padmāvatī occurred the doom of Nāgasena born of the Nāga family, who was foolish enough to have the secrets of his policy discussed in the presence of the *sārikā* bird which declared them aloud."[27] It is interesting here to record the comments of Dr. Bhandarkar on this issue which is as follows:

"The commentator Śaṅkarārya further informs us that this Nāgasena took counsel, in the presence of a *sārikā* bird, to restrain one of his ministers who had possessed himself of one-half of the kingdom but that the minister having come to know about it in confidence from the bird managed to kill the king with a club (*daṇḍa*). It is no doubt possible to argue that as this Nāgasena was killed at Padmāvatī on account of some political intrigue, he cannot be identical with Nāgasena who met with his end on the battlefield. There is nothing, however, in the statement of Bāṇa or his commentator to show that he was murdered in the palace. And the battle in which Samudragupta confronted the confederated kings may have taken place at or near Padmāvatī itself, and the Gupta king may have been here joined by the minister of Nāgasena who perhaps killed his own master and thus helped the Gupta ruler to get rid of his one enemy."[28]

Coins bearing the name of Kota have been found in East Punjab and Delhi and the dynasty may have held sway in the Upper Gangetic Valley regions.[29]

Jayaswal thinks that Nāgasena, Achyuta and the prince of Kota family entered into a league against Samudragupta who defeated their combined force in a battle at Kauśāmbī.[30] Bhandarkar also suggests the confederacy of four Nāga kings against Samudragupta soon after his accession to the throne.[31]

Having secured the Gaṅgā-Yamuna Valley, Samudragupta paid attention to his Dakṣiṇāpatha conquests which is described in lines 19-20 of the Allahabad inscription. This is followed by a description of nine kings of Āryāvarta where he had to conduct a second campaign with a view to exterminate (*unmūla*) the rebellious rulers. The nine kings who became victim of his policy of extermination were Rudradeva, Matila, Nāgadatta, Chandravarman, Gaṇapatināga, Nāgasena, Achyuta, Nandi and Balavarman. As already stated, this description is of the nature of stock-taking one, and at least Nāgasena and Achyuta had already been exterminated in the first Āryāvarta war. Of the five, viz., Rudradeva, Matila, Nāgadatta, Nandi and Balavarman, uncertainty prevails. Some scholars have identified Rudradeva, with Rudrasena I, the Vākāṭaka ruler. But as he was ruling in Dakṣiṇāpatha, this identity cannot be accepted. Possibly he may be identified with one Rudradeva whose coins have been found at Kauśāmbī.[32] About Matila, it has been suggested that he may be identical with Mattila of the seal found in Bulandshahr, but the absence of any honorific on the latter suggests that it is a private seal and not one of the royal personage.[33] Moreover, the seal is of later date on paleographic basis. Nāgadatta, Nandin and Balavarman may have been Nāga rulers. According to Jayaswal, Nāgadatta was possibly father of Maheśvaranāga of 4th century AD whose seal has been found at Lahore.[34] Nandi is possibly identical to Śivanandi and Nandiyaśa of the *Purāṇas*. Balavarman might be a predecessor of Bhāskarvarman of Assam who was contemporary of Harṣa. Majority of scholars do not accept this identification. Possibly he was a successor of Mahākṣatrapa Śrīdharavarman ruling over Eran-Sanchi region. As seen in the preceding chapter, a Nāga family was in existence at Eran during this period.

About Gaṇapatināga, as already stated, his coins in large number have been found in Padmāvatī, Vidishā, Narwar, Kutwār and adjoining regions. He was the Bhāraśiva Nāga ruler with his capital at Padmāvatī. His coins have also been found at Mathurā which must have been included within his dominion. The *Bhāvaśataka* (I.v.800) describes Gaṇapatināga as the Dhārādhīśa, lord of Dhārā, though the authenticity of this statement has been doubted by some scholars.[35] Bhandarkar identifies Dhārā with Kāntipurī, the second capital of the Nāgas where, as per him, Gaṇapatināga ruled.[36] It appears that Gaṇapatināga was a king of considerable importance and might have led the revolt against Samudragupta which forced him to conduct a second campaign in Āryāvarta.

Chandravarman has been identified with king of that name whose record has been found at Susunia in Bankura district of West Bengal.

The kings of Āryāvarta destroyed by Samudragupta were formerly taken to be nine in number, and it was suggested by Rapson that possibly they might all have been Nāgas and denoted the Nava-Nāgas of the *Viṣṇu Purāṇa*, whose expression is taken by him to denote, not a dynasty of nine successive rulers, but rather a confederation of nine princes belonging to the Nāga race.[37] But Bhandarkar believes that the actual number of the Āryāvarta rulers named is not nine, but eight. He thinks that Achyuta and Nandin are not two names, but one; Achyutanandin, wherein Nandin is second component of the name, like Bhutinandin and Śiśunandin of the *Purāṇas*.[38] Secondly, according to Bhandarkar, the *Viṣṇu Purāṇa* speaks of Nava-Nāgā as ruling over Padmāvatī,

Kāntipurī and Mathurā.[39] As these are only three and not nine cities, Nava-Nāgas cannot signify the nine Nāgas but rather new Nāgas, the old Nāgas being those mentioned earlier by the *Purāṇas* in connection with Vidishā.[40] We have already discussed the history of the old Nāgas in the preceding chapter. Samudragupta faced the confederation of the new Nāgas under the leadership of Nāgasena/Gaṇapatināga.

As a result of this war of extermination, existence of the Bhāraśiva Nāgas as an independent power was eclipsed forever. Samudragupta's Garuḍa-type of coins possibly mark his victory over the Nāgas, Garuḍa being the devourer of the Nāgas, i.e., serpents. However, their existence as a political force persisted and this is evident from the fact that Chandragupta II, the successor of Samudragupta entered into matrimonial alliance with the Nāgas. From the Poona Plate of Prabhāvatīguptā it is clear that she was daughter of Chandragupta II by his queen Kuberanāgā, born of Nāga family (*Nāga-Kulasaṁbhūtā*) and was herself the wife of Rudrasena II, the Vākāṭaka king.[41] It is not clear who took the initiative of arranging this politically motivated matrimonial alliance. Possibly it was arranged by Samudragupta himself to pacify the Nāga kings with a view of eliminate the risk of danger from their end in future. To quote Dr. Agrawal, "P.L. Gupta is not inclined to attach any political importance to this marriage and he takes it as an event of Chandragupta's own reign (vide, *Gupta Samrajya*, p. 296). He thinks that there is no ground to believe that this marriage took place in the time of Samudragupta, what the learned scholar has failed to grasp is that it can in no way be ascribed to the reign of Chandragupta II. It is a well established fact that Chandragupta married his daughter Prabhāvatīguptā born of Kuberanāgā to Rudrasena II in c. 380 AD. Even if Prabhāvatīguptā was eighteen years of age at the time of this marriage, the marriage of her parents has to be placed in c. 362 AD which date definitely falls within the reign of Samudragupta, and comes soon after the completion of his conquests."[42] That Chandragupta II took real advantage of this alliance is clear from his war-plans against the Western Kṣatrapas immediately after the accession. To which family of the Nāgas did Kuberanāgā belong is not known. The statement that she was daughter of Nāga ruler Vīrasena[43] is not acceptable in view of absence of any positive evidence. It may be presumed that she came from the most powerful family of them, viz., the Bhāraśiva Nāgas of Padmāvatī.

We do not hear anything about the Gupta-Nāga relations during the post-Chandragupta II Period. The uncertain political situation in which Kumāragupta I died and Skandagupta came to the throne has led number of scholars to propound different theories.[44] An interesting interpretation of the situation wherein the Nāgas played a major role may be narrated in the following words of Dr. D.R. Bhandarkar:[45]

> . . . in stanza 6 (of the Bhitari Pillar Inscription of Skandagupta) which tells us that when he re-established the Fortune of the Dynasty which had turned adrift when his father had repaired to heaven, he saw his mother who was in tears just as Kṛishṇa approached Dēvakī when he had slain his foe. If the comparison of Skandagupta and his mother to Kṛishṇa and Dēvakī has any meaning at all, the foe that had arisen against the Gupta power and made it totter to its foundations was some relative of his through his mother, presumably her brother. In this connection we have to take note of another document of his reign, namely, the Junagadh inscription. The second half of stanza 2 of this record says that 'he forged an order with an effigy, namely, Garuḍa, which rendered devoid of poison, the Serpent (*bhujaga*) Rulers, who had uplifted their hoods in pride and arrogrance.' As bhujaga is synonymous with Nāga, both meaning 'a serpent', and as royal families of the name of Nāga were in existence in the Gupta period, and as, further, Garuḍa was an insignia or signet of the Gupta dynasty, the conclusion is irresistible that there was a rebellion set up by some Nāga rulers which Skandagupta quelled. Further, we know that some Nāgas were related to the Guptas. Thus one queen of Chandragupta II was Kubera-Nāgā, who, we are explicitly informed, was of the Nāga family. His son Kumāragupta may similarly have been married to a Nāga princess from whom Skandagupta was born. This line of reasoning can alone explain why Skandagupta is represented on the one hand as impressing his Garuḍa signet on the Nāgas and on the other as repairing to his mother in tears just as Kṛishṇa did to Dēvakī after he had laid low his enemy. It seems that on the demise of Kumāragupta, Ghaṭōtkacha occupied the Gupta throne. But hardly had he ascended the throne when the Nāgas raised the standard of revolt with such virulence and ruthlessness that the fortunes of the Gupta dynasty sunk to the lowest level. Ghaṭōtkacha was probably killed and his brother Skandagupta who had stood by him had to flee and sleep some nights on the bare earth. Soon, however, he triumphed over all difficulties and was able to re-establish the Gupta supremacy which had for a time been rudely shaken . . .

The Bhitari pillar inscription furnishes us with another item of historical importance connected with the reign of Skandagupta. Stanza 8 thereof describes the terrific conflict into which he came with the Hūṇas. Unfortunately the stanza is very much mangled and further details, if any, which it contained have been lost. With this may, however, be compared the information contained in stanza 4 of the Junagadh rock inscription which says: 'And, moreover, he alone has conquered, whose fame enemies proclaim (being caused to return) to the Mlechchha countries, with (their) pride broken down to the very root.' This is a clear reference to the Hūṇas, because, so far as we know, they alone could be the Mlechchhas who invaded the Gupta territory but were forced to return to their Mlechchha home. This inscription contains three dates, namely, Gupta years 136, 137 and 138. It thus seems that the Hūṇas were defeated and repulsed at least before Gupta year 138=456-57 AD when the inscription was engraved. When there is a rebellion inside a kingdom, that affords a most suitable opportunity for outside powers to encroach upon the neighbouring territory. In many cases the insurgent chiefs themselves seek the help of foreign rulers. It is quite possible that the malcontent Nāga chieftain himself invited the Hūṇa monarch to come to his succour. The result, to begin with, was certainly disastrous, as Ghaṭōtkacha appears to have been killed and Gupta supremacy to have been tottering to its foundations. Skandagupta, however, true to his Gupta heritage, rose to the occasion, put down the Nāga rebellion and drove the Hūṇas back to their own territory.

However, as in the past, following the policy of pacification, some members of the rebellious Nāga community were eventually absorbed by Skandagupta in the ruling hierarchy of the new empire. This is evident from the instance of Śarvanāga whom Skandagupta appointed Viceroy of the big province of Antarvedi (Gaṅgā-Yamuna Doab).[46] Some scholars do not believe in this theory.[47] Others have interpreted the statement in the Bhitari Stone Inscription to identify Puṣyamitras with Nāgas.[48] Nothing definite can be said on this account till further evidences come.

With this the rule and influence of the Bhāraśiva Nāgas came to an end as we do not hear anything about them in the succeeding centuries.

REFERENCES

1. EI, Vol. XXV, pp. 111ff.
2. Jayaswal, K.P., *History of India*, AD 150-350, pp. 19, 20, 35, 50, 90.
3. असंभारसान्निवेषितषिवलिंगोद्वहन –
   – षिवसुपरितुष्टसमुत्पादितराजवंशानाम्
   परामक्रमाधिगतभागीरत्थ्यमलजल –
   – मूर्द्धाभिषिक्तानां दशाश्वमेधा–
   – वभृथस्नातानां भारशिवानां
   महाराजश्रीभवनागदौहित्रस्य,
   गौतमीपुत्रस्य पुत्रस्य।
   -*CII*, V, p. 12
4. *Indian Culture*, Vol. I, p. 115.
5. *Ibid.*, p. 114.
6. *Ibid.*, pp. 635ff; Vol. II, pp. 61ff.
7. *JRASB* (Letters), Vol. V, 1939, pp. 175ff.
8. Chattopadhyaya, S., *Early History of North India* (c. 250 BC to AD 650)
9. *JNSI*, Vol. V, pp. 111ff; *Indian Culture*, Vol. XII, pp. 179ff.
10. *Indian Culture*, Vol. I, pp. 114-118.
11. Sircar, D.C., *Successors of the Sātavāhanas in the Lower Deccan*, Calcutta, 1939, pp. 124ff, 238ff.

12. See *JNSI*, Vol. V, pp. 118-21 for a detailed examination of the numismatic evidence to disprove the view that Nava of the coins was a Nāga ruler of Kāntipurī.
13. *JNSI*, Vol. V, pp. 121-24.
14. Smith, *IMC*, Vol. I, p. 191; *JNSI*, Vol. V, pp. 124-29.
15. Pargiter, *DKA*, p. 53.
16. The only Nāga symbol specifically referred to by Jayaswal as occurring on Yaudheya coins is that of tree with side designs. It is only on the coins of Nava and Vīrasena that this symbol occurs and there is no evidence to show that these were Nāga rulers. The coins of the rulers of Padmāvatī who specifically describe themselves as Nāga on their coins, do not bear this symbol at all. Even if we assume that this tree symbol is a Nāga symbol, we have to note that it is quite dissimilar to the tree symbol that occurs only very rarely on some Yaudheya coins. The Yaudheya coins are quite dissmilar to the Nāga coins in weight, fabric and type. The average weight of the Yaudheya coins is about 163 grams. The weight of the coins of Nava and Vīrasena is about 65 grains and that of the rulers of Padmāvatī varies between 18 to 54 grains. The bull which is a constant symbol on the coins of Nava, is but rarely seen on the coins of the Yaudheyas. Most of the coins of Vīrasena, who was, according to Jayaswal, the leader of the anti-Kuṣāṇa movement, are rectangular in shape; the Yaudheyas never adopted it for their coinage. If the numismatic evidence proves anything, it is the utter absence of any connection between the Yaudheyas and the Nāgas, and not the overlordship of the latter over the former.
17. *Indian Culture*, Vol. XII, pp. 119-121.
18. Trivedi, H.V., *Catalogue of the Nāga Kings of Padmāvatī.*
19. *CII*, III, pp. 6-7.
20. Pargiter, *op cit.*, p. 53.
21. Majumdar and Altekar, *The Vakataka Gupta Age*, Delhi, 1946, p. 27.
22. *CII*, III (revised), pp. 203ff.
23. *Harṣacharita*, (tr. Cowell & Thomas), p. 192.
24. Sircar, D.C., *Select Inscriptions*, p. 256, fn1.
25. Allan, *Catalogue of Gupta Coins*, London, 1914, p. xxii; Catalogue, p. lxxix.
26. *Vakataka Gupta Age*, pp. 36-37.
27. नागकुल जन्मनः सारिका
श्रवित मन्त्रस्य आसीत
नागो नागसेनस्य पद्मावत्याम्
Harṣacharita, Nirnayasagar Press, p. 200.
28. *CII*, III (revised ed.), p. 10.
29. Jayaswal, K.P. *History of India*, p. 113.
30. *Ibid.*, pp. 132ff.
31. *CII*, III (Revised), pp. 10-11.
32. *JNSI*, XI, p. 13.
33. *IHQ*, Vol. I, p. 254.

34. *History of India,* p. 34, 142.
35. *IHQ,* Vol. XII, p. 135.
36. *CII,* III (revised), p. 21.
37. *JRAS,* 1897, p. 421.
38. *CII,* III (revised), p. 20.
39. Pargiter, *DKA,* p. 53, n. 2
40. *Ibid.*
41. Sircar, D.C., *Select Inscriptions,* pp. 411-15.
42. Agrawal, Ashwini, *Rise and Fall of the Imperial Guptas,* Delhi, 1989, pp. 167-68.
43. Sharma, M.L., *Padmāvatī,* M.P. Hindi Granth Academy, Bhopal, 1971, p. 32.
44. Agrawal Ashwini, *op cit.,* chapter XI; Also Altekar, *Vakataka Gupta Age,* pp. 173ff; Gupta, P.L., *Gupta Sāmrājya,* pp. 317ff.
45. *CII,* III (revised), pp. 80-81.
46. Indor Copper Plate Inscription of Skandagupta, yr. 146; Also, *CII,* III (revised), pp. 309-11.
47. Agrawal, Ashwini, *op cit.,* pp. 210, 222.
48. Chattopadhyaya, S., *Early History of North India* (c. 200 BC-AD 650), pp. 168-69.

6

NĀGAS IN THE HISTORY OF KASHMIR

Nāgas have played a very important role in the history of Kashmir Valley. The entire history of the Valley from the proto-historic times till date is in someway or the other associated with the Nāgas. This is evident from the traditional and the dynastic history of the Valley as well as existing remains of ancient monuments, sculptures and lakes, a large member of which are associated with the Nāgas. A summarised account is narrated below.

TRADITIONAL HISTORY

The epics, the *Purāṇas* with special reference to *Nīlamata Purāṇa,* and *Rājataraṅgiṇī* of Kalhaṇa, apart from archaeological, numismatic, epigraphic and other literary works including the accounts of foreign writers are the sources of information for the history of Kashmir. All these sources are unanimous in one respect, viz., in stating that in the Happy Valley, the Nāgas were eminently popular deities. Says Sir Aurel Stein:[1] "From early times, considerable importance must have been attached to their worship, as is proved by the long account given on them in the *Nīlamata*, by the numerous temples erected near the more famous springs, and the popularity and undoubtedly ancient origin of the pilgrimages directed to the latter. The belief in Nāgas is fully alive also in the Muhamaddan population of the Valley, which in many places has not ceased to pay a kind of superstitious respect and ill-disguised worship to these deities. The popular conception of the Nāgas, as now current, represents them under the form of snakes, living in the water of the spring or lakes protected by them."

At the outset[2] Kalhaṇa states that the land of Kashmir within mountainous walls had offered shelter to the Nāgas, who found a refuge there against the attacks of Garuḍa. Among these Nāgas he mentions Śaṅkha and Padma of which the latter appears to be identical with Mahāpadma, the tutelary spirit of the great Vulgar lake which occupies a central position in the Kashmir Valley. The Lord of all Nāgas of Kashmir and the chief guardian of the Valley, as per Kalhaṇa, is not Padma but Nīla who has his abode in Nīlakuṇḍa on the main source of Vyath, the ancient Vitastā. Giving an account of the early rulers of Kashmir, Kalhaṇa says that Jalauka, the son of Aśoka, used to be carried in Kashmir by a Nāga where he entered the lake of the Nāgas and dallied with beautiful maidens.[3] Narrating further, *Rājataraṅgiṇī* relates the fate of the Buddhists who had influenced common people to neglect rites prescribed for the Nāgas as per *Nīlamata Purāṇa*, resulting in heavy snowfall and mass destruction and death. Everything was averted after restoration of the austerities and propitiation of Nīla Nāga.[4]

The *Nīlamata Purāṇa*[5] is a real mine of information regarding the sacred places of Kashmir and legends related to them. At the request of Kashyapa, it is stated, gods had come to Kashmir to fight the water-demon who had infested the big lake and was causing great trouble to the people of Kashmir. It is Baladeva who at the behest of his brother Viṣṇu cleaved the Himalayas with his plough and thus drained the Valley. Then the wicked demon was killed by Viṣṇu. The place where according to popular belief the mountain was pierced by Baladeva is a spot near Vernag at the opposite of the Valley.[6] A Buddhist version of the legend is recorded by Hiuen Tsang wherein the hero of the story is Arhat Madhyāntika who by means of a stratagem rescues the land of Kashmir from the water-demon, a 'dragon-king', i.e., Nāgarāja.

The *Nīlamata* relates in what manner the Valley of Kashmir became inhabited. At first, it states, human beings could live there for only six months. During the rest of the year the land was occupied by *Piśāchas* under their ruler Nikumbha. At the beginning of the spring, the *Piśāchas* left the place and human beings came to live during the summer. However, *Piśāchas* came back during the winters. This continued for *Yugas*. Once a Brahmin, Chandradeva by name, found a refuge in the subterranean palace of Nīla, the *Nāgarāja*. The *Nāgarāja* imparted to his guest the rites which should be observed if the inhabitants wished to live all the year round. The people followed the same and from that time onwards the people were no longer troubled by the *Piśāchas*, and there was no heavy snowfall as long as they observed the rites revealed to them by the *Nāgarāja*. The rites ordained by Nīla has been described in great detail in the *Nīlamata Purāṇa*, two-third of the text of which is occupied by it.[7]

The *Mahābhārata* and the *Purāṇas* contain extensive catalogue of the Nāgas. Such a list is also inserted in the *Nīlamata*.[8] Although it only professes to give the names of the principal Nāgas worshipped in Kashmir, it surpasses in length all the lists known from Sanskrit literature. It contains names of 561 *Nāgarājas* which includes some duplications. Thereafter follows names of four *Dikpālas* of Kashmir.[9] These are Bindusara (Bindusāra) in the east, Śrīmāḍaka in the south, Elāpattra in the west and Uttaramānasa in the north. The *Dikpālas* in question are evidently Nāgas.

The legendary account related to some of the principal Nāgas may be seen still prevailing at some of the sites in Kashmir. Nīla, the principal *Nāgarāja*, was believed from the early times to dwell in the main source of Vitastā. Hence this fine spring was known as Nīla-Nāga or Nīla-Kuṇḍa. In words of Sir Aurel Stein: "The deep blue colour of the water which collects in the spring-basin, may possibly account for the location of the Nīlanāga in this particular fountain. Kalhaṇa's reference to the 'circular pond' from which the Vitastā rises, shows that the spring had already in early times an artificial enclosure similar to the present one."[10]

Nīlamata locates the subterranean palace of the Nāgarāja where the Brāhmin Chandradeva stayed during the six months of cold season and was initiated by his host into the sacred rites to be observed by those that dwell in Kashmir. The abode of Nīla is located under the mountain Dhanada (modern Bānihāl).[11]

In later times the sacred fount of Nīla came to be known by the name of Vera Nāga, which is derived from the district of Ver in which it is situated. Abu'l Faẓl records:[12] "In the Ver tract of country is the source of Bihat (=Vitastā). It is a pool measuring *a jarīb*, which tosses in foam with an astonishing roar, and its depth is unfathomable. It goes by the name of Ver Nāg and is surrounded by a stone embankment and to its east are temples of stone." Jahangir, who was very fond of Kashmir, often speaks of Ver Nāg in his 'Memoirs.'[13]

In Kashmir there is also a small lake known by the name of Nīla Nāga. It is located in the district of Nāgām (ancient Nāgrāma) which is watered by 'Dūdh Gaṅgā' or 'Milk Gaṅgā', a small stream which joins the Vitastā at Srinagar. The spring has also been referred to by Abu'l Faẓl.[14]

Another source of the Vitastā, also situated in the district of Ver (modern Shahbad), some 12 km to the west of Ver Nāg, is consecrated to the great Nāga Vāsuki.[15]

The modern town of Anantnāg in Kashmir situated at the foot of the western extremity of the plateau of Martand derives its name from Nāga Ananta (or Śeṣa). The abode of the Nāga is a great spring which issues at the southern end of the town. Gautama Nāga[16] is situated to the north of the town on way to Bavan. Various sources indicate that Nāga Takṣaka was worshipped in Kashmir Valley from an early date. In the *Mahābhārata, Vana Parva,* is contained a long account of the chief places of pilgrimage (*Tīrthayātrā Parvan*) wherein it is stated[17] that the river Vitastā in Kashmir is the abode of Takṣaka, 'which releases from all sins'. Bilhaṇa in his *Vikramāṅkadevacharita* states that, "At a distance of a *gavyūti* and a half from the capital of Pravarapura (now Srinagar) lies a place with high rising monuments (chaitya) called Jayavana, where a pool filled with pure water and sacred to Takṣaka, the lord of snakes, cuts like a war-disc the head of Kali bent on the destruction of Dharma."[18]

Till today Takṣaka is worshipped in the large pool of limpid water at the village Zevan (ancient Jayavana), three km to the east of the ancient capital Pāndrenṭhan (Skt. *Pūrṇādhiṣṭhāna*). From the Nāga the cultivation of saffron flowers which flourishes in the neighbourhood, is believed to have originated. Abu'l Faẓl also refers to this tradition.[19]

Kalhaṇa the chronicler speaks of the annual festival in honour of the great sperpent king, "frequented by dancers and strolling players and thronged by crowds of spectators." It took place on the 12th day of the waning moon of Jyaiṣṭha.[20] *Rājataraṅgiṇī* has also narrated a fascinating legend about the role of Takṣaka Nāga in the destruction of Narapura. But the Nāga who brought about the ruin of the wicked king was Suśravas whose original home was the lake near Vijayeśvara (modern Vijabror, Vulgo Bij-behara). He is said to have created a lake of dazzling whiteness which is still known by the name of Suśram Nāg. Here a small rock-bound inlet is believed to be the dwelling of Suśravas' son-in-law, the Brahmin Viśākha, who by the miraculous power of the former got converted into a Nāga. On that account it is called Zāmtur Nāg (Skt. *Jāmātṛi-Nāga*), or the lake of the Son-in-law.[21]

The sister of Suśravas, the Nāgī Ramaṇyā, who wanted to assist her brother in his work of revenge but came too late, dropped her load of heavy boulders among the villages. Thus the village-land became a stone waste known as Ramaṇyā's Wilderness (*Ramaṇyāṭavī*). This name is preserved in the Rembyār stream familiar to travellers who enter Kashmir by the Pīr Pantsāl route.[22]

The Nāga Karkoṭaka to whom the royal house of Lalitāditya ascribed its origin must also have had his special *tīrtha.* Its exact position can no longer be fixed, but it must have been somewhere near the mountain-ridge on the Tosha Maidān Road, which is now known as Kākodar. This name is no doubt derived form Kāroṭaka, whence the neighbouring watch-station and village were called 'Kārkoṭa-draṅga.'[23]

Abu'l Faẓl mentions some more Nāgas which were famous in his days on account of the miraculous faculties ascribed to them, and the lakes inhabited by them. Thus, he refers to Kokar Nāg,[24] Shakar Nāg,[25] Balau Nāg,[26] Chatar Nāg,[27] etc. The number mentioned by him are very few as compared to the existing tradition. He recognizes this fact and records: "In seven hundred places there are graven images of snakes which they worship and regarding which wonderful legends are told." This clearly shows how largely the hosts of Nāgas must have loomed in the imagination of the rural population of Kashmir Valley. The sanctity ascribed to the Nāgas and the custom of their divination associated with sacred springs produce a faithful picture of this form of popular worship prevalent amongst a large section of the people of Kashmir Valley even today. We may sum up the importance of the Nāgas in the mythology of Kashmir in the following words of Sir Walter Lawrence: "It is dangerous to discuss so great a mystery as the Hindu religion, yet I cannot help noticing the important part which water-springs and snakes play in the Kashmir mythology. The pretty springs of cold clear water so frequent throughout Kashmir are the abodes of the Nāgs, the old deities who were worshipped in ancient times. When the Nāg visits the world he leaves his home in the heart of some mountain, and creeping through sinuous passages like a snake emerges at the spring. Sometimes he comes with benevolent intent, sometimes on mischief bent, and all agree that he is powerful and to be propitiated. In all the village tales the serpent nature of the Nāg is prominent. When the Nāg assumes the human form he can be detected by the water that drips from his locks. If one has leisure to sit by a spring with the villagers many curious legends may be heard, often full of interest and beauty."[28]

THE KĀRKOṬA NĀGA DYNASTY

The rule of the Kārkoṭa Nāga dynasty in Kashmir coincided with the rise in North India of several Rajput dynasties of the Early Medieval Period, like the Gurjara Pratihāras, the Chandellas, the Pālas, the Kalachuris, the Paramāras, the Chālukyas, the Chāhamānas, the Gahaḍavālas, etc. The primary sources of information for the history of Kashmir is the *Rājataraṅgiṇī* of Kalhaṇa, epigraphic, numismatic and other literary sources including the testimony of foreign writers and travellers.

While inviting attention to the connotation 'Kārkoṭa', appended to the dynasty, it is interesting to note that the word 'Karkoṭa' occurs in the *Ṛg Veda* itself and if Vogel's suggestion is accepted, it finds mention in the *Atharvaveda* also as Śarkoṭa.[29] It should, however, be noted that even during the *Ṛgvedic* period, the legend of the Karkoṭa Nāga was very well known, though terminologically the word can be explained away as referring to a number of plants as well.[30] There are several references to Karkoṭa in the *Mahābhārata* wherein it has been used to denote a non-Āryan tribe, and a Nāga of that name (Karkoṭa) at many places in several *parvas*.[31] It is interesting to note that many of the *Purāṇas* and the *Kathāsaritsāgara* mention a Nāga of that name in different contexts.[32] The *Matsya Purāṇa,* for example, mentions a *tīrtha* of that name on the banks of the Narmadā River.[33] The *Kathāsaritsāgara* refers to a city of that name while the *Nīlamata Purāṇa* lists Kārkoṭa Nāga of Kashmir with other outstanding Nāgas (Nīla, Vāsuki and Takṣaka).[34] Again, a Karkoṭa Nāga is associated with a legend concerning dessication of a lake in Nepal, where it is worshipped even today.[35] All these legendary (and literary) references unimpeachably establish some connection of the Kārkoṭa dynasty with the Nāgas and, possibly, with Nāga worshippers inhabiting the Valley in distant past. Incidentally, the entire *Rājataraṅgiṇī* is full of references to Nāgas and their supernatural powers who, from time to time, had been munificent when pleased and caused harm when annoyed. That Kārkoṭa Nāga commanded an eminent place amongst the Nāga worshippers all over Northern India is apparent from the fact that a shrine dedicated to him at Barha Katra in Banda (U.P.) exists even to this day.[36]

These early notices, it should also be noted, refer to Nāga Karkoṭa and not Kārkoṭa, and this peculiarity has not received sufficient attention from scholars. Grammatically, it is possible to suggest that according to the latter form (i.e., Kārkoṭa), some descendant of Karkoṭa is meant, and not the *Ṛgvedic* serpent. Very possibly, the Valley developed a legend of its own around the name of a descendant of Karkoṭa and not the Vedic serpent itself. On the strength of these literary notices, it is apparent that, with the growth of legends around the Nāga Karkoṭa, the name had achieved considerable importance and was associated with the dynasty in the Valley.

The founder of the Kārkoṭa Nāga dynasty was Durlabhavardhana, who, according to *Rājataraṅgiṇī*,[37] was son of Kārkoṭa Nāga. He succeeded Bālāditya, the last ruler of Gonanda family. His descent from the legendary Nāga Kārkoṭa is yet another instance of supplying haloed pedigree like the origin of the Pālas, Pratihāras, Paramāras, Chandellas, etc. According to *Rājataraṅgiṇī*, Durlabhavardhana was "a man of lowly origin, took service under king

Bālāditya, married his daughter and, after the king's death, succeeded him."[38] It has been expressly stated by Kalhaṇa that he did not come of a royal family and was comely in looks; hence his humble origin may be taken as a fact.[39] The legend of his mother cohabiting with Kārkoṭa Nāga and taking her 'purifying bath' might also offer an inkling of his native place.[40] The Nāga had his abode in some small lake on the Toshmaidan (Tosmaidan) route to Lohara.[41] Evidently, the mother of Durlabhavardhana, a native of the same locality, had gone to bathe in some lake, presumably the same, as the legend has it. It is, however, not specifically stated whether she was married; had she been so, Durlabhavardhana's father would also have been mentioned in the chronicle along with his caste.

According to C.V. Vaidya, Durlabhavardhana belonged to the Vaiśya caste and was not a Kāyastha. The term *Aśvaghāsakāyastha* is indicative of his office and not his caste.[42] It is quite likely that he belonged to the Nāga clan and was a powerful local chief, worthy to be considered by his father-in-law, King Bālāditya, to marry his daughter Anaṅgalekhā to him. Durlabhavardhana was the first historical monarch who laid the foundations of the greater Kashmir. The dynasty which he founded ruled for more than two centuries.

Kalhaṇa tells us little about Durlabhavardhana except that he built a temple of Viṣṇu and granted two villages to Brāhmaṇas. But we may have some idea of his achievements from foreign sources. The Chinese pilgrim Hiuen Tsang, who visited Kashmir in AD 631, says that Takṣaśilā, Uraśa (modern Hazara district), Simhapur (the present Salt Range) and the hill states of Rājapurī (Rājauri) and Parṇotsa (Punch) were subject to Kashmir.[43] It is not unlikely that these territories were conquered and brought under the suzerainty of Kashmir by Durlabhavardhana. The southward expansion of Kashmir seems to have brought it into clash with Harṣavardhana, the emperor of Kanauj, whose authority extended over Jālandhara. Hiuen Tsang tells us that Harṣa marched up to the frontier of Kashmir to demand the surrender of a sacred tooth of the Buddha which was buried in a stupa near Purāṇādhiṣṭhāna, the old capital of Kashmir. The incident took place sometime before AD 643. Behind the apparently religious character of this move on the part of Harṣa, there appears to have been a deeper political motive. It was impossible for Harṣa to permit the ruler of Kashmir to extend his authority to the very frontier of his empire, and the demand for the relic must have served as a convenient excuse for the display of his military might.

Hiuen Tsang gives on the whole a favourable picture of the conditions prevailing in Kashmir. He was particularly impressed with the state of learning in the Valley, and spent two years amongst the Kashmir savants, studying religious texts and holding discussions on points of religious doctrine.

In the Chinese annals also there is a probable reference to Durlabha. We are told that the Indian king Tu-la-pa was charged with having the envoys of Ki-Pin conveyed to their own country sometime between AD 627 and 649.[44] According to the chronology accepted by us, this period falls within the reign of Durlabhavardhana.

The mixed metal coins bearing the legend *Śrī Durlabha* on the obverse and *Jayati Kidāra* on the reverse, belong to this monarch. Kalhaṇa has assigned to Durlabhavardhana a reign of 36 years which came to a close in AD 661.

Durlabhavardhana was succeeded by his son Durlabhaka in AD 661 and he enjoyed a long and peaceful reign of about fifty years during which he consolidated the Kārkoṭa empire founded by his father. He was most popularly known as Pratāpāditya, the *āditya* title having adopted by him from Bālāditya, his grandfather. His copper coins found from Aunjhar fortress in the Mau tehsil of Banda district bear the legend *'Śrī Pratāpa'*.[45] Kalhaṇa has narrated a romantic story of the king's love and marriage with a lady named Narendraprabhā, the wife of a rich merchant named Noṇa of Rauhitaka country (Rohtak in Haryana) who had settled in the Valley.[46] Narendraprabhā gave birth to three sons, namely, Chandrāpīḍa-Vajrāditya, Tārāpīḍa-Udayāditya and Muktāpīḍa-Lalitāditya who succeeded to the throne of Kashmir one after the other. Durlabhaka founded the city of Pratāpapura, modern Thapar, situated between Bārāmulā and Srinagar, and constructed there a Noṇamaṭha (after the name of Noṇa) for the comforts of Brāhmaṇas of Rauhitadeśa, probably as a gesture of goodwill towards Noṇa who belonged to that land.

Chandrāpīḍa-Vajrāditya ascended the throne in c. 711 AD. Scholars have identified him with King Tehen-to-le-pi-li who, according to the annals of the Táng dynasty, sought the aid of the Chinese emperor to fight the Arabs,[47] who, after conquering Sindh, were gradually marching towards the southern borders of Kashmir. Chandrāpīḍa appears to have been a wise and capable ruler. Kalhaṇa has narrated two incidents[48] which exhibit his great love for justice and keen interest in the welfare of his subjects. Abu'l Fazl too testified his benevolent nature.[49] The circumstances under which he was put to death by his brother Tārāpīḍa, are fully detailed by Kalhaṇa.[50] It goes to the credit of noble-hearted Chandrāpīḍa who pardoned the culprit or culprits on his death-bed.[51] He died after a brief rule of about nine years and was succeeded by his younger brother Tārāpīḍa in c. 720 AD.

Tārāpīḍa-Udayāditya ruled the Valley oppressively and derived much pleasure in inhuman acts. According to Kalhaṇa, his antagonism to Brāhmaṇas eventually led the latter to make him a victim of the same plan through which he had disposed off his elder brother Chandrāpīḍa. Falling a victim to their witchcraft, his reign came to an end after a brief period of four years and twenty-four days. He was succeeded by his younger brother Lalitāditya Muktāpīḍa in c. 724 AD.

Under Lalitāditya the Kārkoṭas attained the zenith of their power. During 8th century AD, Lalitāditya proved to be the most illustrious figure of the century, who not only held sway over a large area in North India but also extended his suzerainty over a considerable portion of the subcontient and large tracts of Central Asian regions – probably for the second time in the annals of Indian history, a millennium after the imperial Mauryas. He is remembered in annals of India not only for his wars and conquests but also for his qualities as a champion of justice, promoter of literary and creative activities and for his patronage of art and architecture. Under his benevolent rule the Kashmir Valley rose to heights of unprecedented glory and prosperity which it could never achieve ever after. A crowing achievement of his glory, the Mārtaṇḍa temple, though in ruins, stands to this day as a fitting memorial of his greatness.

When Lalitāditya came to the throne, North India presented a picture of political fragmentation with numerous principalities ruled by weaklings – a factor which helped the ruler of the Valley in his *digvijaya*. Though the account of his conquests as given in *Rājataraṅgiṇī* cannot be regarded as wholly true and reads like the conventional description of Sanskrit epic poems, yet some of the events are undoubtedly historical.

The first task of Lalitāditya was to consolidate his position in the Valley. According to *Rājataraṅgiṇī*, he made extensive conquests in far off regions. Before this, he subdued the neighbouring petty states perhaps on the western and northern fringes of Kashmir. The sovereignty of Kashmir from the Sindhu to the Chenab, testified by Hiuen Tsang, seems to have been maintained by the successors of Durlabhavardhana. Lalitāditya extended it further towards the south-east. Kalhaṇa tells us that Jālandhara was ruled by his feudatory. The assertion of Lalitāditya's authority over the plain between the Beas and the Sutlej as well as the hill tracts of Kangra which were included in Jālandhara, was but a prelude to an attack upon the kingdom of Kanauj.

Having subjugated the petty states neighbouring the kingdom of Kashmir, Lalitāditya directed his forces towards the borders of the kingdom of Kanauj which was ruled by Yaśovarman. That his territories extended as far as the Southern Punjab and the sub-mountainous regions of the Himalayas is fully attested by epigraphic and literary evidences as well as the accounts of the foreign writers.[52] Yaśovarman's conquests brought him dangerously close to the south-eastern extremities of the empire of Lalitāditya and the exchange of arms became inevitable between the two. Jālandhara, because of its strategic location, became a bone of contention between Lalitāditya and Yaśovarman. The advancing forces of Lalitāditya must have clashed with those of Yaśovarman. *Rājataraṅgiṇī* makes it abundantly clear that the tide of events went in favour of Lalitāditya and this is also hinted in *Gauṛavaho*.[53] That Yaśovarman was forced to conclude terms with Lalitāditya is stated by *Rājataraṅgiṇī* in the following words: "The thoughtful ruler of Kānyakubja showed himself as one of the wise, when he first showed his back to the fiercely shining Lalitādiya and then made his submission."[54] Yaśovarman sought for an honourable peace and he drafted the treaty in words which put him at par with the victor. This was explained to Lalitāditya by his minister of war and peace, Mitraśarman, who had strongly reacted to the draft and refused to sign it. Possibly Lalitāditya intentionally made it an excuse to renew conflict with Yaśovarman whom he wanted to defeat finally to have his supremacy established over North India. *Rājataraṅgiṇī* states that Lalitāditya started quick preparations for the second attack in spite of reluctance on the part of his generals.[55] In the protracted struggle that ensued, Yaśovarman was 'completely uprooted.'[56] Lalitāditya thus became master of not only Yaśovarman's dominion proper, but of the entire Gangetic plain from the Yamuna to South-West Bengal. What happened to Yaśovarman after his defeat is an issue of keen controversy amongst scholars. Some believe that he was killed, others opine that he was made a vassal, still others argue that he took to flight.

Kalhaṇa then gives an account of Lalitāditya's conquest of Kaliṅga, Eastern India along the course of the Gaṅgā up to Gauḍa, towards the south up to the river Kaveri including the submission of a Raṭṭā queen of Karnataka, then marching homewards ravaging the seven Konkanas, holy city of Dwārkā and reaching the city of Ujjayinī, the capital of Avanti to pay homage to the Mahākāla.[57]

In view of lack of independent evidence, most of the scholars have accepted Kalhaṇa's Deccan, West Indian and Central Indian conquests as merely a conventional elaboration of the popular belief which attributed to Lalitāditya the customary *digvijaya* of an Indian hero.[58] Some scholars have, however, tried to justify these conquests.[59]

After the successful conclusion of the Gangetic campaign, Lalitāditya turned his attention to the north of Kashmir and conquered the Tuḥkhāras (Tukhāras), Bhauṭṭas, and Darads. The Tukhāras occupied modern Badakhshan and the adjoining territory on the upper Oxus. Perhaps a Tukhāra named

Chaṇkuṇa[60] became Lalitāditya's minister. The memory of this victory survived for a long time as Alberuni records "that the Kashmiris still celebrate the victory of Muttai, i.e., Muktāpīḍa over the Turks." The Bhauṭṭas are the Tibetans of Ladakh and the adjacent territory. The expedition against the Bhauṭṭas was perhaps necessitated by the establishment of the powerful Tibetan empire and its growing spirit of aggression towards the west. The complete success of Lalitāditya's expedition is indicated by the Chinese accounts of Muktāpīḍa's embassy which told the Chinese about the repeated victories of the king of Kashmir over the Tibetans.[61] The Darads occupied the valley of the Kishangaṅgā, the Indus regions of Gilgit, Chilas and Bunji, and Chitral and Yasin beyond the Indus.[62]

Another notable military success of Lalitāditya was the victory over Mummuni whose armies were defeated thrice. Mummuni has been identified with the Caliph who bore the title of 'Amīr-ul Mūmenīn'.[63] The clash between the Arabs and Kashmir is mentioned by the Muslim historian Balādhuri who says that during the reign of the Abbasid Caliph Al-mansur his Governor of Sindh conquered Kashmir and took many prisoners of war. But Indian tradition handed down to Kalhaṇa gave quite an opposite story, viz., Kashmirian monarch's repeated triumphs over the Arabs. The reverses of the Arabs in India early in the reign of Lalitāditya are admitted by Balādhuri himself.[64]

How far the conventional account of Lalitāditya made by Kalhaṇa be regarded as historically true is difficult to say. His defeat of Yaśovarman and conquest up to Bengal and Kaliṅga may be accepted as true in view of wide range of his coins found from Kanauj, Banda, Faizabad, Rajghat, Sarnath, Nalanda and Monghyr. But it is difficult to believe without corroborative evidence that he conquered the Deccan or South India. It is likely that Mummuni was an Arab leader whom he encountered while conquering Kangra. Possibly on account of his presence in the Punjab that the Arabs could not gain any lasting success towards their eastward campaigns. There may also be a great deal of truth in reputed victories of Lalitāditya against Kamboja, Turks, Dards and Tibetans who surrounded the kingdom of Kashmir. Dr. R.C. Majumdar is right when he says that: "Although corroborative evidence is lacking, and final judgement about the nature and extent of Lalitāditya's victorious campaign has to be suspended, there is no valid reason to regard the whole thing as mere fiction. It should be remembered that we have here to deal with not a conventional poetic description in a Kāvya, but a statement of facts made by a historian whose sobriety of judgement and regard for historical truth are vouched for by his work. Making due allowance for the partiality and exaggeration of a court historian and the imperfect knowledge of events which had taken place more than four centuries before Kalhaṇa's time, we cannot but regard Lalitāditya as a great conqueror. His extensive conquest made the kingdom of Kashmir, for the time being, the most powerful empire that India had seen since the days of the Guptas. No wonder that for centuries the Kashmirians celebrated the victories of the great emperor whom, with pardonable exaggeration, they chose to call the universal monrach."[65]

This worthy monarch of Kashmir met his end in one of his expeditions beyond the frontiers of his empire. Kalhaṇa records two traditions regarding the death of Lalitāditya which were prevalent during the time. According to one he died due to heavy snowfall in the region called Āryānaka which may be identified with Ariana of the Greek writers and eastern Iran of the present times.[66] According to the other tradition he committed suicide in order to avoid capture by his enemies when separated from the main body of his army.[67]

Lalitāditya's reign is memorable not only for his glorious conquests but also for his remarkable activities related to art and architecture, administration, patronage to learning, etc. He initiated the scheme of irrigation at Chakaradhara (modern Tsakdar), founded a new capital named Parihāsapura (modern Parspor), built two magnificent Viṣṇu temples named Parihāsakeśava and Govardhanadhara and a Vihāra, surpassing in magnitude the great shrine of Mārtaṇḍa. His queens and ministers also built several temples and monasteries. He also built a monastery at Hushkapura. Kalhaṇa mentions that the cities of Sunischitapura, Darpitapura, Phalapura and Parṇotśa were founded by him. However, these cannot be identified now. He was responsible for founding the Kashmir School of Art which incorporated Greek, Gāndhāra and indigenous (Gupta) traditions in it.[68]

As per Kalhaṇa, Lalitāditya was a compassionate ruler well versed in *Śāstras* and principles of running an efficient government for which he had evolved a 'Code of Ethics' for his ministers and officials. He was also a great patron of learning. If Kalhaṇa is to be believed, Lalitāditya extended patronage to Bhavabhūti and Vākpatirāja, the two court poets of Yaśovarman whom he had defeated.[69] He followed policy of toleration towards all religions and sects though he himself was a staunch follower of Hinduism.

In his old age Lalitāditya appears to have taken to heavy drinking. Once in a state of intoxication he ordered sack of Pravarapura which his wise minister cleverly avoided. A far more serious blemish on his character was his treatment meted to the king of Gauḍa whom he invited with assurance of safe return but got him killed through a hired assasin.[70] As the assurance was made on the oath of Parihāsakeśava (Viṣṇu), the trecherous act invited a band of Gauḍa king's faithful ally to come to Kashmir and destroy the shrine of Rāmasvāmin which they mistook for Parihāsakeśava.

Lalitāditya died in c. 760 AD and was succeeded by a chain of weak rulers whose rule proved to be a period of decline for the Kārkoṭa Nāga dynasty.

Kuvalayāpīḍa, born of queen Kamalādevī, succeeded to the throne in c. 760 AD. His accession was in accordance with an express wish of Lalitāditya in which he instructed his ministers that after his death his eldest son Kuvalayāpīḍa should be his immediate successor. Next, his second son Vajrāditya should succeed. After the death of Vajrāditya, his youngest son Jayāpīḍa should be placed on the throne.[71] The ministers followed his will. The new monarch was of a liberal disposition but was soon called upon to deal with his recalcitrant brother, who, backed by a ministerial party, created trouble and obtained a share of royal authority.[72] Having overcome his initial difficulties, Kuvalāyapīḍa started reorganising his army, but does not seem to have made any conquests. Being a man of sensitive nature, he was disgusted with the conspiracies in the court and decided to abdicate the throne and retire to the forests.[73] Thus ended the short reign of Kuvalayāpīḍa after a period of thirteen months.[74]

He was succeeded by Vajrāditya, also called Bappiyaka. The new king was cruel and cared little for his subjects.[75] Even religious endowments did not escape his greed. He withdrew the grants made by his father Lalitāditya to the religious institutions at Parihāsapura.[76] He spent most of his time in his harems and, as per Kalhaṇa, introduced several *mlechchha* practices in Kashmir including sale of men.[77] He soon became a prey to consumption on account of his excesses and died after a brief reign of seven years (c. 761-68 AD).

The next ruler was Prithivyāpīḍa. He was a man of equally vile disposition and oppressor of his subjects. He ruled for a little over four years (c. 768-72 AD)[78] and was dethroned by his younger brother Saṁgrāmāpīḍa who died after a butterfly existence of seven days on the throne.[79]

Jayāpīḍa Vinayāditya, the youngest son of Vajrāditya and grandson of Lalitāditya, was the next ruler of Kashmir. His good qualities were noticed by his grandfather even when he was a mere child[80] and hence he had selected him as one of his successors. The new king strove to emulate his grandfather in more than one way and succeeded to a great extent in retrieving the fallen fortunes and glory of the family.[81]

Soon after his accession in c. 773 AD, Jayāpīḍa reorgranised his forces and proceeded for expeditions which has been described by Kalhaṇa at a great length. However, the details given by him are, at times, mythical and full of fiction. Many scholars have, therefore, doubted the historical facts stated by Kalhaṇa. To quote Dr. Jagannath, "In Kalhaṇa's account of the reign of Jayāpīḍa fact and fiction have been mixed together and the latter predominates. But for the fact that definite historical data are available for Jayāpīḍa, one might be inclined to regard him as a mythical personality. Kalhaṇa speaks of his expeditions against Bhīmasena, king of the eastern country, but such a king is otherwise unknown so far. Similarly his account of Aramuḍi, a ruler of Nepal, reads more like a romance than sober history. To the same category probably belong the descriptions of adventures in the land of the Amazons and against the Nāga Mahāpadma.[82]

As soon as Jayāpīḍa left Kashmir with a large army to win laurels in war, misfortunes followed in his foot-steps. Jayāpīḍa's brother-in-law (*syāla*) raised a rebellion and usurped the throne by force.[83] He had also to face desertion from his ranks as his soldiers were unwilling to be away for long from their home. Undaunted, Jayāpīḍa proceeded forward with a band of trusted and loyal followers and reached Prayāga. Here he bestowed munificence on the Brāhmaṇas and the worthy.[84] Thereafter he dispatched most of his followers homeward and, eager for adventure, wandered forth all alone and reached Pundravardhana (modern Rajshahi Division in North Bengal), the capital of Jayanta, the king of Gauḍa. Jayāpīḍa's wanderings in distant Eastern India are detailed at great length in Kalhaṇa's *Rājataraṅgiṇī*,[85] and this account has become a matter of great controversy amongst scholars. It is said that Jayāpīḍa's incognito visit to Gauḍa failed soon after his encounter with a lion in which he slew the animal. King Jayanta found out his identity and got his daughter Kalyāṇadevī married to him.[86] Jayāpīḍa is said to have defeated the chiefs of the five Gauḍas (*Pañcha-Gauḍa*) and made his father-in-law the supreme ruler of Gauda. Meanwhile, Devaśarman, the faithful minister and son of Mitraśarman, had been able to collect and reorganise the leaderless forces of Jayāpīḍa and joined him.[87] Devaśarman prevailed upon his master to return back to Kashmir along with his wife and a consort (the latter being a dancing girl who had gained Jayāpīḍa's confidence and favour).[88] Enroute Kashmir, Jayāpīḍa defeated and seized the royal throne of the king of Kānyakubja (Kanauj) who, in all probability, was Vajrāyudha. When he reached Kashmir, Jajja, the usurper of the throne came forward with his followers and gave battle to Jayāpīḍa at Śushkaletra (modern Hukhaliter), which continued for several days finally leading to the defeat and killing of Jajja. Thus Jayāpīḍa regained possession of his ancestral throne. To commemorate the victory, Jayāpīḍa's queen Kalyāṇadevī founded a town named Kalyāṇapura (modern Kalanpor).

The irrepressible spirit of adventurism in Jayāpīḍa did not allow him to remain qutie for long and he set out to subdue a chieftain named Bhīmasena whom he defeated and killed in spite of being taken a prisoner in the campaign.[89] His next target was the invasion of Nepal which was under the rule of a king named Aramuḍi.[90] Here also he is said to have succeeded in defeating the ruler after initial failure and capture.[91] The conquest of *Strī-rājya* (kingdom ruled by a woman, i.e., queen) was his next target. All these adventures of Jayāpīḍa have been vividly described by Kalhaṇa and it reads like a romantic tale. Stein, Smith and many other scholars have seriously doubted the historicity of the entire account of Jayāpīḍa's above-mentioned invasions.

Towards the latter part of his reign, Jayāpīḍa turned a tyrant and an oppressor of his people, and thought of enriching the royal treasury through heavy and extortionate taxation.[92] This turning point in his career seems to have occurred after his breach of etiquette with some legendary Nāga Mahāpadma, and the story is related at great length in *Rajātaraṅgiṇī*.[93] Little credence can be placed on the story, but it seems that Jayāpīḍa, acting on the advice of some Kāyastha officials, levied and exacted taxes to the disgust of his subjects.[94] He even tried to confiscate *agrahāras*, but desisted from doing so when 99 Brāhmaṇas committed mass suicide by drowing themselves.[95] The unrest in the country was further aggravated by harsh actions taken by his revenue officials.[96] According to Kalhaṇa, the curse of a Brāhmaṇa led him to receive an injury which ultimately proved fatal and he died after a rule of 31 years.[97]

Soon followed the decline of the Kārkoṭa Nāga dynasty; the successors of Jayāpīḍa were licentious and weak rulers who, far from redeeming the fallen prestige of the family, hastened its eclipse.

Jayāpīḍa was succeeded by his son Lalitāpīḍa, born of his queen Durgādevī. He was a weak ruler of licentious habits.[98] The administrative machinery became loose but the king had no time to look into the problems. His inglorious reign came to an end after a rule of 12 years.

Lalitāpīḍa was succeeded by his step-brother Saṅgrāmāpīḍa II, born a queen Kalyāṇadevī,[99] daughter of Jayanta, king of Bengal. Of his reign of seven years, no events have been recorded.[100]

Sangrāmāpīḍa II was succeeded by Chippaṭajayāpīḍa, also known as Bṛhaspati, and a son of Lalitāpīḍa from his concubine Jayādevī, who came of a family of spirit-distillers (Kalyapāla).[101] Since he was a minor, the affairs of the state were looked after by his maternal uncles and his mother.[102] During the period of this regency, the royal treasury was systematically looted by the cunning regents, cleverest among them, Utpalaka by name, chose for himself the highest honour (*pañchamahāśabda*) and conferred upon his brothers other high titles.[103] Being ambitious, the regents managed to kill Chippaṭajayāpīḍa after a brief rule of 12 years and were soon themselves involved in a struggle for supremacy.[104]

Henceforth, the history of Kashmir is a continuous struggle for supremacy, till the firm establishment of the Utpala dynasty. The principal actors in the drama were the five regents, viz., Padma, Utpalaka, Kalyāṇa, Mamma and Dharma. They had managed to seize and concentrate all powers amongst themselves. Jealous of each other, they found it expedient to seat Ajitāpīḍa on the throne, as he served as a convenient screen for their design and machinations. In doing so they disregarded the claim of Tribhuvanāpīḍa, born of queen Meghāvalī, by King Bappiya.[105] Vaidya is right in saying that these king-makers played a role similar to that of the ambitious and unscrupulous officers during the closing years of Abbasid Caliphs and Mughal dynasties.[106] Since Ajitāpīḍa was a very weak ruler, he failed to control the activities of his five regents, the former liquor-sellers, who, during 26 years of their supremacy, tried to outdo each other by founding towns after their names, building temples and similar acts of charity and munificence all at the cost of the royal treasury and their ill-gotten gains.[107]

Kalhaṇa gives an account of such activities conducted by each regent.[108] Naturally such a state of affair could not last long and open hostilities flared up between Utpalaka and Mamma.[109] The latter, however, emerged victorious through the gallantry of his son Yaśovarma, dethroned Ajitāpīḍa, who was a protege of Utpalaka, and seated Anaṅgāpīḍa, a son of Saṅgrāmāpīḍa II on the throne.[110]

Anaṅgāpīḍa could not last long as Sukhavarman, son of Utpalaka, was constantly conspiring against him. After three years of successful intrigues, he deposed Anaṅgāpīḍa and enthroned Utpalāpīḍa, a son of Ajitāpīḍa.[111] His brief rule of two years was marked by disintegration of the empire. The rulers of dependencies like Parṇotsa and Dārvābhisāra threw off the yoke. The authority of Kashmir was now confined to the valley of Vitastā only.

The fortunes of the Kārkoṭa Nāga dynasty were waning rapidly.[112] The minister Sukhavarman was himself aspiring to the royal position. His ambition remained unrealised as he was killed by a relative named Śuṣka.[113] Śūrā, a minister and a partisan of Sukhavarman, deposed Utpalāpīḍa and placed Avantivarman, son of Sukhavarman on the throne.[114] With Avantivarman was founded the line of Utpala dynasty. Thus came to an end the dynasty of the Kārkoṭa Nāgas, after a rule of a little more than two centuries and a quarter.

The Kashmir Valley did not ever rise to such heights of glory and prosperity as under some of the rulers of this dynasty and never before or after did the empire reach up to such extents in territories. For some time, during the reign of Lalitāditya and also under Jayāpīḍa, it was the supreme power in Northern India and even Kanauj had to bow twice before its might. These kings had established an efficient system of administration; the empire had, from the earliest times, been divided into two broad divisions, viz., the *parganas* of Kramarājya (regions below Srinagar and on both side of the Jhelum) and Maḍavarājya (those above it) with the sole authority vested in the king who ruled with a council of ministers, many of whom were greatly respected for their devotion and intelligence. The kings, though themselves professed Śaivites, showed no religious bias, and Śaivism, Vaiṣṇavism, Buddhism and numerous minor sects flourished together. It may be noted here in passing that many kings of this dynasty did not, as Kalhaṇa hints at in a veiled and indirect way, show enough respect to the Brāhmaṇas, but one may safely look on such pointers as the author's partiality towards them.

Another noteworthy contribution of the Kārkoṭas in the politics of the times was their desire and endeavour to establish and maintain friendly relations with foreign countries, as related above. Also, their contributions in the spheres of art and literature cannot be left out, for many kings of this dynasty were responsible for the foundation and embellishment of numerous cities, palaces, temples and works of public utility and welfare.

Thus, though the power and fame of the rulers of the valley reached its zenith during the rule of the Kārkoṭas, the rather inglorious rule of the later rulers, who proved mere weaklings, brought about the dissipation of the royal family and its pristine glory. Given to pleasure-seeking, they turned tyrants and were themselves promoters of court intrigues through their favourites. Events of far-reaching consequences were happening in the neighbouring countries and only Lalitāditya seems to have realised their importance. Lacking in political vision and wisdom, his successors, could not rise to the occasion and the empire fell to pieces.

REFERENCES

1. Kalhaṇa's *Rājataraṅgiṇī* or *Chronicles of the kings of Kashmir*, ed. M.A. Stein, Bombay, 1892. Eng. tr. by Stein in two volumes, Westminister, 1900.
2. *Rāj*, II, 28-31, Stein's tr., Vol. I, pp. 5ff.
3. *Rāj*, I, 111 and 114; Stein's tr., Vol. I, pp. 21ff.
4. *Rāj*, I, 177-84; Stein's tr., Vol. I, pp. 32ff.

5. *Nīlamata Purāṇa*, ed. R.L. Kanjilal and Pt. J. Zadoo, Lahore, 1924. A Nāgrī manuscript of the same exists in the Indian Institute at Oxford.
6. *Ibid.*, 430 (MS. 331).
7. *Ibid.*, 781-89 (MS. 670-79).
8. *Ibid.*, 896-902 (MS. 772).
9. *Ibid.*, 116-18 (MS. 969-70).
10. Stein, *Rāj*, tr., Vol. II, pp. 469 ff.
11. *Nīlamata*, 432 (MS. 333).
12. *Āīn-i-Akbarī*, tr. Vol. II, p. 361.
13. *Tūzuk-i-Jahāngīrī*, tr. Vol. I, p. 92; cf. also Vol. II, p. 174.
14. *Āīn-i-Akbarī*, tr. Vol. II, p. 363; cf. Stein, *Rāj*, tr. Vol. II, pp. 474ff.
15. Stein, *op cit.*, Vol. II, p. 470.
16. *Ibid.*, p. 466.
17. *Mahābhārata Vana-Parva*, lxxxii, 90.
18. *Vikramāṅkadevacharita*, XVIII, 70 (Buhlar's tr.).
19. *Āīn-i-Akbarī*, (tr. Jarrett), Vol. II, p. 358.
20. Stein, *op cit.* Vol. I, p. 37.
21. *Ibid.*, Vol. II, p. 409.
22. *Ibid.*, p. 415.
23. *Ibid.*, p. 399.
24. *Āīn-i-Akbarī*, Vol. II, p. 356.
25. *Ibid.*, p. 361.
26. *Ibid.*, p. 362.
27. *Ibid.*, p. 365
28. Walter R. Lawrence, *The Valley of Kashmir*, London, 1895, pp. 295-99.
29. *Atharvaveda*, VII, 56: 5 and 7.
30. Vogel, J. Ph., *Indian Serpent-Lore*, p. 214.
31. *Mahābhārata*, I, 35, 1550; I, 123, 4828; II, 9, 316; III, 66, 2611; III, 72, 2828; III, 79, 3072; VIII, 44, 2066; XVI, 4, 119; cf. Sorensen, S., *An Index to the Names in the Mahābhārata*, p. 384.
32. *Bhāgavata Purāṇa*, xii, II, 42; *Matsya*, 6, 18, 29, 33, 39, etc; *Vāyu*, 17, 26, 52, 69, 70, 94; *Viṣṇu*, I, 221, 22; II, 14, 22; *Brahmāṇḍa* II, 17, 23; III, 7, 34; IV, 20, 33, 36, 50; Tawney, C.H., *Ocean of Stories*, Vol. II, pp. 67, 73, 78; IV, pp. 245-50.
33. *Matsya Purāṇa*, 36, 196.
34. Tawney, C.H., *Ocean of Stories*, II, pp. 67, 73, 78. Further, dealing with the story of Nala, Kārkoṭa Nāga has been mentioned (IV, pp. 45-46, 48, 50); *Nīlamata Purāṇa*, 901; *Rāj*, III, 490 (Stein's note).
35. Vogel, J. Ph., *Indian Serpent Lore*, p. 215.
36. *Ibid.*
37. *Rāj*, I, iii, 490, 530, iv, 2.
38. Ray, S.C., *Early History and Culture of Kashmir*, p. 38.
39. *Rāj*, I, iii, 488-89.
40. *Ibid.*, 490.

41. *Ibid.*, Stein's note; II, viii, 1596, 1997.
42. Vaidya, C.V., *History of Medieval Hindu India,* I, p. 203.
43. *Buddhist Records of the Western World*, tr. from the Chinese of Hiuen Tsang, by Samual Beal, I, pp. 136, 143, 147, 164; Hiuen Tsang says that Kashmir's suzerainty over Taxila was of recent date.
44. A Remusat, *Nouveaux Melanges Asiatiqus,* I, p. 212.
45. Agrawal, V.S., *JNSI*, X, pt. I, p. 31.
46. *Rāj*, IV, 17-37.
47. Remusat, *op. cit,* p. 196ff.
48. *Rāj*, IV, 55-109.
49. *Āīn*, II, p. 175.
50. *Rāj*, IV, 82-118.
51. *Ibid.*, 115-16.
52. Vakpati, *Gauḍavaho*, (ed., S.P. Pandit & N.P. Utgikar, Poona, 1927), Intr. pp. xx-xxxiii, verse 484; Smith, V.A., *JRAS*, 1908, p. 784; *The Indo-Asian Culture*, XII, No 3, pp. 177-90.
53. *Gauḍavaho*, vs. 827-31.
54. *Rāj*, I, iv, 135.
55. *Ibid.*, 39.
56. *Ibid.*, 40.
57. *Ibid.*, 147-62.
58. Stein, *Rājataraṅgiṇī*, I, p. 90.
59. Saxena, K.S., *Political History of Kashmir*, Lucknow, 1974, pp. 61-80.
60. Stein thought that Chankuna was the Sankritized form of Turkish name. But Sylvain Levi pointed out that the Sanskrit name is a transcription of a Chinese title, Tsiang-kiun meaning 'general' which had found its way into the Tukhara country; See Stein's note on *Rāj*, IV, 211.
61. cf. Chavannes and Levi, *JA*, 1895, p. 382.
62. cf. Stein's note on *Rāj*, I, 312-16.
63. *JA*, 1895, p. 382, Stein's view on this point (cf. Stein, IV, 167, note) is not justified in view of the Arab historian Balādhuri's account of the Arab raids in India. cf. R.C. Majumdar, 'Arab Invasion of India,' *JIH*, X, part I, Supplement, pp. 40-43.
64. cf. ch. XIX, Saxena, K.S., *op cit.*
65. Majumdar, R.C. (ed.), *Classical Age*, pp. 134-35.
66. *Rāj*, I , iv, 367.
67. *Ibid.*, 368-69; vii, 1428-49.
68. *Journal of the Bombay University*, XXI, pt. 2, pp. 63-94.
69. *Rāj*, I, iv, 144.
70. *Ibid.*, 323-30.
71. *Ibid.*, 353, 356.
72. *Ibid.*, 373-76.
73. *Ibid.*, 378-87.
74. *Ibid.*, 392.

75. *Ibid.*, 394.
76. *Ibid.*, 395.
77. *Ibid.*, 397.
78. *Ibid.*, 399.
79. *Ibid.*, 400-401.
80. *Ibid.*, 359.
81. *Ibid.*, 403.
82. Majumdar, R.C. (ed.), *A Comprehensive History of India,* Vol. III, pt. I, p. 535.
83. *Raj*, I, iv, 410.
84. *Ibid.*, 415.
85. *Ibid.*, 420-69.
86. *Ibid.*, 462-67.
87. *Ibid.*, 469.
88. *Ibid.*, 422-44.
89. *Ibid.*, 521-29.
90. *Ibid.*, 531.
91. *Ibid.*, 533-50.
92. *Ibid.*, 620ff.
93. *Ibid.*, 592-615.
94. *Ibid.*, 621.
95. *Ibid.*, 638-39.
96. *Ibid.*, 629.
97. *Ibid.*, 638-56.
98. *Ibid.*, 662.
99. *Ibid.*, 674.
100. *Ibid.*, 675.
101. *Ibid.*, 676-78.
102. *Ibid.*, 679.
103. *Ibid.*, 680.
104. *Ibid.*, 687-88.
105. *Ibid.*, 689-90.
106. Vaidya, C.V., *History of Medieval Hindu India*, Vol. I, p. 218.
107. *Rāj*, I, iv, 693-702.
108. *Ibid.*, 695-702.
109. *Ibid.*, 704-06.
110. *Ibid.*, 707.
111. *Ibid.*, 709.
112. *Ibid.*, 713.
113. *Ibid.*, 714.
114. *Ibid.*, 715.

7

THE CHHINDAKA NĀGAS OF CHAKRAKŪṬA (BASTAR), NĀGAS OF KAWARDHĀ AND BHAṬGĀON

THE NĀGAS OF BASTAR

The ancient name of Bastar (district headquarter of the same name in Chhattisgarh state) was Chakrakoṭṭa, also called Chakrakūṭa, Chakrakoṭa, etc. Epigraphic and numismatic evidences prove that a Nāga dynasty was ruling over this region for more than five hundred years between c. 8th and 14th century AD. They designated themselves as the Chhindaka Nāgas and the capital of their territory was at Barasur, modern Barsur, about 70 km from Jagdalpur. They belonged to the *Kaśyapagotra* and had the snake-banner and 'tiger-with-cub' crest. One of their significant titles was "the lord of Bhogavatī, the best of the cities." Bhogavatī was the mythical capital of the snake-demons, called Nāgas, who lived in *Rasātala* forming a part of *Pātāla* or the sub-terranean world.

Regarding the origin of the Chhindaka Nāga family of Bastar, great uncertainty prevails as different views have been expressed by scholars. Scholars like R.B. Hiralal[1] and D.C. Sircar[2] have suggested that the expression 'Chhindaka' is a variant of Sindaka or Sinda; consequently the Chhindaka Nāgas of Bastar belonged to the stock of the Sindas of Bagalkot in the Bijapur district, Yelburga in the formerly Nizam's dominion and of Hallavur and

Belagutti in the Mysore area. According to D.C. Sircar, "The above information about the Chhindaka Nāgas of Bastar clearly points to their close relationship with the Sindas of the Kannad country. The land of the Sindas, called Sindavāḍi, comprised parts of northern Mysore, Bellary, Dharwar, and Bijapur, and is mentioned in a record of AD 750. The Sinda families ruled from Bagalkot and Yelburga in Bijapur and Hollavur and Belagutti in Mysore. There is no doubt that the family name Chhindaka, preferred by the Nāgavaṁśīs of Bastar, is the same as Sinda, although the Sindas fabricated a mythology to explain their family name as derived from the name of the river Sindhu. The fabricated genealogy of the Sindas sometimes says that the eponymous progenitor of the dynasty was a 'long-armed' Sinda who was the human son of a snake king named Dharaṇīndra and that he was born at Ahichchhatra near the Sindhu and was reared by a tiger. Elsewhere, however, the same mythical Sinda is described as the son of the god Śiva from the river-goddess Sindhu and as brought up by the snake-king with tiger's milk. We have no such explanation of the family name in the inscriptions of the Chhindakas; but it is quite significant that, like them, the Sindas also claimed the Nāga lineage, the snake-banner (sometimes explained as the banner having the figures of the Nāga-chiefs Ananta, Vāsuki and Takshaka represented on it), and the hereditary title 'lord of Bhogavatī, the best of cities.' It may be suggested that the Chhindakas left their original home in the Kannada country before the fabrication of the above genealogy by the Sindas, sometime after the middle of the eleventh century."[3]

Against this view it has been suggested that the original home of the Chhindaka Nāga family of Bastar was not the Kannada country, but Padmāvatī (in modern Gwalior district) which was situated on the 'Sindhu' (modern Kali Sindh) River where a major Nāga dynasty ruled during the post-Kuṣāṇa to Gupta Period, as already discussed in a preceding chapter. After their defeat in the hands of the Guptas the Nāgas of Padmāvatī migrated southwards and for a short period stayed in the forest areas of modern Hoshangabad and Jabalpur districts, as suggested by K.P. Jayaswal.[4] Their stay in the Hoshangabad district is proved by the existence of a later Nāga dynasty at modern Bhatgaon, as revealed by the inscription of Nāga king Pratāparudradeva (discussed below). Their subsequent migration to Jabalpur region is noted by Dr. H.L. Shukla who says that "Parenthetically I may note here that the name of 'Dharaṇīdhara' is found in the vulgar form of 'Dharen' with similar story in the Jabalpur district of M.P. in connection with the descent of another royal family tracing its origin from snake. We find that the Bagalkota branch of the Nāgavanshīs owned the tiger crest and 'Phaṇiketana' or banner of hooded serpents. This proves that next to Padmāvatī, the Sindhu dweller Nāgas during their migration to south, stayed for sometime in the Jabalpur region."

"The same mythical Sinda is also described as the son of the god Shiva from the river goddess Sindhu and as brought up by the snake king with tigress milk. We have no such explanations of the family name in the inscriptions of the Chhindakas; but it is quite significant that like them, the Sindas also claimed the Nāga lineage, the snake-banner, and the hereditary title 'lord of Bhagavatī, the best of cities.' Thus there can be no doubt that the dynasty was not connected with the Sinda's family of the Karnataka. The 'tiger-crest' was common to all branches of 'Sindakula'; while the Bagadage branch had simply the tiger-crest and 'phaṇiketana' or banner of hooded serpents, the Chakrakoṭa branch had a tiger with a calf or child (*savatsa*). Thus they were depicting probably the story of their origin in a cleaner way. The Bastar Sindas were sub-divided into two houses, the minor having the bow and tiger-crest and the banner of lotus flower and plantain-leaf (EI, X, 181). One point of striking contrast between the Sindas of Karnataka and those of Bastar is that latter, to judge from their titles '*Paramamaheshwara Parama Bhaṭṭāraka Mahārāja*' were independent monarchs without recognising the overlordship of any emperor."[5]

It may be suggested in this context that the presence of Nāgas in Jabalpur region is further confirmed by the wide prevalence of the legendary account of a king named Śālivāhana of Nāgvaṁśa who is supposed to have built the temple of Chausaṭha Yoginī at Bheraghat (for details of the legend, see Cunningham, ASI Report, Vol. IX, pp. 75-76).

A good number of the inscriptions of the Chhindaka Nāga rulers of Bastar have come to light. These inscriptions supported by literary evidences and other contemporary inscriptions have helped in reconstruction of the history of this dynasty.

The earliest known inscription of this Nāga dynasty is on a copper-plate found from Upet, a village situated on the road to Chitrakut and close to Chhapar Bhanpuri. The record is yet unpublished and is preserved in the Collectorate at Jagdalpur. As per information recorded by Dr. V.D. Jha, the inscription which is datable to AD 760 refers to one Vallabharāja who seems to be the first known ruler of this dynasty.[6] No details are known about him. The ruler Rājamalla, the Nāga ruler of the Southern region referred to in the Dhenkanal inscription as ruling in the first quarter of the 9 th century AD, seems to be a successor of Vallabharāja.[7] Another fragmentary inscription datable to later half of 9 th century AD found by Dr. Jha from Chhote Dongar refers to Vankhāditya and his crown prince.[8] Possibly he was successor of aforementioned Rājamalla. Nothing is known about the successors of

Vankhāditya till Śaṅkhapāla, the contemporary of the Paramāra ruler Sindhurāja (AD 995-1000) of Malwa with his capital at Dhārā.

Reference to the Chhindaka Nāga ruler Śaṅkhapāla is found in the historical *Kāvya Navasāhasāṅkacharita* composed by Padmagupta, the court-poet of Sindhurāja. The work narrates how a king of the Nāga dynasty, whose kingdom lay two hundred miles south of the Narmadā, sought help from Sindhurāja against a neighbouring demon-king named Vajrāṅkuśa. Sindhurāja along with the Vidyādharas, reached the country of the demons after crossing the Godavari and killed the demon-king in a battle. In gratitude the Nāga ruler Śaṅkhapāla gave his daughter Śaśiprabhā in marriage to Sindhurāja. Scholars have admitted that the outline of this story, narrated by Padmagupta, is based on historical facts.[9] It has been suggested that the Nāga king was a chief of the Nāga dynasty ruling in the Bastar region and the demon-king was either a chief of the non-Āryan Māna tribe of Vajra, modern Wairagarh in the Chaṇḍa district of Vidarbha (Maharashtra)[10] or the *Asura* chief of Komomaṇḍala in the Bilaspur district of M.P.[11] The Vidyādharas were the Śilāhāras of Thana, whose ruler at that time was Aparājita.

Nṛapatibhūṣaṇa was successor of Śaṅkhapāla. His fragmentary stone inscription in Telugu dated in Śaka era 945 (AD 1023) has been found from Errakot, 15 km from Jagdalpur.[12] His mutilated name '............tibhūṣaṇa' has been restored by scholars to read as 'Nṛapatibhūṣaṇa'. It was probably during his reign that the mighty Chola emperor, Rājendra I invaded Bastar and conquered Sakarakottam, which has been generally accepted to be a variant of Chakrakoṭa. The Nāga chief possibly acknowledged the supremacy of the Chola power.

The next ruler was Dhārāvarṣa *alias* Jagadekabhūṣaṇa whose four inscriptions have been found. His Telugu inscription found from Barsur, about 75 km from Jagdalpur, is dated in the Śaka era 983 (AD 1060).[13] It refers to the king as Mahārāja Jagadekabhūṣaṇa and records that a feudatory chief *(mahāmaṇḍaleśvara)* Chandrāditya Mahārāja, lord of Ammagrāma, excavated at the capital town of Bārāsuru, a tank which is called Chandrāditya Samudra, on whose bank he constructed a Śiva temple, naming it after himself as Chandrādityeśvara Shrine. For the maintenance of the temple he made grant of a village, Govardhanāṇḍu, which he had purchased from King Dhārāvarṣa. The transaction was effected in the presence of the ruling king. Chandrāditya claims descent from the Karikāla family who held sway over the Kaveri and had their capital at Orayuru. They belonged to the Kāśyapa *gotra* and to the Chola race and had a lion for their crest. This proves that Chandrāditya was connected with the ancient Cholas of Cuddapah district, who probably invaded

Bastar country and left him or his ancestor in charge of the conquered territory. Hiralal is of the opinion that "we know from other inscriptions that Kulottuṅga I (who ascended the throne in 1070 AD) attacked the Bastar country in his youth, and it is suggested that probably Chandrāditya followed Kulottuṅga in his campaign and settled down in the newly conquered country as a subordinate to Dhārāvarṣa. The pride of the victor could hardly have allowed his kith and kin to accept such a position, and it must have taken a long time for an enemy's follower to settle himself as a *Mahāmaṇḍaleśvara* of an aggrieved party, unless the terms of peace stipulated that the latter should accept a relative of the conqueror in that position."[14]

Of the three other inscriptions of the reign of Jagadekabhūṣaṇa, the one is from Potinar, about 100 km from Jagdalpur.[15] It is almost a duplicate of the above-mentioned Barsur inscription with the only difference that the village granted is different and the gift was meant to cover the expenses of a garden, also named Chandrāditya-nandanavana, planted in the vicinity of the aforementioned Śiva temple.

The second inscription is from Dantewada, about 60 km from Jagdalpur.[16] The name of the king is effaced in the inscription, but its date, viz., Śaka year 984 (AD 1061) falls in the reign period of Jagadekabhūṣaṇa. The inscription records that the king, while encamped at Dattavāḍā (Dantewada), purchased a village from a cultivator and presented it to the god Bhairava to meet the expenses of offerings to him.

The third inscription is from Bhairamgarh.[17] This is an incomplete inscription in Telugu, carved in 35 lines, which gives the usual *birudas* of the Nāgavaṁśī kings and introduces the Mahārāja Jagadekabhūṣaṇa (the worshipper of Māṇikyadevi's feet) and his feudatory Rāṅgayādeva, together with his son. Here the inscription breaks off, leaving us in dark as to its objective.

Dhārāvarṣa Jagadekabhūṣaṇa did not continue to have survived long after AD 1060 as the Chhindaka Nāga throne was occupied by another member of the family, named Madhurāntaka sometime before the fifth of October, AD 1065 (Śaka year 987) which is the date of his Rajapur plates.[18] The purpose for which the grant was made is somewhat obscure but interesting. It records the grant of Rajapura village, situated in the *Bhramarakoṭya maṇḍala* (alternate name of *Chakrakoṭya maṇḍala*), to one *Meḍipōta* or a *Chhurikara Meḍipōta* and his descendants, together with 70 *gadyāṇaka* (it is a weight) gold. It is stated that "nobody enters the *Chhuriprabandha*. There is no place for the preceptor of *Yoginis*. For this purpose this village is taken with a view to do good to all living beings."[19] Hiralal has interpreted the passage to mean that it refers to compensation given for supplying a victim for human sacrifice.[20] He points out that the grant was not made for any spiritual purpose such as the increasing of the religious merit of the king and his ancestors, but with a practical earthly aim, viz., in order to secure the welfare of the general public including cattle and other animals. Hiralal notes that in Bastar and the adjoining tracts, human sacrifices were rampant even during recent past and human victims were offered to the goddess Dantesvari, enshrined at Dantewara in Bastar. He quotes Col. Macpherson of the Madras Army, who was appointed agent for the suppression of Meriah sacrifices and female infanticide in the hill tracts of Orissa adjoining Bastar. According to Col. Macpherson: "In the worship of Pennu or Earth Goddess the chief rite is human sacrifice. It is celebrated as a public oblation by tribes both at social festivals held periodically and when occasions demand extraordinary propitiation, such as the occurrence of an *extraordinary number of deaths* by disease or by tigers, or should very many die in childbirth, or should the *flocks or herds* suffer largely from disease or from wild beasts, or should the greater crops threaten to fail, or the occurrence of any marked calamity to the families of the tribal chiefs. Victims are called Meriah and are acceptable only when they have been acquired by *purchase* or were born as such, that is, of a victim father. Victims are generally supplied to the Khonds by men of the two races called Panwa and Gahinga, who are attached in small numbers to almost every Khond village for the discharge of this and other peculiar offices. The Panwas purchase the victims without difficulty or kidnap them from the poorer classes of Hindus, procuring them either to the order of the Khonds or on speculation, and they moreover constantly sell as victims their own children and children of whom as relatives they are the guardians. Khonds when in distress, as in times of famine, also frequently sell their children for victims, considering the beatification of their souls certain and their death for the *benefit of mankind*, the most honourable possible. The Meriah grove, a clump of deep and shadowy forest trees, usually stands at a short distance from the village by a rivulet which is called the Meriah stream. It is kept sacred from the axe and is avoided by the Khonds as *haunted ground*."[21]

The arguments advanced by Hiralal to arrive at the conclusion seems to be quite convincing, particularly in view of the fact that human sacrifice was prevalent among the tribals of the region even a hundred years ago, till it was banned by the British government. In fact, nobody can convincingly say that incidents of this nature do not occur even now.

The king Madhurāntaka was a Śaiva and had the banner bearing the representation of a lotus and a plantation leaf on the back of Airāvata, instead of the snake-bearer used by the other members of the family. He was soon ousted from the throne by Someśvara I, son of Dhārāvarṣa, and his earliest known date is AD 1069, as recorded in his Kuruspal stone inscription of Śaka era 991. The names of these two rivals of the same family suggest that Someśvara was supported by the Chālukyas of Kalyāṇa, while Madhurāntaka received help from the Cholas, who, as noted above, had conquered Sakkarkottam (Chakrakoṭa) under the leadership of Kulottuṅga I at an early date.

The most important record of the reign of Someśvara I is the fragmentary stone inscription from Kuruspal.[22] The inscription records the name of Kanhara, who was the king's son and therefore it appears that the inscription was engraved late in his reign. The inscription states that he had a tiger crest and snake banner and he had acquired the sovereignty of Chakrakūṭa through the favour of the Goddess Vindhyavāsinī. It is recorded that his father was Dhārāvarṣa and that he had killed the powerful king Madhurāntaka in battle. This Madhurāntaka was none else than his predecessor, the issuer of the Rajapur plates of AD 1065. It is clear that taking advantage of the situation, he had usurped the throne after Dhārāvarṣa but was finally ousted from his position by Dhārāvarṣa's son.

The Kuruspal stone inscription also credits Someśvara with many other military activities, viz., the burning of Veṅgī, subjugation of Bhadrapaṭṭana and Vajra and seizure of six lakhs and ninety-six villages of Kosala country (South Kosala). Vengī, the kingdom of the Eastern Chālukyas, was the name of the territory between the Godavari and Krishna, and it was now a part of the Chola-Chālukya empire. Kuruspal stone inscription mentions the name of Vīrachoḍa, who, as we know from other sources, was the Viceroy of this country during AD 1078-84 and 1088-92 and was appointed by his father Kulottuṅga I (AD 1070-1120). The Vengī and the Chakrakoṭa kings appear to have always in feud with each other and to have burnt each other's towns whenever there was an opportunity. Bhadrapaṭṭana of the inscription has been identified by scholars with modern Bhandak in the Chaṇḍa district of Maharashtra. Vajra is generally identified with Wairagarh, also in Chaṇḍa district. Regarding the taking of six lakhs and ninety-six villages of Kosala, there is no doubt that it is an exaggeration. The Kosala referred to in the record must be taken as South Kosala (modern Chhattisgarh) country and it is very unlikely that it ever contained so many villages. Even if it did, there is nothing to justify the boast that Someśvara ever became the king of that country. It is possible that he may have raided a part of South Kosala and may have held it in his possession for some time as is also evidenced by discovery of gold coins issued by Someśvara from Sonsari in Bilaspur district of M.P.[23] This success might have been achieved at the expenses of the Kalachuris and the Somavaṁśīs who were ruling over the territory. It is to be noted that Yaśorāja I, father of the Telgu-Choḍa chief Chandrāditya who was ruling at Ammagrāma, as a feudatory of Someśvara's father, also claims to have carved out a kingdom in Kosala. It is not unlikely that Yaśorāja I entered Kosala as a lieutenant of Someśvara I and was rewarded the governorship of a part of the country he had conquered on behalf of his overlord. Another interesting fact is that Kumāra Someśvara of Suvarṇapura and Paschim Laṅkā, who belonged to the Somavaṁśa that was overthrowned by the descendants of Yaśorāja I, was probably named after the Chhindaka-Nāga king Someśvara I. This may suggest that for a time the later Somavaṁśīs had to acknowledge the supremacy of the Chhindakas. This suggestion is supported by the influence of the Telugu-Choḍa grants on the style of the copper-plate charter of Somavaṁśī Someśvara. The Kuruspal inscription also mentions the King of Ratanpur (the capital of the Kalachuris of South Kosala) as one of his antagonists as well. Some scholars suggest that King Someśvara, referred to in the Ratanpur stone inscription of Jājalladeva I dated in Kalachuri year 866 (AD 1114), who was seized by him in a battle and his capital city "was burnt by him after slaying (his) immense army; and by whom was captured and then released at his mother's words, the group of (his) ministers and wives,"[24] refers to the Chhindaka Nāga ruler Someśvara I. However, in the light of latest discoveries, Dr. A.M. Shastri believes that Someśvara referred to in the inscription of Jājalladeva I is "the homonymous Somavaṁśin chief who came to power in Kosala after Abhimanyu and issued his charter from Suvarṇapura."[25]

According to the Kuruspal inscription, other rival kings of Someśvara I with whom he conflicted were the kings of Uḍra (Orissa), Lāñjī (in Balaghat district) and Lemnā (Lavana in Raipur district). The king of Uḍra was possibly the Somavaṁśī ruler Uddyotakesarī.

Kuruspal has yielded two more inscriptions of Someśvara.[26] These record donation of village, by his queen Dhāraṇa Mahādevī to god Kāmeśvara (Śiva). The first inscription is dated in Śaka era 991 (AD 1069) but the second is undated. An inscription each from Kuruspal and Gadia,[27] both dated in Śaka era 1019 (AD 1097) record donations given by Someśvara.

An inscription found from Narayanpal which is dated in Śaka era 1033 (AD 1111) records the grant of a village Narayanpur by Guṇḍa Mahādevī, the chief queen of Mahārāja Dhārāvarṣa, the mother of Someśvara and the grandmother of Kanharadeva who was then ruling after the death of his father.[28] Thus, Someśvara I must have ended his reign sometime before AD 1111.

An inscription from Barsur records that Gaṅgamahādevī, the chief queen of Someśvara, gave a village as grant to two temples of Śiva built by her.[29] It is dated in the Śaka era 1130 (AD 1208), which, according to Hiralal is a mistake on the part of the scribe. It should be read as Śaka era 1030 (AD 1108) as the details mentioned in the inscription tally with the reign of Someśvara I. D.C. Sircar, however, suggests[30] that the King Someśvara mentioned in this inscription should be identified with King Rājabhūṣaṇa Someśvara II, known from Gadia inscription.[31] Rājabhūṣaṇa Mahārāja is also known from an undated inscription from Dantewada.[32] It is an interesting inscription, recording a notification to the general public by Māsakadevī, younger sister of Rājabhūṣaṇa Mahārāja. The notification runs as follows:

"In view of the fact that every member of the agricultural classes have been troubled by the king's officer while collecting rents which have been exacted even before they were due, the elders of the five great assemblies and the agricultural classes, in meeting assembled framed the following rules: 'That in future those villages which at the time of the coronation of any king may be required to render service shall collect the taxes etc., only from such residents as had been settled long there.' Māsakadevī has therefore set up this pillar recording the rules to regulate the position of the several classes. They shall be traitors to the king and Māsakadevī who, living in Chakragoṭṭa (will) violate these rules."

The record is interesting as it throws light on the administrative procedures of the Chhindaka Nāga rulers of Bastar.

An inscription from Barsur[33] mentions a king named Kanharadeva, who seems to be a later member of the family and may be styled as Kanhara II.

There are two inscriptions, one from Jatanpal which is dated in Śaka era 1140 (AD 1218)[34] and the other from Dantewada which is dated in Śaka era 1147 (AD 1224).[35] Both of them refer to a Chhindaka Nāga king Jagadekabhūṣaṇa Mahārāja Narasiṁhadeva.

Another member of this family is known from an undated inscription found from Sunarpal which refers to the grant of a village by the queen of Jayasiṁhadeva.[36] His relation with Jagadekabhūṣaṇa Narasiṁha is not known.

Another ruler of Chakrakoṭa named Hariśchandradeva is mentioned in a Sati inscription found from Temara.[37] It records that one of his officers' wives immolated herself on the death of her husband. The record belongs to the Śaka year 1246 which is equivalent to AD 1324. It shows that even in the 14th century AD the interior of Bastar went by the name of Chakrakoṭa which is recorded in the inscription. Though the name of the dynasty to which Hariśchandradeva belonged is not indicated in the inscription, but apparently he was a descendant of the old Nāgavaṁśī kings. Nothing is known about this dynasty after Hariśchandradeva.

The Chhindaka Nāgas of Bastar had innovated several new measures to enrich governance of their tribal dominated country. In words of Dr. H.L. Shukla,[38] "In early medieval period, a tribe in Bastar was divided into a number of multi-village groups called 'parganā' and there were 84 parganās in whole of the district in later medieval period. The pargana-headman or the chief of the villages termed as 'Grāma-Nāyaka' in Nāga Inscriptions, no longer worked at all. The social hierarchy had three levels: The parganā-headman's families, headed by a supreme chief; the level of administrators, generally distant relatives of the Mājhīs or the Rājā or men of high rank in the society; lastly the Commoners who formed the mass of the population and were distant relatives of the Mājhīs and their councillors. A considerable number of toboos surrounded the person of supreme chief. A commoner might not touch any object used by the Chief: his shadow might not fall on the clothes of the Rājā, special adornments and perhaps special language distinguished the latter from other men. The King descended directly from the semi-god head (recorded in all the inscriptions) and had special natural functions including the consecretation of temples. Official ceremonies celebrated the birth, marriage and death of the aristocracy (Hiralal, 1916:166). The supreme chief controlled the use of land. The 'Grāma-nāyaka' (Village chief) kept watch over the use of his plot of land. He might be dispossessed if he refused to contribute to collective works or managed his land in an unproductive way. Redistribution was, in fact, redistribution of control in local groups between king's entourage, after the accession to power or following a war. This entourage constituted a kind of 'primitive bureaucracy' of the 'heads of 12 ministers' (Dvādasapātra) supervising production."

"The king had the means of coercion at his disposal and punished those who infringed his rights, the punishment varying with the status of accused. Sometimes he was declared as 'mēdipota'. The King's will in short, was the supreme law. Assassination, rebellion, emigration limited the tyranny of his, or his servants' powers and made for an alternation in the periods of decentralisation and centralisation of the political history of Bastar. The land and the factors of production were no longer the property of direct producers alone. The latter must produce surplus used partially for enterprises of collective interest which exceeded the possibilities of local communities. The mobilised surplus, for certain ceremonial occasions as Kutumbajātrā assumed considerable proportions. Figures such as buffaloes (*El*, X, 40) have been quoted in an inscription. On the basis of the appropriation of excess products in local communities and the unequal control of production factors, a class division had been built up. A central government existed. It had, as one of the essential characteristics of the State, the right to levy tribute on the ceremonies, but the State remained embryonic in so far as a veritable public force did not appear to exist and the territorial organisation of the population was but little developed. Revolts occurred, not in order to abolish the system but to restore it to a bearable limit."

"Thus in Bastar we find a fully developed state structure. The population of state was divided administratively and the central authority was effected through territorial subordinates who were either appointed or hereditary. The State had a public force at its command and the power of levying taxes on commoners was considered one of its essential tributes. Local groups, organised according to kinship relations had, in part, lost control of land. The State decided on land occupancy and usage. In the economic and political spheres the State organised activities on a level unattainable by local groups, but these always assured protection and co-operation among members. Autonomy in local groups was more or less reduced by new obligations to authorities and local communities. A network of new relations was developed mainly outside kinship relations and this constituted the framework of new forms of social promotions and status. The state was responsible for peace within, and defence against attack from outside."

Regarding economic conditions Dr. H.L. Shukla is of opinion that "the Nāgas promoted agriculture to an extent not known before. The people supported their efforts whole-heartedly. The lands were measured and divided into various categories, and on the basis of their fertility taxes were levied and collected. Some tanks named 'Chandrāditya Sarovara' were constructed in Barsur and the different parts of the state."

"In 1076, Māsakadevī, to enthuse the peasants and infuse confidence among them, issued the proclamation to the people of Bastar (Hira Lal, 1916; 166): 'bureaucrats levied some unjust taxes on you. The collection of these dues is unjust. Now we have exempted you from the payment of the taxes.'"

"The tradition of granting whole villages to Brahmin families who were the residents of the area continued through the ages. To promote agriculture the Nāgas on special occasions granted villages rent free to inhabitants themselves. Right of ownership of land was comprehensive and all embracing. It was also laid down that one should either cultivate the land by himself or give it to another for cultivation. If one failed to do either, tax was collected on the same. With land becoming private property, land disputes became natural. The disputes were settled with the help of five chiefs."

"Regarding taxation, we have no information about the preparation of the land and the produce which the state claimed its share. As pointed out, taxes were levied by the state as well as village organisation. They were collected either in cash or in kind."

"Nāga mode of production can be classified into two categories:

(a) 'Mēriyā' mode of production.

(b) Feudal mode of production.

These two modes of production explain the primitive as well as the feudal emergence of the society."

As for village organisation, Dr. Shukla says that during the Nāga regime "the basic political society was the village. Even the most powerful kings mainly exercised their authority over their villages and only secondarily over their 'Maṇḍala' (district). The village community as a whole cultivated the gardens, went to war, performed religious ceremonies, undertook commercial expeditions. Its political and economic autonomy was important. It was directed by the 'Pañcha Pradhāna' (five chiefs) or five members of the dominant clan. The chief of the village (*grāma-nāyaka)* might or might not be a man of rank. When he combined these two titles, his position was much stronger. He then exercised a certain authority over a 'Parganā', that is to say a group of villages which adjoined his own, for purposes of war and the great religious ceremonies. All men of rank belonged to a hierarchy, the head of which was the Nāga King. He was the most powerful ritual expert (*Epigraphia Indica*, IX:164), controlling rain and sun. Men of rank wore distinctive adornments, but were mainly differentiated from commoners by the existence of special taboos, the number of which increased as the hierarchy was ascended. People of high rank and the kings, possessed no judicial or executive authority over people of inferior rank from villages unconnected with their own."

"When a king or the Middle man (Mājhī) asked for help from members of his village, he compensated them. The necessary resources were furnished by him through polygamy, the king's or Middle man's privilege, and the gift which each brother-in-law must give to his sister's husband. The numerous kings of Bastar from 760 to 1947 used to marry a girl or sister from each tribal group, such as Dhurvā, Dorlā, Māriā, Halbā or Bhatrā etc. and these tribal groups in turn owed their brother-in-law a significant part of their harvest and valuables. The Kings and 'Mājhīs' of Bastar were, thus seen as 'glorified' and glorious brother-in-laws to the whole tribal communities. The use of word 'māmā' (maternal uncle) for a tribe denotes the same historical and social meaning. His exceptional wealth was used to promote grand ceremonies and, generally, to integrate a number of tribal communities with the 'State economy'. The king 'mājhī' was, therefore the instrument of a much greater economy than that of village and a fortalice of the domestic units of production."

"The king had no public force at his disposal to regulate conflicts, these remained the concern of the lineages. The king availed himself of a single weapon, sorcery, and the best sorcerers were at his disposal. Tribal society of Bastar therefore, did not recognise any central government in action. What then was the meaning of 'hierarchy' which reigned there, linking all political and territorial units on the region, i.e. the local lineages?"

"The reality is that the rank of local lineage of the Nāga time may be considered as the combined result of three factors:

(a) an economic advantage signifying that a village had fertile fields, such as Halbā-pattis;
(b) The degree to which this village played role of integrating centre with its economic powers;
(c) Its position in the network of external alliances and its role in the famous inter-regional exchange cycle.

I think it was these three factors which combined to determine the relative status of the different villages and the local lineages dominant therein. When two Māṛiās or Halbās met who were not related by kinship or marriage, and one bents his knee to the other, this behaviour had to be understood as a symbolic recognition of the relative standing of their villages in the past. In the same way, the Daṇḍāmī Māṛiā region was the most fertile area on the district actively participating in Dusserā-festival and controlling the largest network of Dusserā-festivities, while at the opposite end we find Abujhmāṛiā who had the worst fields and no participation in Dusserā-festivities."

"In tribal societies of Bastar we had the example of a hereditary hierarchy (Mājhī, Chālkī etc.) which bound different lineages and local communities without functioning as a unique, integrating political structure. The 'Majhi's' power lay in supporting economic and religious relations which extended the framework of particular village communities, without, however, integrating them into a single economic or ceremonial network covering the whole region (because it was the role of the king to integrate the whole region). 'Mājhīs' were those who possessed the most potent magical powers and they must use these on behalf of their community. Their privileges were thus, the obverse of their duties and the reward for exceptional services rendered to the community at every level, imaginary or real."

Regarding society, Dr. Shukla says that "Social life at the time of Nāgas was not as static as we find at the present time. Restrictions in social contact between the different classes were not deep rooted. It was the age of tribal feudalism, and this was why the social conditions were influenced by the tribal ideologies. Religion was a dynamic force and anyone was free to choose any path or creed."

"The king occupied a dominant role in tribal economy. He had ultimate control over the land. He was the 'titular owner' of the land and he had the supreme control of the fertility. He was the privileged intermediary between the clan, his ancestors and the gods. In the production processes, he took interest in agricultural activities, ensuring the direction of cooperative exercises, sago-cultivation etc. He controlled the correct utilisation of most of the basic natural resources. He made sure of their conservation by imposing taboos which protected them from immediate consumption (to do this he invented many new eating festivals). He received and distributed a large quantity of goods, encouraging their accumulation by organising big ceremonies which integrated the society into something bigger than clan-state society. He had the right to material assistance from members of different clans but could not exercise any material sanction against those who refused this assistance. He settled differences and, in some cases, resorted to forced help by the members of other lineage against serious offenders, as is the case with the Chālukya King Daryao Deva (1780 AD)."

"The later mediaeval rulers of Bastar enjoyed a twofold inequality, i.e. social and spiritual. The inequalities were natural and irreducible, while in economic sphere they were chiefly by degree. Within his domestic unit, the king and his family never participated directly in production. In communal undertakings, he played a guiding role. He was not responsible for any losses. The harvests were gathered by the land-labours (*bhutiyār*). He never cooked his food and appointed cooking experts called 'Suar Brāhmanas.'

"It was on the 'Meḍipoṭa'-based (*Epigraphia Indica*, IX, 160) forms of dependence that the majority of primal class societies developed together with Chakrakoṭa-State. The Nāga-empire grew up in between 760-1324 AD and this growth was exceeded only by Annamadeva who, when entering Bastar from Warangal in 1324 AD was a warrior, having no kin-relations with the tribes. Before the conquest of Annamadeva and Chālukyan integration to a new state, the modes of production of many Dravidian tribes of this part of the country was based on the production of tubers. There was also a from of communal labour, based on mutual help among the villages in the performance of various productive tasks. The 'Parganā Mājhī' was the first beneficiary of the village mutual aid, and the communal land was especially cultivated for maintaining the temples of local divinities."

"When the tribes of Bastar fell under the Nāga domination, these communities underwent a profound change. A section of these lands was definitely expropriated and became state or temple property. The remainder was returned to them through the kindness of the Nāgas, on certain conditions.

Relations of production were, therefore, thrown into confusion on those lands returned for subsistence the communities lost their former right of communal ownership, controlling rights of possession and use only. On these lands, production and customary forms of soil and usage still assumed the same communal form as before the Chālukya conquest, nevertheless, a new mode of production was established on a regime of forced labour since 1324 AD."

"Forced labour was not an individual matter; the whole village participated in it and the Chālukya-State provided the food drink, in the same way, as in the traditional tribal social structure; the beneficiary of communal mutual aid had provided for those who helped him. The state provided the tools and seeds and insisted that the people go to work with music and song. In this way the Nāga-forms of economic reciprocity together with the ideology and ritual linked with them, were now after 1324 AD, used for the functioning of economic relations of exploitation and servitude, characteristic of a new form of production. In order to organize its own economic basis on a stable level and to ensure growth, the Chālukya-State checked all lands, peoples, their customs, animals and produce. For this, it needed to create an administrative organisation of Zamindars which would cover the population and control it directly or indirectly; it also needed to popularise the cult of Danteswari and maintain an Halbā army to suppress revolts etc. This body of institutions corresponded to the new mode of production; and it is known that this mode of production was by 1379 AD (*Epigraphia Indica*, XII, 242) fully developed. To control the local population a new development occurred in which Halbās were given the military status and different military colonies of Halbās were set in the different parts of the state. Thus, Halbās were attached to an aristocratic master and remained in the service of Chālukyas up to 1777 AD (*Epigraphia Indica*, IX, 166). The descendants of Halbā generally inherited this military position. This form of exploitation (the one tribal group exploiting the other group) certainly existed before Chālukya conquest when the Māṛiās held a superior position, but assumed greater social significance with the development of a kind of individual ownership of lands given by Chālukya- State to certain strata of nobility."

"By compelling the peasants to come and work on lands of the State and Danteśwarī, by providing them with food and drink, the Chālukya rulers were employing the former mode of production based on reciprocal obligations between members of local communities, where both the form of obligation were known and understood by all; in this way they shaped new relations of production, founded on oppression and domination, since the producers had now lost part control of their labour and its product. Moreover, the

Chālukyas while retaining the cult of local gods, added the cult of Danteśwarī, in honour of whom the peasant would offer his labour, as was already demanded by his own traditional and local divinities. The old kinship relations and the former village and tribal political relations without a change in either form or structure, had now changed their function, since they were required for furthering a new mode of production."

"The practical problem confronting the Chālukyas after their conquest, was two fold: to allow the subjugated people to continue to produce their means of subsistence in accordance with traditional practice; and to oblige them to produce for the state in forms of production which they would understand and which, upto a certain extent, would be justified in their eyes. In order to resolve this problem, exceptional efforts of political and social invention were required, both collectively and individual - tradition has credited the almost legendary kings."

"Among these means, there were firstly, the fact that production was based on different forms of simple cooperation; secondly, the fact that the land was owned by the community as a whole and that the individual possessed only rights of using to the plots, which were redistributed more or less periodically; thirdly, the fact that – equally in the sphere of the material process of production as in the individual's relation to the basic means of production – the land and the community existed and appeared as a reality superior to the individual and as the practical condition for his survival; fourthly, the fact that the function of representing the community, of controlling the process of its reproduction as such was the responsibility of a particular family, and in this family, of the individual, who could best fulfil this function. This person was the *Mājhī*, the chief of the tribal community, and also chief of war in early mediaeval Bastar. By this function, the *Mājhī,* and his family, personified the community more than any other person; he in same way incarnated the society in so far as he was in reality superior to others and he personified his superior unit; fifthly, in organising the process of production, their labour force, taken from the members of the local community, the Māṛiā, was utilised to reproduce their own existence and that of other members of the community in need. Finally, supplementary land and labour were devoted to the cult of ancestors and local divinities, and to the upkeep of temples."

"These five elements belonging to the old mode of production did not disappear after the Chālukya conquest. The Nāga mode of production continued to ensure both the subsistence of local communities and these five elements provided the operational bases and shape of the new mode of production. The victorious community appropriated all lands and natural resources from the conquered communities. All that the victors needed to do was to apply traditional law: so long as the individual was a member of the community he was entitled to his rights. If he did not belong he was deprived of all rights. The superior community, personified in the Chālukya king, who represented both the community and the state hence, became the collective landlord, and all conquered territory became the 'Crown' property. It meant that the State took the place of the local community as landlord and this constituted for the individual, a new community superior to his traditional one and upon which he depended for survival."

"We can now grasp the ideological consequences which arose as a result of the fact that the Nāga-relations of production (village mutual aid, surplus labour etc.) gave their form to the Chālukya-relations of production (forced labour). The fundamental consequence was that the Chālukya relations could only come about in a form, an appearance, which marked the economic agents, in spontaneous ideological representations, making the new, real content, the exploitation of man by man."

Regarding religious conditions, Dr. Shukla says that "during the Nāga-period (760-1324) Vīra Shaivism held the hearts of the people and enjoyed royal patronism. Shaivism consisted of three sects – Kāpālikas, Kaulas and Shāktas. While each recognised Shiva as the supreme lord of the Universe and 'bhakti' as the only way of salvation, they differed from one another in their emphasis on one or other of its tenets, in their forms of worship, mode of discipline and practice of rituals. Vīra Shaivism distinguished itself by its militant opposition to atheistic religions like Jainism. It opposed renunciation or 'sanyāsa', condemned castes distinctions and advocated equality of sexes."

"Thus, Vīra Shaivism showed an illusory way to the thoughts and actions of the tribal people who were absolutely ignorant of the laws of social development. It prevented rational outlook, spirit of enquiry, and creative thought. It thus contributed to the stagnation and backwardness of the self-sufficient village. The tribal people tended more and more to escape from reality, seeking refuge in spiritual forces, which were supposed to do for man what he could do for himself."

"Contemporary literature throws much light on the religious life of the tribal people. The devotees manifested their feeling more through gymnastic and daring feats of heroism than the prayer and penance. Jātrās or Kakśāṛas or religious festivals were widely prevalent. Local deities such as Vindhyavāsinī or Danteśwarī were commonly worshipped. Human sacrifice was the order of the day. In different types of sacrifice (human sacrifice, animal sacrifice etc.) the series of natural species played the part of intermediary between two polar terms, the sacrifices and the deity, between where there was initially no homology, nor even any sort of relation. For the object of the sacrifice precisely was to establish a relation not of a resembling but of continuity, by means of a series of successive identification. These could be made in either direction depending on whether the sacrifice was expiatory or represented a rite of communion. Its object was to bring to pass the fulfilment of human prayers by a distant deity. Its claim to achieve this by first bringing together the two domains through a sacralised victim and then eliminating this connecting term. The sacrifice thus created a lack of contiguity and by the purposive nature of prayer, it induced a compensating continuity to arise on the plane where the initial deficiency experienced by the sacrificer traced the path which led to the deity, in advance and as it were, by a dotted line."

"Among the tribes, religious practice took the form of a Shākta-cult. It was observed every day and in all their actions. The more exceptional circumstances in the life of individuals or bands – birth, girl's puberty, death, were occasions for ritual. The most important were the puberty festivals for girls and the great 'anal' festival for the dead. In case of epidemic, a success of poor hunts, serious accidents, the band carried out 'hele'. In all , every day or more exceptional events in the life of both the individual and the community, the tribes turned to deities and worshipped them, that is to say, they danced and, especially, sang in their honour."

"The mystical power lay in the forest. So the forest was 'everything' to the tribes. It was ensemble of all inanimate and animate beings. It was a higher reality which existed as person, a divinity to whom one spoke as to father, mother, friend, even lover. It was Life. Death overtook men and other living things because the forest was asleep and, therefore, it must be awakened to persuade it to carry on providing nourishment, health, goodwill – in short, happiness and social harmony for the tribes in whatever band they might happen to be."

"Tribal religion, therefore, was an ideological instance where the conditions of reproduction of their mode of production and their society was represented; but they were represented upside down, as 'fetished', mythical."

"Tribal religion, then, was not the domain of fantastic shadows projected into the depths of their consciousness of reality existing in itself – solid and material, a reality which was their social relations in the production of the material sources of the existence. Far from being a ghostly reflection – both passive and derisory – of a reality which might move off elsewhere, these representatives and religious observances drew their content."

Regarding the language policy of the Nāga rulers of Bastar, Dr. Hiralal says that "from the point of view of the tribal society of Bastar, Telugu was the first official language (760-1224) and the hybrid Sanskrit (1065-1324) was the second official language of the State. Sanskrit was introduced and imposed on the society by Madhurāntaka Deva's (1002-1069) feudal administration (*Epigraphia Indica*, X, 26). As the language of the North Indian feudals, the cultural language, it was naturally the language of administering the State from 1065 to 1324 AD. Sometimes having the independent status and sometimes a bilingual state language, it continued upto the conquest of Bastar by Annama Deva (1324 AD). The stronger the Āryan influence, the more powerfully the language was forced on the society. Although indirect rule through local chieftains and Zamindars was the characteristic administrative procedure, the more potent agents of administration were judiciary, the civil service and legislature. All these instruments were run in Hybrid Sanskrit and Hybrid Telugu. Thus, although Telugu was widely known with its local Dravidian dialects and Sanskrit was very much restricted, and although Hybrid Sanskrit minority was not evenly spread throughout the state, Sanskrit became the first and only language of Bastar Government in the year 1224 AD. To know and use the language was prestigious to somebody, indeed; the importance of knowing it was so great that a person who did not know, it was erroneously considered by the society to be an illiterate, even when he could read and write very well in his Telugu, which developed diglossic bilingualism. It was also usual for the society to regard, whoever could not use Sanskrit, as an 'uncivilised person.' "

"Largely because fedualism thrived on the doctrine of the superiority of the North Indian culture over the tribal culture: the cultural language was also considered to be superior to the tribal language. It was, therefore not surprising to find that it was really the only means of communication in the State that qualified to be called a language, while all of its indigenous Bastar counterparts were mere tribal dialects."

The overall pattern has been summed up by Dr. Shukla in the following words: "The early mediaeval formation which took a concrete shape in the course of six hundred years, beginning from 760 AD, was characterised by the rise and growth of feudalism. It was the fedualism from the tribal group."

"Powerful intermediaries wielding political power grew in the countryside as a result of extensive fiefdoms granted to them. These intermediaries developed into a hierarchy with differences in status, privileges and jurisdiction – a phenomenon characteristic of fedualism. Besides fiefdoms, the lords and nobles acquired marginal lands as private property with rights of sale and purchase. They got them cultivated through labours or tenants and earned additional income on them."

"Political decentralisation – a result of wars and civil wars, not only between suzerain states but also between chiefs and their suzerains – was another feature common to the region. In these struggles Bastar state got weakened and paralysed, until a single power like Someswara Deva came out successful."

"The village assembly, which consisted of all the high-ups of the village, was also owning lands. As an important part of the feudal set-up, the assembly discharged vital functions like maintaining the union between agriculture and industry, acting as a bridge between the state and its subjects in fiscal matters, dispensing justice in minor disputes and balancing the interests of various sections of the people."

"Caste system, which in its early phases, had fulfilled in varying degrees, the needs of the society within the framework of self-sufficiency, lost its original rigidity and developed on tribal lines."

"The rise of the 'bhakti' cult, expressed in the worship of a personalised god, reflected the impact of feudal relations on human mind. It offered the best solace to the frustrated and showed the easiest way of attaining happiness. There arose a plethora of beliefs and practices which sought to achieve man's liberation from the world of woes through sensualism on the one hand and self-torture on the other, both of which manifesting a degenerate mind. Even human sacrifice came to be considered an act of the highest order of devotion."[39]

Chhindaka Nāga contributions in the field of art and architecture comprised building of a number of temples and secular structures and promotion of sculptural art. Abundance of evidence is available in the inscriptions of the Nāga rulers as well as existing remains. Thus, the Barsur Telugu inscription of the time of Jagadekabhuṣana[40] states that a feudatory chief Chandrāditya Mahārāja, lord of Ammagrāma, excavated at the capital town Barasuru, a tank which he called Chandrāditya-Samudra, on whose bank he constructed a Śiva temple, naming it after himself as Chandrādityeśvara Shrine. A garden planted in the vicinity of the same temple and by the same person, who named it as Chandrāditya-Nandanavana is referred to in the Potinar inscription of the same ruler.[41] Reference to construction of two temples of Śiva by Gaṅgamahādevī, the chief queen of Someśvaradeva, appears in her Barsur stone inscription.[42] That the royal ladies of the Chhindaka Nāga rulers were quite active in religious activities is evidenced by two other inscriptions. An inscription of Guṇḍamahādevī, the chief queen of Mahārāja Dhārāvarṣa, the mother of Someśvara and the grand-mother of Kanharadeva, found from

Narayanpal records the grant of the village Nārāyaṇapura to the god Nārāyaṇa and some land near the Khajuri tank to the god Lokeśvara.[43] Two more inscriptions from Kuruspal states that Dhāraṇa Mahādevī, queen of Someśvaradeva, had donated land to god Kāmeśvara.[44] Reference of land grant to another temple by the queen of Jayasiṁhadeva of Nāga Vaṁśa is referred to in a stone inscription found from Sunarpal.[45]

The epigraphical evidences have been supported by archaeological finds. Early medieval temples and other remains have been found at several places in Bastar district. There are remains of brick temples and Śiva liṅga at Khamargaon (7 km from Jagdalpur), *Chaitya* and sculptures at Jaitagiri Pahurbel (29 km north-east of Bastar village), Nṛisiṁha sculpture in a huge cave at Pala (8 km from Kokri on Kondagaon-Narayanpur road), brick temples, two huge and one small stupas, remains of a city at Gubarhin-Garhdhanora (10 km east of Keskal), huge stupas of bricks and sculptural remains at Bhongapal, the temple of Danteśvarī built in eleventh century AD at Dantewada, small stupas at Edka (on Narayanpur-Bhainsgaon road), temple remains and sculptures at Deo Dhanora on Kondagaon-Keskal road, remains of forts and temples, Śaiva and Vaiṣṇava sculptures at Podagarh (in Koraput district on the boundary of Bastar), and a huge Śiva liṅga at Guptesvara (42 km from Jagdalpur).[46]

Centres from which remains of temples, sculptures and inscriptions datable to medieval period have been found are: Deurgaon, Gadia, Narayanpal, Garhbothra, Kuruspal, Sataspur, Madhota, Bastar, Kesarpal, Mavlibhata, Mavlipadar, Tirathgarh, Kondagaon, Amravati, Bhangaram, Bade-Dongar, Alor, Bangoli, Farasgaon, Balpeth, Nagphani, Barsur, Samlur, Bhairamgarh, Bade Tumnar, Gudma, Patakutru, Toinar, Eramnar, Bijapur, Murdand, Pamer, Talanar, Chintagupha, Kanker, Gadiapahar, Kogera, Murpar, Anjani, Deogaon, Sarangpal, Sihawa, Jagdalpur and Kangoli. Majority of architectural and sculptural remains at the above-mentioned places are assignable to the Chhindaks Nāgas. Detailed discussion on them is beyond the scope of the present work.[47]

THE NĀGAS OF KAWARDHĀ

Another branch of the Nāga rulers was ruling over the territory around Kawardhā. Whether they were related in one way or the other with the Nāgas of Bastar cannot be determined in the present state of our knowledge. They ruled over this area at least for twenty-four generations, roughly covering a period of about 500 years, but they never came in prominence. Their status was much more of a feudatory of the Kalachuris. The genealogy and chronology

1. Ahirāja
2. Rājalla
3. Dharṇīdhara
4. Mahimadeva
5. Sarvavandana (Śaktichandra?)
6. Gopāladeva
7. Naladeva
8. Bhuvanapāla

- 9. Kīrtipāla
- 10. Jayatrapāla
  - 11. Mahipāla
  - 12. Viṣamapāla
  - 13. Ja (nhu)
  - 14. Janapāla or Vijanapāla (or Jvapāla?)
  - 15. Yaśorāja
  - 16. Kanhaḍadeva (Vallabhadeva)
  - 17. (La)kṣmavarmā

- 18. Khaḍgadeva
  - 19. Bhuvanaikamalla
  - 20. Arjuna
  - 21. Bhīma
  - 22. Bhoja
- Chandana
  - Vijjana
  - Malugideva
  - 23. Lakṣmaṇa
  - 24. Rāmachandra
    - Arjuna
    - Haripāla

of the rulers of this Nāga dynasty is known from a long inscription found from the temple of Mandwa Mahal situated at Chaura, a village about 16 km from Kawardhā.[48] The inscription records the construction of a Śiva temple by King Rāmachandra, born of the Phaṇi or Nāgavaṁśa, and married to Ambikādevī of Haihaya lineage. It gives the legend of the origin of the Nāgavaṁśa, stating that a serpent got enamoured of Mithilā, the beautiful daughter of the sage Jātukarṇa. He therefore assumed human form and had intercourse with her. Their issue was Ahirāja, who, having conquered the neighbouring chiefs, set himself up as a king. The kings who followed him are shown in the genealogical table given on page 140.

It would appear that the succession deflected twice from the direct line. For nine generations up to Kīrtipala it went in a direct line. The 10th king Jayatrapāla was a brother of Kīrtipala, who apparently had no son to succeed him. Twelve descendants of Jayatrapāla succeeded one after the other, the last king Bhoja being succeeded by Lakṣmaṇa, a great-grandson of his great-great-granduncle. Lakṣmaṇa's son was Rāmachandra, the 20th descendant from the original ancestor Ahirāja.

The inscription is dated in Vikrama Śaka 1406, bearing the name Jaya, which makes it clear that the year intended was that of the Vikrama era, as the cyclic year Jaya was current in Vikrama Saṁvat 1406 (AD 1349). This record shows that Kawardhā and the neighbouring country were under the sway of the Nāgavaṁśā kings for a period of about 500 years, connecting from the beginning from the 9th century AD, a little before the advent of the Kalachuris or Haihayas to Chhattisgarh. Apparently, the Nāgavaṁśīs became the feudatories of the Kalachuris and continued to rule under their protection for a long time. Amongst the kings of this dynasty we find two names, Gopāladeva (6) and Yaśorāja (15), with which we are familiar from other inscriptions found in this locality. Gopāladeva's name occurs in the Boramdeo temple, about a mile away from our inscription slab. It is dated in the Kalachuri year 840, or AD 1088, while at Sahaspur, only 21 miles away from Chaura, there is a record of Yaśorāja, dated in the Kalachuri year 934, or AD 1182. These kings must evidently belong to the dynasty which our record describes. Between Gopāladeva and Yaśorāja there was an interval of only 94 years according to the dates of their inscriptions, but our record gives eight intervening generations, giving an average of less than 12 years to a generation. This throws a doubt on the accuracy of the genealogy, to swell which it is possible a number of fictitious names may have been inserted.

The geographical names mentioned in the record are Chavarāpura, the Śaṁkarī River, Rājapura and Kumbhīpurī. Chavarāpura, to the east of which the temple was built, is undoubtedly the village Chaura, within whose limits the temple still lies, and Śaṁkarī is the Sankari River which is about a quarter mile away. Rājapura was a village granted for the supply of offerings to the god, and may be identified with a village of the same name three miles from Chaura. Kumbhīpurī is not traceable.

Nothing is known about the subsequent history of this Nāga dynasty.

THE NĀGAS OF BHAṬGĀON

Bhaṭgāon is a village in the Sohagpur *tehsil* of Hoshangabad district in M.P. It was during 1978-79 that a stone inscription was discovered from this village which revealed the existence of a Nāga dynasty which was ruling over this region during 14-15th centuries AD.[49] The inscription belonged to the reign of Pratāparudra and is not dated. However, on palaeographic grounds, it can be assigned to 14th-15th centuries AD. The record is not complete as the stone bearing the inscription has broken off at the beginning of line 26 and consequently the object of the inscription has been lost. The existing part bears the following details:

The inscription commences with the obeisance to Śrī-Rāmachandra. This is followed by two imprecatory verses in praise of gods Śiva (*Bilvapāṇi*) and Rāmachandra. The third verse introduces king Chaṁdrasena who was verily the moon to the ocean of Nāga family *([Phaṇi]-vaṁs-āvdhi-chaṁdramāḥ)*. Verse 4 describes his father (Janaka) whose name however is not given, who with his stout and strong hands bore the burden of the earth and was indeed another Mount Meru. Verse 5 mentions his mother Dasamāṁvikā who begot her valiant son for protecting the entire world. She is first compared to Aditi who gave birth to Devas and to Indra (*Jiṣṇu*) who had Kṛṣṇa (*Naṁdakī*) as his younger brother. Verse 6 refers to his (Chaṁdrasena's) queen *(rājñī)* Karpurāṁvā who was known for her chastity *(pātivratya)*, illustrious family (*kula)*, munificence *(oudārya*), compassion *(karuṇā)* and largeness *(parināhinī)*. Verse 7 states that a son was born to king Chaṁdrasena and queen Karpurāṁvā by the name Pratāparudra who was renowned not only by name but was also in deed so. True to his name, he won many a battle in the battlefield that brought fame to him which looked like the rising of the legendary tree Pārijāta from the Ocean of Milk. Verse 8 tells that while King Pratāparudra was ruling, righteousness (*dharma*) got support (*ālaṁvana*) in him and the miserable (*dīna*) and virtuous people (*sajjanāḥ*) got protection. Verse 9 describes that the earth, due to its burden being borne by the strong hands of King Pratāparudra which is whitish in colour like the camphor, became really immovable *(achala)* (as it could not be shaken by any other alien king) and also got rid of its suffering from exposure to the poisonous breath emanating from the myriad and multiple hoods of the serpent Ādiśeṣa.

Verse 10 then proceeds to describe Bhaṭṭi-grāma, which is stated to be a divine city (*divyā-nagarī*) and a place of holy deeds (*sukṛita-dharā*). Verse 11 states that lord Indra though satisfied with the drinking of ambrosia (*amṛita*) (in the heavens) looked suppliantly at the hands of the Brāhmaṇa residents of the city for tasting the sacred rice *(haviḥ)* perpetually offered by them in the sacrifices. This verse suggests that the Brāhmaṇas of Bhaṭṭi-grāma were very religious and were regularly performing various sacrifices. Verse 12 says that the Brāhmaṇas of the city, well known for their penance and amiable nature, were always repeating Vedas in beautiful *maṇḍapas* that are appealing to the mind both in *krama* and *pada pāṭhas.* The prose passage that follows speaks of the courtesans residing in the city of Bhaṭṭi-grāma drawing their fanciful portraits on the sky for the damsels of the capital city of Indra to see. Verse 13 states that the main thoroughfares of the city were frequented by slowly walking courtesans smitten with passion who appear to teach the elephants the art of walking stately. Verse 14 describes a person named Āhava who was residing in the city of Bhaṭṭi-grāma at that time. He was an emigrant from Muṅga-purī and he belonged to Bhāradvāja Kula. By profession he was a priest in a temple. He had a son named Harigaṇa who was renowned throughout the world. He was always interested in the worship of Śiva. The inscription abruptly ends here. It is quite evident from the long description of the city of Bhaṭṭi-grāma that it was the capital of the kingdom of Pratāparudra. The same is no doubt identical with modern Bhaṭgāon from where the inscription has been discovered.

Nothing more is known about this Nāga dynasty and its connections, if any, with the Nāga ruling families of Bastar and Kawardhā.

REFERENCES

1. *IHQ*, IX, pp. 92ff.
2. *QJMS*, Vol. 44, p. 2.
3. Sircar, D.C., in: *The Struggle for Empire* (ed. R.C. Majumdar), pp. 214-15.
4. Jayaswal, K.P., *Andhakār Yugīn Bhārat*, Sam. 1995, p. 59.
5. Shukla, H.L., *Tribal History: A New Interpretation*, Delhi, 1988, p. 72.
6. Jha, V.D., *Bastar Kā Mūrtishilpa*, Bhopal, 1989, pp. 18-19.
7. *Ibid.*, p. 19.
8. *Ibid.*, p. 19.
9. Mirashi, *CII*, IV, pt. I, Introduction, p. cxviii-cxx. Ganguly, D.C., in: *The Age of Imperial Kanauj*,(ed. R.C. Majumdar), pp. 98-99.

10. Ganguly, D.C., *op cit.*, p. 98.
11. Mirashi, V.V., *op cit.*, pp. cxix-cxx.
12. *Hiralal List*, No. 285, p. 166.
13. *Ibid.*, No. 269.
14. *Ibid.*, pp. 158-59.
15. *Ibid.*, No. 270.
16. *Ibid.*, No. 283.
17. *Ibid.*, No. 289.
18. *Ibid.*, No. 278.
19. *Ibid.*, lines 26 to 28.
20. *EI*, IX, pp. 176-77; *Hiralal List*, No. 273.
21. *Ibid.*
22. *EI*, X, pp. 25ff.
23. *JNSI*, XVII, pt. II, p. 54-57.
24. Mirashi, *CII*, IV., pt. II, p. 416; Also *Ibid.*, pt. I, pp. cxxiii-iv.
25. Shastri, A.M., *Inscriptions of the Śarabhapurīyas, Pāṇḍnduvaṁśins and Somavaṁśins*, pt. I., Delhi, 1995, p. 220.
26. *Hiralal List*, No. 275 and 276.
27. *Ibid.*, No. 274, 277.
28. *Ibid.*, No. 272.
29. *Hiralal List*, No. 271.
30. Sircar, D.C., in: *Struggle for Empire*, (ed. R.C. Majumdar), p. 218.
31. *Hiralal List*, No. 293.
32. *Ibid.*, No. 284.
33. *Ibid.*, No. 292.
34. *Ibid.*, No. 280.
35. *Ibid.*, No. 279.
36. *Ibid.*, No. 281.
37. *Ibid.*, No. 282.
38. Shukla, H.L., *Tribal History – A New Interpretation*, Delhi, 1998, pp. 88-101.
39. *Ibid.*, pp. 104-105.
40. *Hiralal List*, No. 269.
41. *Ibid.*, No. 270.
42. *Ibid.*, No. 271.
43. *Ibid.*, No. 272.
44. *Ibid.*, No. 275, 276.
45. *Ibid.*, No. 281.
46. Jha, V.D., *Bastar Kā Mūrtishilpa*, Bhopal, 1989, pp. 51- 52.
47. *Ibid.*, pp. 52-57. For details of sculptural remains, see *Ibid.*, pp. 59-133.
48. *Hiralal, List* No. 305.
49. *Journal of the Epigraphical Society of India*, Vol. IX, 1982, pp. 94-97.

8

NĀGA ASSOCIATION WITH ŚRĪ LAṄKĀ, SOUTH INDIA, DECCAN, EAST INDIA AND GREATER INDIA

From the earliest times, in addition to North India, the remaining part of the country was also associated with the Nāgas and the impact had reached even up to Śrī-Laṅkā and South-east Asian countries where Hinduism had migrated. We may briefly discuss this in the following account.

ŚRĪ-LAṄKĀ, SOUTH INDIA AND DECCAN

Śrī-Laṅkā, South India and the Deccan are rich with Nāga associations from very early times. It has been discussed above that *Pātāla* or the nether region said to have been occupied by the Nāgas in the *Purāṇas*, has been tried to be located in South India and Ceylon, probably on account of their distance from Āryāvarta. The land of Rāmaṇīyaka to which the Nāgas migrated according to the *Mahābhārata* has been sought to be identified with Malabar, not only on account of its distance and charm, but also on account of the existence in it of people associated with the Nāgas. According to the *Bhāgavata Purāṇa,* the original home of Kāliya was Ramaṇaka.[1]

If the *Rāmāyaṇa* mentions that Ceylon and South India were peopled by the *Rākṣasa*, the *Mahāvaṁsa* says that Ceylon was the home of the Nāgas and Yakṣas. It is said that Vijaya was met by them when he landed in Ceylon on his conquering expedition. Buddhist tradition has it that Nāgadīpa (North Ceylon) had a number of Nāga kingdoms even in the life-time of the Buddha. In one of his earlier births, when the Buddha was born as Akkitti, he is said to have gone to Ahidīpa, perhaps the same as Nāgadīpa, near the island of Tambapanni (Ceylon) where he reached omniscience. It is recorded that the Buddha visited Nāgadīpa thrice in the ninth months, fifth and eighth years, respectively after he attained Buddhahood. The story is told that on the second of the three occasions, when he visited the island, its king Mahodara, and his nephew Chulodara who was ruling over Kannavadhamāna (Gandhamādhanam near Rāmeśvaram) were quarrelling among themselves for the possession of a gem-set throne. The Buddha appeared on the scene, settled the dispute, seated himself on the throne and preached to the rivals the sermon of reconciliation, and converted them along with a number of Nāgas to Buddhism.[2] This story is told in the Tamil epic *Maṇimekalai* also, where the scene of the episode is laid in Maṇipallavam, identified with Jaffna, the Nāgadīpa of the Mahāvaṁsa.[3]

The Nāgas are mentioned in some of the early Tamil works. The *Pattuppāṭṭua* contains interesting details about a prince called Tiraiyan who was washed to the Indian shore by the waves of the sea.[4] The commentator explains this by referring to a legend. According to it a Choḷa chief of Nāgapaṭṭiṇam went to *Pātāla* and fell in love with a Nāga lady in it. Later she sent him the child of their union floating on the waves (*tirai*) of the sea.[5] In the *Maṇimekalai* is told the story of the Choḷa king Neḍumkiḷḷi, the ruler of Kāverippūmpaṭṭiṇam, who fell in love with a Nāga lady whom he by chance met in a grove near his capital. She disappeared after a month. Sometime later she sent to the king in a ship the son born to them. But the ship was wrecked near the coast. When the Choḷa king heard of it he was so much worried and absorbed in searching for the child that he forgot to perform the annual Indra feast. This roused the anger of the god and the city was destroyed by the waves.[6] Another story in the work reads that a Tamilian Cheṭṭi named Sāduvan who wanted to trade with Vanga was driven to the shore of the naked nomads, the Nāgas, but he was able to make good his escape because he had mastery over their language.[7] Whether there can be much truth in these stories or not, one thing is clear: the northern part of Ceylon was the land of the Nāgas in the centuries preceding and succeeding the dawn of the Christian Era, and there was communication by sea between the east coast of South India and the Nāga land of Ceylon.

From the evidence of early Tamil literary works it appears that Kāverippūmpaṭṭiṇam, the Choḷa capital at the mouth of the river Kāverī, was in more ancient times the capital of the Nāgas and the Nāganāḍu.[8] It is believed that Toṇḍaināḍu, to the north of the Choḷa country, was the land of the Kurumbar, Aruvar or Aruvāḍar (Tamil *Arivāḷ* = Bill-hook) according to early Tamil literature and a Mackenzie manuscript. The region seems to have been divided into two halves, Aruvānāḍu, and the Aruvāvaḍatalaināḍu.[9] The former of the two extended between Bāhūr near Pondicherry in the South and Kāñchī in the North and the latter between the region about Kāñchī in the South and the river North Peṇṇār in the North. Beyond that was the country of the Vaḍugas who spoke a language different from Tamil. The Vaḍugas called the Tamil-speaking people *Aravar*. The word means 'Nāgas' in Tamil. The region appears to have been known also as Oymānāḍu. From later inscriptions one finds that the Oymānāḍu lay in the region of the present Tindivanam taluk.[10] According to the Śirupāṇaṟṟuppaḍai among the chief towns in it were Āmūr, Eyilpaṭṭaṇam and Mālangai. The chiefs ruling over the region are said to have belonged to the Oliya Nāga family.[11] One of the members of the family was known as Nalliya Kōdan (Kārkoṭa?).

Considering the paucity of reliable information about the geography and peoples of South India in the early centuries of the Christian Era, the notices contained in the *Periplus Maris Erythraei* and the writing of the geographer Ptolemy are of much interest and value. Among the list of countries, cities and important places mentioned in the geography of Ptolemy the following are of interest to us:

(a) Coast of Soringoi (Choḷas) with its capital at Orthoura 130° 16″ 20′ ruled by Sornagos;
(b) Arouarnoi with its capital at Malanga 130° 13″ and ruled by Basaronagos; and
(c) District of Moisoloi (Masolia-Masalia in the *Periplus*) with its metropolis at Pitundra.[12]

It is not difficult to identify Moisoloi with Masulipatnam. To its south was Arouarnoi, the Aruvāvaḍatalai of early Tamil literature, the country in which Kāñchī grew into a great city in later times. According to Ptolemy the capital of this country was Malanga. Opinion is divided among scholars as to its exact location. Cunningham thought that it was the same as Masulipatnam. But the place lay in the Tamil country only, and may probably be identified with Kīḷmāvilangai in the Tindivanam taluk.[13] Another Mālanga mentioned by Ptolemy as an emporium of trade has been sought to be identified with Mallai,[14] the future Māmallapuram or Maylapore in the city of Madras. These attempted identifications apart, it is of interest to note that the region according to Ptolemy was ruled by a Basaronāga. Cunningham thought this Basaronāga was the same as Pāli Mājerika Nāga of Amarāvati, according to the *Mahāvaṁsa*. But since we are identifying Arouarnoi with Aruvāvaḍatalai, Basaronāga must have ruled only in the Tamil country. Though it is not easy to find out the Indian equivalent to the word Basaro (it may be *Vajra* or *Varṣa*) the fact that it ends with the suffix Nāga shows that the Nāgas were in the occupation of the country during the time of Ptolemy.

According to the same geographer farther south in the coat of Soringoi ruled Sornagos with Orthoura as his capital. Apparently Orthoura is the same as Uraiyur or Uragapura of the early Choḷas. The region lay to the south of Aruvānāḍu, and during the time of the Greek geographer it was ruled by a king named Sornago (Sūryanāga or Suranāga?) or something like that. Uragapura appears to have also been known as Argaru. Thus the region seems to have been dominated by the Nāgas in the early centuries of the Christian Era.

The Pallavas who had an important place in the early history of India are not mentioned in the lists of the kings of the Tamil country in the Sangam age; from the provenance of their early inscriptions it may be presumed that they were mainly in the occupation of the Telugu country south of the river Krishnā till they established themselves at Kāñchī. The Velurpalaiyam plates (ninth century AD) say that Vīrakūrcha, the first well-known Pallava king obtained a kingdom by marrying a Nāga princess.[15] The Nāgas and Pallavas had become so much united by that time that myths tracing the origin of the Pallavas themselves to their ancestor Aśvatthāman by a Nāga princess had grown. Whatever may be the basis for the myth, it was a historical fact that like the Guptas of North India who gained political position and influence by Chandragupta's marriage with Kumāradevī, the Lichchhavī princess, the Pallava Vīrakūrcha had to seek the hand of a Nāga princess for gaining political position in the country round about Kāñchī, where, as seen above, the Nāgas appear to have been flourishing. Rasanayagam is at great pains to work out the theory of the Choḷa-Nāga origin of the Pallava, and make Toṇḍaimān Iḷamtiraiyan, the son of a Choḷa king by a Nāga princess of Manipallavam, the founder of the line. But it is not supported by epigraphy. The Nāga princess married by Vīrakūrcha, probably belonged to the family of the Oliya Nāgas which ruled over the Oymānāḍu, Aruvā and Aruvāvaḍatalainādu etc. The Pallavas who became matrimonially connected with the Nāgas came to be considered a mixed caste or group of people and were known as Kayavar, Nisar (low caste), etc.

It may be mentioned in passing that some scholars who are inclined to think that there was close connection between the present Nayars of Malabar and the Nāgas of ancient times, say that it is suggested among other things by the way in which the Nayars of old times combed their hair and made a knot of it over their head and thereby made their face look like the expanded hood of a cobra. The hypothesis however looks more fictitious and fanciful than real and tenable, for the Nayars of Malabar appear to have risen as a military class and were something like the Nayakas and Nayudus of the Tamil and Andhra areas.

Sufficient evidence is available to show that there was a Nāga population in the Deccan also. The Chūṭus or Nāgas were feudatories under the Sātavāhanas, and they declared their independence on the latter's fall. A Chūṭukulānanda Sātakarni, the king of Vaijayanti, is recorded to have established the sway of the Nāgas farther south.[16] The Kanheri inscription of Nāga Mūlanikā, wife of a *mahārathi*, daughter of a great king and mother of Skanda Nāga, takes the Chūṭu realm to Aparānta, north of modern Bombay.[17] The early Nānāghāṭ inscriptions mention the Andhra queen Nāganikā and a Nāga general Nākāyiro.[18] Karli has an iron pillar of an Agnimitra Nāga.[19] His niece, the Nāganikā, is mentioned in an inscription from Kuda.[20] A careful reading of the inscription in the Deccan found in Luder's list of Brahmi inscriptions gives many similar names. The inscriptions at Amarāvati and Jaggayyapeṭa also contain a large number of Nāga names. Though it is true that no definite conclusion can be reached merely from the find of such place and personal names, it must be recognised that the numerous names with 'nāga' either as a suffix or prefix make the surmise irresistible that there was a large Nāga element in the population of the Deccan.

Some Buddhist stories mention a Nāga king called Kāla (a name which resembles the name Kālabhartṛ Pallava) ruling in Majerika. Some Buddhist traditions of Ceylon and Siam refer to a Nāga country on the coast near the 'Diamond sands' between the mouth of the Ganges and Ceylon and to the south of Dantapura.[21] The country is called Majerika. The region appears to have been in the lower valley of the river Krishnā. Majer and Pātha Majer are two ancient places in the Divi taluk, Krishna district. It is not known if the country came to be called after the names of those two places, or after the name of the river Manjhirā, a branch of the river Godāvarī or probably it was the same as Masulika or Masulipatam. Whatever may be the exact identification of the Majerika, it seems pretty certain that in the region about the Krishna district there was a Nāga population.[22] But with regard to the period to which the Ceylonese and Siamese traditions relate there is some difference. The Ceylonese tradition gives the date as 157 BC while the Siamese tradition gives AD 310-13. But if there is any basis for the tradition preserved in both the countries probably the Ceylonese tradition is more dependable. This kingdom of Kāla was also called Pallava Bogga. When Duttagāmini of Ceylon performed his coronation a number of people from Pallava Bogga seem to have attended it. There were maritime and cultural relations between Pallava Bogga and Ceylon from early times.

It is generally believed that the Satavahanas were Brāhmaṇs with an admixture of Nāga blood. The Dvātṛmśatputtalikā represents Sālivāhana (or Sātavāhana) as of mixed Brāhmaṇa and Nāga origin.[23] The Nāga connection is suggested by names like Nāga-nika and Skanda Nāga-Śātaka. The Brāhmin origin of the Sātavāhanas or their support to the Brāhmaṇas is suggested by the Nasik *praśasti* of Gautamīputra Sātakarṇi, where he is called *Eka Bamhaṇa*.[24] Dynasties of rulers who claimed to belong to the Nāgavaṁśa ruled over parts of the Deccan in later times also.[25]

Though the Nāgas were kept under check under the Guptas they lingered on then and in subsequent periods. As already noted, during the days of Skandagupta one Sarvanāga is mentioned as the governor of Antarvedī.[26] In the neighbourhood of Surāṣṭra and Bharukachchha they appear to have been influential in the sixth century. From the Junagadh inscription of Skandagupta one may infer that a Nāga rebellion was suppressed by him.[27] About AD 570 Dadda I Gurjara uprooted the Nāgas who have been sought to be identified by Fleet with the forest tribes ruled over by Nirihullaka of Broach.[28]

In the Deccan the Nāgas regained much of their influence and power in the seventh century. Even in the medieval period there were a few dynasties in the Deccan that claimed to be of Nāga descent.

The Sendrakas

An important Nāga dynasty that appears to have ruled over contiguous parts of the present Bombay and Mysore states was that of the Sendrakas. The Sendrakas flourished in the fifth, sixth and seventh centuries and were feudatories first of the Kadambas and then of the Western Chālukyas of Vātāpi. Some of the rulers of the dynasty claim to have been of the lineage of the Bhujagendras (*Bhujagendrānvayaḥ*).[29] The country over which they ruled is mentioned as Sendrakaviṣaya in an inscription of the Kadamba king Kṛṣṇavarmā.[30]

According to an inscription of the fifth year of the Kadamba king Śrī Harivarmā one Bhānu Śakti was a chieftain of the Sendraka family.[31] Subsequently, the Sendrakas appear to have become the feudatories of the Chālukyas of Vātāpi. A Sedrakarāja, Śrī Vallabha Senānandarāja is said to have been the maternal uncle of King Pulakeśin II.[32] Probably there were different branches of the Sendraka family, as may be seen, for instance, from an inscription of Pulakeśin II which mentions a Sāmiyara of the Rudranīla Saindraka family who was a feudatory ruling over the Kuhundi district.[33] The Bagumra (Nausari district) copper-plate grant dated 406 probably of the Kalachuri or Chedi era (AD 655) gives the genealogy of the Sendraka kings and furnishes the names of a Bhānu Śakti (different from the one mentioned above), his son Āditya Śakti and his son Pṛthvī-vallabha Nikumbhalla Śakti.[34] From this inscription it appears certain that the Sendrakas who were settled exclusively in the Karnāṭaka country held later a portion of southern Gujarat. In the south one Durga Śakti, son of a Kunda Śakti, who was himself the son of a Vijaya Śakti of the Sendraka family, is said to have been a contemporary of a Satyāśraya who was possibly Pulakeśin II himself.[35] In AD 664 there was a rāja Deva Śakti in the Sendraka family at whose request the Western Chālukya king Vikramāditya I made a grant of the village of Raṭṭagiri.[36] Again under the Western Chālukya king Vinayāditya a Sendraka chieftain called Mahārāja Pogili is mentioned as a feudatory ruling over the Nāyarkhaṇḍa district, i.e., the Nāgara khaṇḍa division of the Banavase province.[37] The Sendrakas, however, appear to have declined as a political power after the seventh century, though their name was associated with a small territory in Mysore in much later times.[38]

The Senāvāras

Another Nāga dynasty about whom some information is available is that of the Senāvāras, who were a Jain family of rulers ruling over parts of the Kadur and Shimoga districts in Mysore. The first mention of a Senāvāra is in about AD 690 during the time of the Āluva king Chitravāhana[39] and of the Western Chālukya king Vinayāditya.[40] For nearly three centuries thereafter, there is, however, no mention of them. But from the beginning of the eleventh century we get some account of them again. They were of the Khachara *vaṁśa*, had the *phaṇidhvaja* (serpent flag), and the *mṛgendralāñchana* (lion crest).[41] The first known member of the dynasty was Jīvitavāra. His son was Jimūtavāhana, and his son was Māra or Mārasiṁha. The last of them ruled about AD 1058. He is said to have received homage from all the kings of the Vidyādharaloka and been master of Hemakūṭapura.[42] Sūrya and Āditya, the sons of Senāvāra, were ministers in the court of the Western Chālukya Virakmāditya in AD 1128.[43]

The Sindas

The Sindas were an important dynasty of Nāga chieftains who ruled over certain parts of the Deccan in the tenth, eleventh and twelfth centuries. Some scholar believe that there were at least four branches among them, namely, those of Bagadage (Bhagalkot in the Bijapur district), Erembarega or Erambirage (identified with modern Yelburga in the old Hyderabad state and lying about twenty-five miles in a south-easterly direction from Pattadakal), Bastar, Halavūr and Bellary. These branches were distinguished from one another by some variations in their crests (*lāñchanas*) and banners (*dhvajas, patākas* or *ketanas*). The common crest for all the branches was the *vyāghra lāñchana* or a tiger with a calf or child, thus indicating probably their origin in a clearer way. However, their banner is not mentioned. The other which belonged to Bharmarkoṭya *maṇḍala* had the *lāñchana* of a *dhanurvyāghra* (bow and tiger) and the *dhvaja* of *kamalakadali* or lotus flower and plaintain leaf. The Halavūr branch of Banavāsi had the *vyāghramṛgalāñchana* (the crest of a tiger and a deer) and the *nīladhavaja* (blue banner).[44]

The Sindas of Bhagalkot

Of the above different branches of the Sindas that of Bagadaga (Bhagalkot-Bijapur district) may be taken up first. The legendary origin and history of this branch are contained in an interesting stone inscription at Bhairanmatii in the Bhagalkot taluk.[45] According to it the Sindas belonged to the Nāgavaṁśa or the race of hooded serpents and the eponymous founder of the family was a certain 'long-armed' Sinda, a human son of the serpent-king Dharaṇendra, born at Ahichchhatra in the region of the river Sindh, i.e., the Indus. Perplexed at the birth of a son in human shape he bade a tiger nourish the child. The tiger transferred the child to the care of the lord of the snakes. In due course the child grew of age and became the king of the Sinda country. He married a daughter of the lord of the Kadambas and had by her three sons. From them sprang the Sindavaṁśa or the race of the Sindas. It seems there were thirty-one rulers in the dynasty without any break after which there was born a prince named Sinda. In this lineage of the Sindas of Bagadaga there was a chieftain called Kammara. His wife was Sangarabbaraśi. Their son was Pulikāla who is described as 'an ornament' of the family of the serpents (i.e., the family of those who have poison in their glances [*dṛṣṭiviṣakula*] 1.6.). He married a Revakabbe and to them was born Nāgāditya. He was a feudatory of the Western Chālukya king Jayasiṁha II and ruled about Ś. 955 (AD 1033-34). To him and his wife Polayyabbaraśi was born Polisinda, an ornament to the Sinda race. His wife was a Bijjaladevi, daughter of the Khāṇḍava Maṇḍaleśvara and their son was Mahāmaṇḍalesvara Sevya or Sevyarśa. He was a feudatory of Bhuvanaikamalla Someśvara II, the Western Chālukya king.

The Nāga lineage of the family is further borne out by the fact that Pulikāla is described in the inscription as having had a *nāgadhvaja* or *phaṇipatākā* (hooded serpent banner) which bore representations of the Nāga kings, Ananta, Vāsug(k)i and Takṣaka, *Vyāghra lāñchana* (tiger crest) and the hereditary title of Bhogavatīpura-Parameśvara or 'Supreme Lord of the Town of Bhogavatī', a place which, according to Hindu mythology, was the capital of the Nāga king Vāsuki in Rasātala, one of the seven divisions of *Pātāla* or the subterranean regions.

The exact relationship between this family and the family of Sindas of Yelburga, is not known. But the Sindas of Bhagalkot appear to have been slightly earlier than those of Yelburga.

The Sindas of Yelburga

Another branch of the Sindas was that of Yelburga, who in the eleventh, twelfth and thireenth centuries ruled over the region covered in ancient times by the political divisions of Kiśukāḍ seventy and 'several other towns' and feudatories of the Western Chālukya king Vikramāditya VI. Hence some members of the dynasty were called Tribhuvanamalladeva Kesarin or 'the lion of Tribhuvanamalladeva'.[46] Some of the later inscriptions of the dynasty credit them with a number of achievements. One of the members of the dynasty, Sinda Āchugideva, is said to have been "a very hand-mill for grinding the wheat which was an enemy named Jaggu" and plundered the country of a person named Hallakavaḍikeya-singa,[47] to have at the command of Vikramāditya VI, pursued and prevailed against the Hoysalas, taken Goa, put Lakṣmaṇa to flight in war, caused the Pāṇḍyas to retreat, dispersed the Mālapas or people of the Western Ghat and seized upon the Konkan,[48] and put to flames Goa and Uppinakaṭṭe and repulsed a Bhoja who invaded his territory.[49] Though it is difficult to identify many of the names mentioned above, it seems that Bhoja was the same as Bhoja I of the family of Śilāhāras of Karad.

The next ruler of the dynasty was Achugi's son Mahāmaṇḍaleśvara Permāḍi I, also called Perma, Pemma, Paramarḍi and Hemmaḍi. One of his inscriptions dated Rākṣara, Ś. 1067=1144 AD seventh year of the Western Chālukya king Jagadekamalla II gives him the title Jagadekamalla Permaḍi and shows thereby that he was his (Jagadekamalla's) feudatory. According to it he vanquished one Kulaśekharānka, besieged and decapitated Chaṭṭa, pursued a certain Jayakeśin (probably of the family of the Kadambas of Goa), seized the royal power of the Hoysalas, penetrated to the mountain passes of "the marander Biṭṭiya (Visṇuvardhana) besieged his city of Dvārasamudra, pursued him as far as the town of Belapura which he took and followed him beyond that place as far as the mountain pass of Vāhadi."[50]

His successor was his brother Mahāmaṇḍaleśvara Chāvuṇḍa or Chāvuṇḍa II. Of him we have one record from Paṭṭadakal dated Subhānu Śaka 1084 (5) = AD 1163. It mentions that he was (or rather had been) a feudatory of the Western Chālukya king Taila III, and was then ruling over Kiśukāḍ Seventy, the Bagadage Seventy, the Kelavadi Three Hundred and 'several other districts', and records that his senior wife Damaladevī and his son Achideva (Anegi III) were governing as regents at Kisuvolal or Paṭṭada Kisuvolal (Paṭṭaḍakal), the chief town in the Kiśukāḍ district.[51] He had another son by her, named Permaḍi (Permaḍi II).

It seems that Chāvuṇḍa II had another wife called Siriyadevī, daughter of the Kālachūrya king Bijjala and Vikrama or Vikkayya. They are said to have been ruling over their country in AD 1169-70 in the ninety-fourth year of the era founded by Vikramāditya VI,[52] while in a record of Ś. 1102 (AD 1179) Vikramā alone is mentioned as ruling over the Kiśukāḍ Seventy as a feudatory of the Kālacūrya king Śankama.[53]

THE SINDAS OF YELBURGA

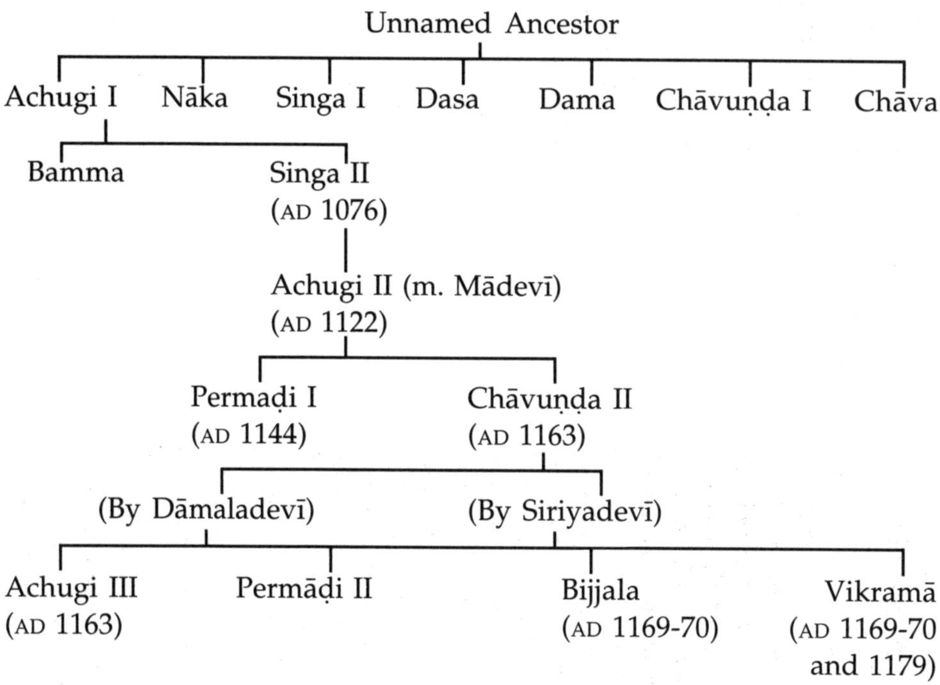

Again, during the days of the Western Chālukya Vikramāditya VI, mention is made of Mahāmaṇḍaleśvara Muñja Mahīpati of the Sinda race. He was the son of a Sindarāja and grandson of Bhīma, the governor of the Pratyaṇḍaka Four Thousand. This chieftain who was entitled to the privilege of the *pañchamahāśabdas* is mentioned as the lord of the city of Bhogavatī, born in the serpent chief's race (*phaṇīndra vaṁśodbhava*) and the frontal ornament of the Nāga family (*nāgakula tilaka*).[54]

The Nagpur museum inscription of Someśvara dated Ś. 1129 (1131?) = 1210 AD refers to a Someśvara Chakravartin who claimed to be a descendant of the Nāga of thousand hoods, i.e., of the serpent Śeṣa, to be the lord of the city of Bhogavatī, to have for his crest a tiger with a calf (*savatsavyāghralāñchana*), to belong to the Kāśyapa *gotra* and to be worshipper of the god Maheśvara and of the goddess Māṇikyadevī.[55] Though these two chieftains belonged to the Sinda family their mutual relationship or their relationship with the other branches of the Sinda family are not known.

The Sindas of Belagavartti or Belagavatti

Another branch of the Sindas ruled over parts of the Shimoga and Chitaldurg districts of Mysore, which along with parts of the Dharwar, Bijapur and Bellary district formed part of the Sindavāḍi province, and their inscriptions are largely found in the Honnali taluk of the Shimoga district and the Davanagere taluk of the Chitaldurg district. A few inscriptions contain interesting information about the origin and early history of a branch of the Sindas. According to them from the union of Śiva and Sindhu[56] (the river Indus) was born a son to whom Bhava (Śiva) with affection gave the name Saindhava saying, "be a king in the earth" and appointed the king of the serpents as his guardian. Saying that unless his son drank tigress' milk he would not become brave, Śiva created a tigress the milk of which the child drank and grew of age. Moreover, Parameśvara directed the Goddess Mālati to help his son in war and gave him a second name of Nidudol (long-armed) Sinda. Being told that Karahaṭa (modern Karad in the Satara district) was to be his residence he went there, drove out the king of the place and acquired the earth and began to rule over many districts in the Karahaṭa Four Thousand. He and his successors were known by the titles of 'Mahāmaṇḍaleśvara', Lord of Karanāṭa-pura and obtainer of a boon from Mālati. They claimed descent from the Phaṇirājavaṁśa (the race of the king of serpents) and were distinguished by the *nīladhavaja* (blue flag) and had the *vyāghra-mṛga lāñchana* (tiger and deer crest). They were further entitled to the sounds of the musical instruments of the *mallai* and *tūryya*. The Sindas had also the titles of 'Sindha', 'Govinda' and 'Pātāḷa Chakravarti'.[57]

An early member of the dynasty, Kerasinga Nanniya Sinda is mentioned in an inscription of the time of the Rāṣṭrakūta king Akālavarṣa dated AD 968.[58] When the Western Chālukya power was established, the Sindas appear to have accepted their overlordship as may be seen from an inscription of a Mulguṇḍa Sinda dated AD 992, during the time of the Western Chālukya king Āhavamalla. Towards the close of the eleventh century there was a Piriya Chaṭṭarasa in the dynasty. His grandson, also called Chaṭṭarasa, ruled about AD 1117. Between AD 1164 and 1180 ruled an important ruler of the dynasty named Īśvaradeva. His Nāga lineage is well borne out by an inscription of his, which says that at his coronation the sound of the drums and conches roused up Uragendra, the king of serpents, who, saying "this is a glorifiation of my line: Oh! I must see this" came there with haste, the jewels in his head appearing like a great illumination. Saranadī (Gaṅgā), Rudrāṇi (Pārvati), Śaṁbhu and Heramba (Gaṇapati) are said to have blessed him on the occasion.[59]

Among the territories included in his kingdom were the Edevetty Seventy, Bellave Seventy, Muduvalla Thirty and Narivalige Forty.[60]

While till the days of Īśvaradeva the royal residence was at Hallavur (Hulloor in the Rani-Bennur taluk in Dharwar on the Tungabhadra) from about his time the capital seems to have been Bellagavartti or Belagavatti now called Belagutti in the Honnali taluk in the Chitaldurg district, Mysore. The Sindas appear to have been attacked frequently by Umā Devī, the queen of the Hoysala king Ballāla II. But they were able to maintain their position, though the invader gained a lot of booty.[61] By AD 1198 the Hoysalas were, however, in the ascendant.[62] From about AD 1215 the Sinda country appears to have been under the control of the Yādavas of Devagiri. In AD 1245 and 1247 the Sinda chieftains fought severe battles at Kuḍali and Nematti (Nyamti) against the Seuṇa general Śrīdhara whom they appear to have driven away in confusion.[63]

The Nāgas of Bellary

Another branch of Nāga rulers appears to have flourished in the region of the Bellary district and enjoyed some political power during certain periods. The earliest reference we have to them is in the Velūpāḷaiyam copper-plates of Pallava Vijaya Nandivarman where it is said that the Pallava king, Nandivarman, a predecessor of Siṁhavarman, the father of Siṁhaviṣṇu, "with the favour of the God Pinākapāṇi (Śiva) caused to dance the powerful snake (*phaṇindraḥ*) whose poison was in (its) eyes (*Dṛṣṭiviṣah*)."[64] The term has to be interpreted here as a Nāga king rather than as 'lord of snake' while the term 'Dṛṣṭiviṣa' may be taken to be the name of a person rather than "a snake whose poison was in (its) eyes". This becomes apparent from the reference to a 'Dṛṣṭiviṣa' in whose family a Sinda chieftain ruling over parts of the Bellary district in the eleventh century AD is said to have been born.[65]

From about the close of the first half of the twelfth century two Nāga chieftains ruled over the area and were probably feudatories of the Western Chālukas. An inscription at Sindigeri in the Bellary district belonging to the (Dumati) fourth year of the Western Chālukya king Jagadekamalla II mentions a Sinda chief Mahāmaṇḍaleśvara Ballarāya Rāchamalladevarāsa during whose time a subordinate of his made a grant to the Śaiva teacher Nirvaṇideva of the E(l)koṭi Chakravarti-maṭha at Sindagere.[66] Another inscription of the tenth year of the Western Chālukya king Jagadekamalla mentions that Rāchamalla was the younger brother of an Irumaḍi Bhīma and both of them were ruling the Ballakundanāḍu when a certain individual built village temples for Śiva, Viṣṇu, Āditya (Sun), Vighneśvara and Bhairava.[67] A feudatory of his was Lākkeya Nāyaka who called himself the supporter of the kingdom of Immaḍi Rāchamalla.[68] This chieftain appears to have had a long rule, and became a feudatory of the Kalachūrya king Rāyamurāri Savideva (1168-78), elder brother of Śankama.[69] When the Kalachūri power was put to an end and Western Chālukya power was restored under Vīra Someśvara (Someśvara IV), Rāchamalla who is also called Sinda Govinda transferred his allegiance to him.[70] But of his successors no information is available.

There were some Nāga chieftains even in the late Vijayanagar period, as for example the Haratti chiefs who ruled over Nidugal under the Vijayanagar emperors.

EAST INDIA: ORISSA, BENGAL AND ASSAM

Nāga worship in Orissa is confirmed by the availability of a number of literary and antiquarian remains dating back to 1st-2nd centry AD. The twin hills of Khandagiri and Udayagiri, famous for the celebrated Hathigumphā inscription of Khāravela, contain a few sculptures of the Nāgas. Serpents are represented on the facade of the Anantagumphā flanking the door arches and near the artificial cave of the second full spandril of the upper main wing of Ranigumphā. In the Alakāpurigumphā, at the pilaster top a serpent is seen effectively entwined with a huge tusker in a tree and is about to strike at his head. Though the representation appears to be decorative in nature, it reminds us of the idea of Nāgapāśa,[71] popular in Pauranic legends, as well as the association of the Nāgas with Jaina religions reflected in the legend of the giant serpent king. In the cave of Khandagiri, images of Pārśvanātha, canopied by seven-hooded snake, are found in ten places, two in Navmuni Guṁphā, two in

Bārabhūji Guṁphā, one in Māhavīra Guṁphā and five in Lalāṭendukeśarī Guṁphā. It appears to be an exact replica of the Buddhist story of Muchalinda. In addition, there are two life-size anthropomorphic images of Nāgas in broken condition kept in the State Orissa Museum.[72] Three more anthropomorphic images of Nāga and Nāgīs may be seen at Sunderpara (near Bhubaneswar).[73] These are independent cult images datable to the period of Khāravela.

From 4th century AD onwards we find epigraphic references to the Nāgas and their association with the dynastic rulers. The Asānpat inscription of Nāga king Śatrubhañja in the Keonjhār region of Orissa is datable approximately to 4th century AD.[74] In this connection mention may be made of the presence of a carved serpent at Rāvaṇachāyā, Sītābinji in the district of Keonjhār belonging to Mahārājā Deśibhañja (c. 5th century AD)[75]. The Kanasa copper-plate grant[76] of King Lokavigraha, the king of Toṣali dated in G.E. 280 (AD 600) throws light on the worship of Maṇināga.[77] Two officials, Bhavanāga and Nāgadatta, possibly of Nāga lineage are also referred to in the same inscription. Also, there are temples of Maṇinageśvar on the bank of the river Langulia in Southern Orissa[78] and Suvarnarekha in North-Eastern Orissa. A small mountain in the shape of a coiled serpent is worshipped as Maṇināga in Ranpur region of Puri district.[79] Reference to Śeṣa rescuing the earth in the two Midnapur plates, Somadatta[80] and Śubhakīrti, feudatories and Mahārāja Mahāsāmata Śaśāṅka in the first half of 7th century AD hint at the place of Nāga in the religious faith of the contemporary people of Orissa.

During the 8th century AD the Bhauma-Karas came into power in Orissa. Tribhuvana-Mahādevī was a powerful queen of this dynasty. In the Talcher plate dated 141, it is said that after the death of Kusumahāra, his mother Tribhuvana Mahādevī took up the burden of administration of the entire kingom and abdicated in favour of her grandson Laoṇabhāra when he had come of age. In the inscription she is called "the crest jewel of Nāga dynasty, the ornamental mark of the southern Rājamalla's daughter."[81] It is clear that the Bhaumas were matrimonially related to the Nāga rulers of South India.

From post-Gupta Period onwards independent Nāga cult images are found in various parts of Orissa. At Bhubaneswara, in front of the Suvarṇajāleśvara, the bust portion of a Nāga figure datable to this period is found.[82] The cult, however, gained greater strength around Mayurbhanj region with the ascendancy of a Nāga dynasty, known as Vairāṭa Bhūjaṅga dynasty, who worshipped Nāga as their tutelary deity, the original seat of which is traced at Paṭāmuṇḍi hill near Puradihāris. The image of the tuletary deity is still preserved in the house of the Sarbarākhār of the dynasty of Koptipada.[83]

The sculpture of Kiñchaka Nāga carved on the Paṭāmuṇḍi hill is still another proof of Nāga worship by this dynasty. The image known by the name Kiñchakeśvarī or Khichiṇgeśvarī, now at Khiching, appears to be identical with Pāṭā Thākurānī of this dynasty.[84]

The Vairāṭa Rājās performed the worship of Nāgamātā and of eight Nāgas in their respective hearths. In all possiblility, the worship of Nāgamātā has come down to modern times as the worship of Manasā in Orissa, Bengal and Assam.

A beautiful Nāga icon found at Kuchiparā in Kalahandi district on the bank of river Jonk in the Maraguda Valley is a cult image locally worshipped by the people as Yogisunder.[85] The area formed a part of the Somavaṁśī territory who were closely associated with Nāga worship. The Bilhari stone inscription of Kalachuri ruler Yuvarājadeva II of Tripurī, dated c. 980 AD states[86] that Lakṣmanarāja (c. 945-970 AD) defeated the king of Kosala, who was most probably Mahābhavagupta-II Bhīmaratha of Somavaṁśī dynasty and obtaiend from him the effigy of Kāliya wrought in jewels and gold. He then worshipped Śiva at the well-known temple of Somanātha in Kathiawad and presented the aforementioned deity of the serpent Kāliya to the God.

In 11th century AD at Kalahandi was established the rule of a Nāga dynasty. Raghunāth Sai, one of the brothers of Gajānand Rai, the Nāga ruler of Chhota Nagpur (in Bihar) became the king of Kalahandi in Saṁvat 1062 (AD 1005) after his marriage with the princess and heiress of Kalahandi named Surekhā Devī, the daughter of the last Gangavaṁśī ruler, Jagannath Deo. The Nāga rulers of Chhota Nagpur trace their origin from the mythical serpent Puṇḍarika; they worship and propitiate Nāga in royal occasions. The worship of Māṇikeśvarī as their tutelary deity may be said to have been a derivative of Maṇināgeśvarī, a Nāga deity. The ruling family of Himgir in Sundergarh district also worship Māṇikeśvarī as their Iṣṭadevī. It may be worth noting here that Māṇikeśvarī was the Iṣṭadevī of the Chhindaka Nāga rulers of Chakrakūṭamaṇḍala (Bastar district of Chhattisgarh and Koraput district of Orissa) also and this is known from the inscriptions of the Chhindaka Nāga ruler Someśvara.[87] From the historical background of this region it appears more plausible to believe that the Nāgas of Kalahandi were related to Chhindaka Nāgas of Chakrakūṭa Maṇḍala rather than to the Nāgavaṁśīs of Chhota Nagpur. The territory of the Chhindaka Nāgas was close to the state of Kalahandi. The proximity of Kalahandi and Bastar, the synchronism of the rise of the Nāgas of Kalahandi region, the decline of the Chhindaka Nāgas of Bastar and the religion and religious faiths of both the families indicate that the Nāgas of Kalahandi were probably the descendants of the Chhindaka Nāgas of Bastar.

We have mentioned above some details about the Vairāṭa Bhūjaṅga dynasty of Mayūrbhañja. The early history of this dynasty is shrouded in obscurity whereas the Nāga rulers of Kaṭipada bearing the title 'Jaya Bhūjaṅga' are known to have flourished in the late medieval period.[88] The state of Kaṭipada was founded by the Nāga chief Phaṇī Mukuṭa during the rule of Gajapati king Kapilendra Deva (AD 1425-66) about the middle of 15th century AD. He was succeeded by his son Vasanta Virāṭa. It is said that Vasanta Virāṭa was one of the generals of Gajapati Puruṣottama Deva. During the war of Puruṣottama Deva against Kāñchī and Vijayanagar, Vasanta Virāṭa exhibited great courage and chivalry for which he obtained the title of 'Jaya Bhūjaṅga' and got sanction of the Gajapti king for the use of the titles of 'Jaya Bhūjaṅga', 'Virāṭa Bhūjaṅga', 'Abhinava Bhūjaṅga' and 'Parikṣita Bhūjaṅga' one after the other by his successors. Kiñchaka Nāga was the tuletary deity of this dynasty. The rulers of the dynasty believed that their achievements were due to the blessings of the Nāga; therefore they added 'Bhūjaṅga' with their titles.

Thus the association of many ruling dynasties of Orissa with Nāgas is apparent. Most of them traced their lineage to the Nāgas. That the cult of the Nāgas was very popular in Orissa is proved by the availability of large number of Nāga sculptures of all ages throughout Orissa.[89] Traditions, folklores and legends related to the Nāgas are abundant in Orissa where Nāga festivals are observed in various forms even today. In Western Orissa, the folk-cult of Nāgabāchā still exists prominently.[90]

As far as Bengal is concerned, we come across two references to Nāgas in the inscriptions of Bengal. The Ramganj record of Mahāmāṇḍalika Īśvara Ghoṣa introduces us to a Ghoṣa-Nāga family of Dhekkari, which is assigend to c. 11th century AD.[91] The *Bhuvaneswar praśasti* of Bhaṭṭa Bhavadeva, the minister of Harivarmadeva in c. 12th century AD[92] also refers to the destruction of Nāga kings by him. The *Rāmacharita* mentions the conquest of Utkala, the kingdom of Bhava-bhūṣana-Santati, by Rāmapāla, but it is not clear whether in this case the Nāgas were meant though there is every possibility of it.

In Bengal the goddess Manasā, or Biṣaharī holds the foremost place. The goddess is still regarded as an object of popular worship in Bengal and its neighbouring regions in Bihar and Assam. Like other folk deities, viz., Sitala, Shashthi, etc she was originally worshipped by primitive peoples but gradually found a place in the orthodox pantheon of Hinduism. It is only in the later *Purāṇas* like the *Padma, Devī Bhāgavata, Brahma Vaivarta*, etc that the name 'Manasā' as the serpent goddess is found.

It may be noted that the dominant position of the serpent goddess in Bengal is possibly on account of non-Āryan cultural influences. A. Bhattacharya thus observes: "The eastern provinces of India and the peninsula of the Deccan are the places where Āryan influence could not spread so effectively. Hence it is this part of India that possess some of the pre-Āryan cultural characteristics. Śakti worship or the worship of the goddess power of some specific nature is one of them. This is why in no other place in India except Bengal, some parts of Bihar and Assam and the South can the worship of the anthropomorphic serpent goddess be met with. In all places subject to the direct influence of Āryan culture the serpent too is worshipped but as *Nāga-rāja* or the king of serpents who is obviously a male deity."[93]

A close scrutiny of the worship of Manasā in the present day reveals its strong association with the non-Āryan mother goddess worship of India. In fact, the worship of Manasā is prevalent all over Bengal especially the rural Bengal and neighbouring regions among the people of the lower stratum of the society like the Dom, Bauri, Keot, Mal, Bagdi, etc mostly Hinduised aboriginals. There is hardly any village in the district of Birbhum where the worship of Manasadevī is not performed. In some parts of the district of Bardwan the higher caste Hindus observe *arandhana* or abstinence from cooking on the *Nāga-panchamī* day and place a few leaves of milky hedge plants inside the oven in order to worship the deity. An account of the worship of the goddess Manasā in the district of Burdwan was given by Risely nearly a century earlier. The deity is believed to be the serpent goddess and is primarily worshipped to get rid of snake bites during the rainy season. She is also worshipped for other purposes, like, to cure chronic diseases and to get a child showing the association of the deity with fertility cult. She is accredited with occasional violent anger manifested in snake-bite and other curses as depicted in the medieval *Manasā-mangal Kāvyas*. The rites and rituals relating to the worship of Manasā have variations in different parts of Bengal, but the basic elements are almost the same and identical.

According to some scholars Mahāyāna or the Tantric Buddhist School of Eastern India witnessed the worship of the serpent-goddess in the name of 'Jāñgulī'. It is believed that Buddha taught some of his chief disciples the mystical formula of the worship or this goddess.[94] The *Sādhanamālā* informs us that "The Hindu Manasā or Viṣahari has a marked resemblance to the appearance of Jāñgulī, and some of the meditative verses in the Hindu Tantric works for the goddess distinctly give her the epithet of Jāñgulī."[95] In the description of the images there are also conspicuous resemblances which also lead to believe that: "the influence of Mahāyāna Buddhist continued almost till the times of the Pāla kings in Bengal. Therefore, there is sufficient reason to believe that the worship of this most ancient anthropomorphic serpent-goddess Jāñgulī was widely prevalent in Bengal up to that time. When with the decline of the Pāla kingdom there was a revival of Brahmanism in the hands of the Sena kings many Buddhist priests left this county for Nepal where Mahāyāna Buddhism was still very popular, but those who stayed on preferred to introduce their gods and goddesses in new names so as to avoid any suspicion of their Buddhist affiliation. It seems that the name Jāñgulī for the snake-goddess was dropped at that time and a new name Manasā was taken instead."[96] The Jains regard Padmāvatī as the serpent-goddess. A.K. Bhattacharya has discussed this issue in a paper entitled 'Tārā as a Serpent Deity and its Jaina Counterpart Padmāvatī.[97]

While dealing with the origin of the name of goddess Manasā, Acharya Kshitimohan Sen points out that the serpent-goddess Mane Manchamma of the Canarese country is a source of the Bengali snake-goddess Manasā.[98] The earlier Sena kings who hailed from this region possibly carried the tradition of Mane Manchamma to Bengal. In fact, there are many other views relating to the origin of the name of goddess Manasā.[99] But there is no denying the fact that the present form of the deity originates not earlier than the eleventh-twelfth centuries AD.

A large number of sculptural representations of the deity have been found from different places of Bengal and its adjoining states. The general type of the stone image of Manasā has been described thus : "The deity is seated on a lotus in the *lalitāsana* pose, with hoods of seven snake spread over her head, her left hand holding eight Nāgas (mythologically, eight Nāgas are associated with the goddess). Her right hand in the *Varada* pose holds a fruit, and she is attended on either side by a seated emaciated figure and a crowned male person."[100] A beautiful bronze figure of Manasā, probably belonging to the Pāla Period, is now in the Indian Museum, Calcutta. "It shows the goddess seated under the usual snake-hoods in the *lalitāsana* pose, with child on her left lap and her right hand holding a long leafy branch."[101]

Innumerable images of the deity have been discovered from different places of Bengal and adjoining regions and they are now housed in the Indian Museum, Calcutta; in the museums of Decca and Varendra Research Society of Rajshahi in Bangladesh.[102] Almost all the images are assigned not earlier than eleventh-twelfth centuries AD and by that time the conception of the anthropomorphic serpent-goddess with Brahmanical attributes found expression in the sculptural representations. Thus from this time onwards goddess Manasā is being worshipped by all sections of Hindu society. In the concept of the present-day Manasā goddess an amalgamation of Brahmanical deities (like Sarasvatī, Lakshmī, etc.), Buddhist Jāṅgulī-Tārā and Jaina Padmāvatī is distinctly manifested. A synthesis of both Brahmanical and non-Brahmanical elements is discernible and it is very much in vogue even in the practices of rites and rituals as well as in sculptural representations.

The Nāgas of Assam, now settled in Nagaland state of the north-eastern part of India, were racially of a stock different from the Nāgas of the remaining part of India. Some scholars have tried to trace the Nāgas of this region from the Dravidians who first went from South India to Burma by sea and thence to Assam. In these matters there is such a wise difference of opinion and free play of imagination that it is just impossible to be sure on any point.[103]

In the political history of north-eastern India, there is hardly any evidence to show that the Nāgas had any contribution. This is in spite of the existence of the *Mahābhārata* tradition of Manipur being the seat of Nāga king Chitravāhana, whose daughter Chitrāṅgadā was married to Arjuna. Even at the present day, the ancestral god of the royal family is a snake called Pākhaṅgba. As a cult, however, the Nāga worship was widely distributed and developed in more interesting forms among the various tribes of Assam. Among the Khasis of Assam the most remarkable form of serpent-worship is that of the U-Thleṅ, a gigantic snake which demands to be appeased by the sacrifice of human victims, and for whose sake, even in recent items, murders have been committed.[104] Among the Meitheis, the ancestors of one clan, Pākhaṅgba, manifests himself as a snake.[105] Among the Lusheis, a man acquires the right to heaven by slaying certain animals, when a snake coils round the antlers of a sambhar stag, the man sitting on the coils is conveyed to heaven.[106] The Rabhās worship a snake-god which once dwelt in a cave and was propitiated by the annual sacrifice of a boy and a girl.[107]

The Hindus, however, worship it under the iconographic form of goddess Manasā, as in case of Bengal. The tradition of this may be traced in this region at least upto c. 10th century AD. The earliest image of this deity, in bronze, datable to c. 10th century AD, comes from Guwahati and is preserved in the Assam State Museum. The second in stone from Narakasur hill is also preserved in the same museum. A very fine specimen of the goddess, in stone, is at Barangabari. A stone image carved in the same style may be noticed at Phulbārī Devālaya in Sonitpur district. A very interesting stone image of the goddess is from the tea-garden near Silghat. It is datable to c. 12th century AD. At Sri Surya Pahar a rock-cut, twelve-armed image of the deity has been recovered.[108] Many more sculptures of the goddess may be traced in Assam.

The Manasā Pujā, which is celebrated during the rainy months *Jaiṣṭha, Āṣāḍha, Śrāvaṇa* and *Bhādra* is a popular festival in Assam, especially in the districts of Kamrup and Darang. In these festivals, offering are generally made to the deity without any image being made. The festival lasts for 2-3 days during which songs connected with legends of Chānd-Sadāgar are recited.

GREATER INDIA

When we pass from India to Greater India, interesting facts come to our notice. In Cambodia and East Indian Archipelago, we meet with the same association of the Nāgas with the royal families. Down to the 7th century AD, a tradition was strongly current in the Kambuja court of the origin of the ruling line from the marriage of a Nāga princess Somā with a Brahmin Kauṇḍinya.[109] It was believed that Funan, or the major portion of modern Cambodia, was once under a Nāga king, the marriage with whose daughter conferred the ownership of Funan on the Kambuja rulers. The old Tamil poem *Manimekhalai* mentions a town Nāgapuram in Java[110] which was apparently founded by the Nāgas. According to Chu-fan-Chi of *Chao-Jou-Koua*, a work on Chinese trade in the 12th century AD, the people of Śrīvijaya gave the title of 'long-tsing or the seed of the Nāgas,' to their king. This would appear to point to an association of the Śailendra dynasty of Eastern Sumatra also with the Nāgas. The early history of Pegu is similarly connected by tradition with the Nāga race.

The motif of snake-god finds a place in art forms in Greater India too. In the Khmer art of Kampuchea (Cambodia), the many-headed serpent is employed as a decorative device. One is carried away by the sight of the pair of enormous snakes, each carried by a row of fifty-four stone giants placed outside the Gate of Victory of Angkor Thom.

In the Isle of Java it is the human-shaped Nāga which has received special favour. At Borobodur the Nāga is shown in the human form even in those scenes in which the legend clearly required an animal-shaped creature. The most striking example is the well-known episode of the serpent Muchalinda sheltering Buddha under his hood against the inclemency of the weather. From the Buddhist sculpture it is perfectly clear that Muchalinda, in order to perform his benevolent and pious act, appears as a serpent, whereas, only when his services are not required he assumes human form. The Javanese artist adheres to the principle of representing his Nāgas as human beings, their serpent nature merely indicated by snake-hood.

REFERENCES

1. *Bhāgavata Purāṇa*, V, 24, 29, X ch. 16.
2. *Mahāvaṁsa*, I.
3. *Canto*, VIII, 11, 43-63.
4. *Perumbāṇāṟṟuppaḍai*, 11, 30-31.
5. *Pattuppaṭṭu*, p. 153.
6. *Maṇimekalai*, XXIV, 11, 23-24; XXV, 11, 178-192.
7. *Ibid.*, XVI, 11, 60-61.
8. *Śilappadikāram*, canto I, 11, 19-20.
9. *EI*, XVIII, p. 8, n. 3; also *SII*, ii, p. 27.
10. 353 of 1900; 246, 247 of 1901; 279 of 1909; 303 of 1910; 253 and 256 of 1913, etc.
11. *op cit.*, 11, 111-126.
12. Cunningham, *Ancient Geography of India*, p. 439; Caldwell, *Comparative Grammar*, p. 93.
13. *MAR*, 1919-20, p. 26.
14. S.K. Aiyanagar, Introduction to Gopalan's *Pallavas of Kanchi*, pp. xi-xii.
15. *SII*, II, p. 50
16. *EI*, X, Luder's List, No. 1195.
17. *Ibid.*, Nos. 935, 1021, 1196, etc.
18. *Ibid.*, Nos. 1114, 1116.
19. *Ibid.*, VII, p. 49
20. *Ibid.*, X, Luder's List, No. 1078.
21. Cunningham, *Ancient Geography of India*, pp. 534-5.
22. See *JASB*, VI. p. 856; XVII, pt. ii; *JRAS*, 1906, p. 685; 1907, pp. 341-6; *IA*, XVI, p. 4.
23. Raychaudhuri, *Political History of Ancient India*, p. 280.
24. See Ep. Ind., VIII, No. 2.
25. A dynasty of rulers who styled themselves Ālpuas, Āḷuvas, Āḷvas, or Ālus ruled over parts of the Deccan from about the sixth century. It has been suggested by Fleet that the cognomen is derived from the word Āluka – an epithet of Ādiśeṣa, the chief of the serpent race, and so they were a branch of the Nāgas (*Bombay Gazetteer*, I. ii, p. 309). But the word seems to be derived from the root *āḷu* which means to govern, and so it appears to be a technical expression to indicate subordinate government. This is indicated by such expressions as Kongālvas and Changāḷvas, rulers respectively of the Kongāḷnād and Changanād in the Kannaḍa country and *nāḍ-āḷvan* (ruler of a small territory in the Tamil country).
26. Fleet, *Gupta Inscriptions*, p. 68.
27. *Ibid.*, p. 59.
28. *Bombay Gazetteer*, I, i. p. 115; *IA*, XIII, pp. 82ff.
29. *IA*, VII, p. 106, 1.54.
30. *EC*, V. Bl. 245. The Mercara grant of Avanīta Kongaṇi mentions a Sendrika as

a witness to a grant (Rice, *Coorg Inscriptions*, No. 1, 1.52). It has been suggested that the term refers to a Sendraka chieftain. But that is very doubtful, because the word used in the inscription is Sendrika and not Sendraka (See Fleet, *Bombay Gazetteer*, I, ii, pp. 292-3, n. 10).

31. *IA*, VI, p. 31.
32. *EI*, III, pp. 50ff.
33. *Ibid.*, VII, p. 110.
34. *Ibid.*, XVIII, pp. 266-7.
35. *Ibid.*, VII, p. 110.
36. *JBBRAS*, XVI, p. 228.
37. *IA*, p. 142. The term 'Nāyarakhaṇḍa' is the *Prākṛit* form of Nāgarakhaṇḍa and denoted the territorial division of the Nāgas (See Fleet, *Bombay Gazetteer*, I, ii, p. 281, n. 3). It is strange that while the inscriptions of the Nāgas bear among others the emblems of the Nāga or serpent, this particular inscription bears the emblem of an elephant. It is hard to explain it, though Fleet thinks that it may be due to the fact that 'however authentic may be the contents of it, (the inscription) this Lakhmeshwar inscription was not engraved till after AD 967, (*Ibid.*, p. 292, n. 9).
38. The country to the south of Basavapaṭṭaṇa was called the Sendraka country so late as the seventeenth century.
39. *EC*, VI, KP. 36.
40. *Ibid.*, VII, Sk. 278.
41. Usually the rulers in Mysore who claimed Nāga lineage had the tiger crest only.
42. *EC*, VI, Cn. 61, 62, 75, 94. 95.
43. *Ibid.*; XI, Dg. 90.
44. *EI*, IX, pp. 312-3.
45. *Ibid.*, III, pp. 230ff.
46. *JBBRAS* (old series), XI, p. 247-52.
47. *Ibid.*, p. 243.
48. *Ibid.*, p. 244.
49. *Ibid.*, p. 269.
50. *JBBRAS*, (old series), XI, p. 244.
51. *Ibid.*, p. 259.
52. *Ibid.*, p. 274; IA, IX, p. 96.
53. See *Bombay Gazetteer*, Vol. I, ii, p. 576.
54. *EI*, III, pp. 306ff.
55. *EI*, III, pp. 314ff. The Chhinda Nāgas of Bastar were also worshippers of Goddess Māṇikyadevī.
56. In *EC*, VII, H. 29-Sindu is referred to as Sura Sindu (the river of the gods, the Ganges).
57. *Ibid.*, HI, 20, 50; XI, Dg. 43; also *Bombay Gazetteer*, I, ii, pp. 577-8 and *EI*, III, pp. 231-2.

58. *EC*, VII, Hk 23.
59. *Ibid.*, XI, Dg. 43.
60. *Ibid.*, XI, Hl. 26, 27 and 28.
61. *Ibid.*, XI, Hl. 37, 38, 40 and 28.
62. *Ibid.*, VII, Sk. 315.
63. *Ibid.*, XI, Hl, 54 and 55.
64. *SII*, III, p. 508, e. 9.
65. *ARSIE*, 198 of 1913.
66. 211 of 1913.
67. 69 of 1901.
68. 69 of 1904.
69. 56 and 58 of 1904.
70. Kielhorn, *List of Inscriptions of Southern India*, No. 253; *Asiatic Researches*, IX, p. 431; Colebrooke, *Miscellaneous Essays*, Vol. II, p. 271.
71. Mohapatra, R.P., *Udayagiri and Khandagiri Caves in Orissa*, 1980, pp. 260-61.
72. Panda, S.C., *Naga Cult in Orissa*, New Delhi, 1986, figs. 2, 3.
73. *Ibid.*, figs. 4a and 4b.
74. *OHRJ*, Vol. III, No. 2, p. 1
75. Sahu, N.K., *Odia Jatir Itihasa*, (Oriya), Bhubaneswar, 1975, p. 190.
77. *JKHRS*, Jan. 1950, pp. 262-66.
78. Francis, W. *Gazetteer of Vizagapatnam* Dist. Vol. I, 1915, p. 10
79. Panda, S.C., *op cit.*, p. 19.
80. *JASB*, XI, 1945, No. I, pp. 7-9.
81. *JAHRS*, IV, pp. 189-94; *JBORS*, XVI, pp. 79-83.
82. Panda, S.C., *op cit.*, p. 19.
83. Senapati, N. (ed.), *Orissa District Gazetteers* (Mayurbhanj), Cuttack, 1967, p. 84.
84. Fig. 7 of Panda, S.C., *op cit.*
85. Fig. 21, of Panda, S.C., *op cit.*
86. *CII*, IV, pt. I, p. 205.
87. *EI*, III, p. 318.
88. Senapati, N. (ed.), *Orissa State Gazetteers* (Mayurbhanj), Cuttack, 1967, p. 84.
89. For details, See, Panda, S.C., *op cit.*
90. *Ibid.*, pp. 39ff.
91. *Bhandarkar List*, No. 2100.
92. *Inscriptions of Bengal*, III, pp. 30ff.
93. Bhattacharya, A., *The Sun and the Serpent Lore of Bengal*, Calcutta, 1977, pp. 131-33. For a detailed study of the Manasa Cult see Maity, P.K., *Historical Studies in the Cult of the Goddess Manasa*, Calcutta, 1966.
94. *Sadhanamālā*, 120.
95. Bhattacharya, B., *Buddhist Iconography*, Calcutta, 1924, p. 180.
96. Bhattacharya, A., *op cit.*, pp. 137ff.
97. Sircar, D.C. (ed.), *Sakti Cult and Tara*, Calcutta, pp. 158-59.

98. *Prabasi*, 1329 B.E., *Ashadha*, pp. 391ff.
99. Sircar, D.C., *Religious Life in Ancient and Medieval India*, New Delhi, 1971, p. 137.
100. Majumdar, B.C. *History of Ancient Bengal*, Calcutta, p. 536.
101. *Ibid.*
102. Bhattashali, N.K., *Iconography of the Buddhist and Brahmanical Sculptures in the Decca Museum*, Dacca, 1929, pp. 220ff; Majumdar, R.C., *History of Bengal*, Decca, pp. 460ff.
103. Choudhury, P.C., *History of the Civilization of the People of Assam*, pp. 81-114.
104. Gurdon, P.R.T., *The Khasis*, London, 1914, pp. 98ff.
105. Hodson, T.C., *The Meithesis*, London, 1908, pp. 100ff.
106. *Census of India*, 1911, iii, Assam, pt. I, pp. 140ff.
107. *Ibid.*, p. 145.
108. For details of these images, see Choudhary, R.D., *Archaeology of the Brahmaputra Valley of Assam*, Delhi, 1985, pp. 100-103.
109. Chatterjee, *Indian Influence in Cambodia*, pp. 3ff.
110. *Ibid.*, p. 5.

9

CONCLUSION

In the preceding pages we have discussed the rise and growth of the Nāgas as a political force in the history of North India from the earliest times to c. 15th century AD. If we look at the problem in the national perspective, several interesting features emerge and we may sum up these in the following words:

I

To a student of Indian history, it appears as if there lay a complete veneer of a belief in the divinity of the Nāgas and of the Nāga racial blood over the length and breadth of India. From Kashmir, Tibet or Nepal to the Malabar and Konkon coast in the South; from Gujarat to Bengal and Assam; from Ceylon to Java, Sumatra and Cambodia, there are very few places indeed, where we do not meet frequently with individual or local names of which the word 'Nāga' forms a part, or where the ruling dynasty is not believed sometimes to have been associated with a Nāga clan. Such peculiarly Nāga names as Nāgadatta, Nāgāṁbikā, Nāgasena, Nāgapāla, Nāgarjuna, Bhavanāga, Nāgabhaṭṭa, Nāgarāja, Nāganikā, or more simply Nāga and Nāgī, occur alike in the dynastic lists of Southern as well as Northern India. Individual names including the word 'Nāga' appear in the votive inscriptions of Sanchi and Bharhut as well as of Amrāvatī. The Sātavāhanas, the Guptas, the Valabhī kings and the Pālas employed Nāga officials. Nepal is said once to have been known as the Nāgahṛada; the old capital of Kashmir was Ananta Nāga; and we hear of a city called Nāgapuram on the river Gomati in the Naimiṣāraṇya. Ahichchhatra or Ahikṣetra in Rohilkhand undoubtedly seems to denote that it was the field or home of Ahis = Nāgas. The belief that Ceylon was the habitat of a Nāga race was so strong that even down to a very late period it continued to be known as the Nāgadvīpa. Besides, such local names as Nāgakhaṇḍa, Nāgavāḍi, Nāgoda, Nāgāvi or Nāgamaṅgalaviṣaya and Nāgpura, Nāgercoil, Nagarkoṭa, Nāgapaṭnam, Nāgāṇādu, Nāgardhana, Nāgārjunikoṇḍā, etc which occur so frequently in the inscriptions of Central and Southern India bear indubitable traces of association with the Nāgas.

II

An interesting fact is the association of the royal dynasties with the Nāgas. This appears in two forms, viz., (a) in the form of matrimonial alliances with the contemporary Nāga tribal chiefs, and (b) claiming their origin from the Nāga racial stock themselves.

The instances of royal dynasties having matrimonial alliances with the contemporary Nāga chiefs, with a view to strengthen themselves, are more than one. The Devagiri record of Kadamba king Kṛṣṇavarmma I connects the beginning of the Kadamba-kula with the Nāgas.[1] Rayakota grant of 9th century[2] mentions the marraige of Aśvathāmā with a Nāgī and the foundation of the Pallava line by Skandaśiṣya, the issue of this marriage Vīrakūrcha, who according to another Pallava inscription dated in the 9th century AD was the ruler of the dynasty and who is also mentioned in the same inscription as having married a Nāgī and "obtained from her the insignia of royality."[3] The marraige of Gautamīputra, the son of the Vākāṭaka king Pravarasena, with the daughter of a Bhāraśiva king Bhavanāga, is a historical fact. So is the marriage of Chandragupta II with Princess Kubera Nāgā of the Nāga *kula*.[4] A Tamil poet asserts that Kokkili, an early king, had married a Nāga princess.[5] Rājendra Chola is also credited to have won "by his rediant beauty the hand of the noble daughter of the Nāga race."[6] The *Navasāhasāṅkacharita* describes the marriage of the Paramāra king Sindhurāja (who seems to have reigned towards the later part of 10th century AD) with the Nāga princess Śaśiprabhā, in such exhaustive details as to make us almost certain that there must have been some historical basis for this assertion.[7] From the history of the Chāhamānas, we know on the evidence of *Prithvīrājavijaya* that during the regency of Prithvirajā III, Bhuvanaikamalla, the commander of the army had exterminated the Nāgas who proved dangerous to the safety of the prince. The location of the Nāgas is not known.[8] Śāntikara of the Bhauma Dynasty of Orissa, one of whose dates was most probably AD 921, is mentioned as having married Tribhubana Mahādevī of the Nāga family in an inscription of his son.[9]

When we pass from India to Cambodia and the East Indian Archipelago, we meet the same association of the Nāgas with the royal families. Down to the 7th century AD, a tradition was current in the Kambuja court of the origin of the ruling line from the marriage of a Nāga princess Somā with a Brāhmin in Kauṇḍinya.[10] It was believed that Funan, or the major portion of modern Cambodia, was once under a Nāga king, the marriage with whose daughter conferred the ownership of Funan on the Kamboja rulers. The old Tamil poem *Manimekhalai* mentions a town Nāgapuram in Java[11] which was apparently founded by the Nāgas. According to *Chu-fan-chi* of Chao-Jou-Koua, a work on Chinese trade in the 12th century AD, the people of Śrīvijaya gave the title of 'long-tsing' or 'the seed of the Nāga,' to their king.[12] This would appear to point to an association of the Śailendra dynasty of Eastern Sumatra also with the Nāgas. The early history of Pegu is similarly connected by tradition with the Nāga race.

When we consider those dynasties that claim or are reputed to have belonged to the Nāga tribal stock themselves, we find there are also a considerably large group of varied interest and importance. A list of such families would take us through all the centuries from the later Vedic Age down to 15th century AD. The earliest among these are the Pañchālas and Kṛivis, the etymology of whose names seems to connect them with serpents. The name of Pañchāla in particular would warrant such an assumption since it is difficult to explain its origin otherwise than as a confederacy of five *ala* or serpent-tribes.

If we pass over the vague half-mythical and half-historical references to the Nāgas contained in the epics and the *Purāṇas*, the next in point of age among the kings who should be associated with the Nāgas would perhaps be the rulers of Ayodhyā, who are believed to have ruled sometime between 150 BC and AD 100 and whose coins are discussed on pp. 148-150, in V.A. Smith's *Catalogue of the Coins in the Indian Museum*. It will be noticed that on the coins of three kings of this group Viśākhadeva, Dhanadeva and Kumudasena, the snake occurs as one of the symbols. King Parvata of Kosam who ruled about 2nd BC (*ibid.*, p. 155) also has a similar snake on his coin. Snake similarly occurs on two of the Taxila coins mentioned in the same *catalogue* (p. 156, nos. 6 and 7) and attributed to about the 4th or 3rd century BC as well as on two if not three coins of the Mālavas who ruled during the first centuries of the Christian Era (p. 171, no. 5, p. 174). A Yaudheya coin of early age (no. 31, p. 183) also contains a symbol composed of two snakes. The full significance of such symbols is difficult to determine at the present state of our knowledge. It is interesting, nevertheless, to take note of a few curious features. In the first instance, we know that excepting Nāgarāja Śeṣadatta, the founder of the earlier Vidishā branch of the Nāgas which reigned during the later half of the 1st century BC, neither the coins of the Nava Nāgas of Padmāvatī and Kāntipurī, nor those struck by the Sātavāhanas, who are credited by some to have been Nāgas, are known to bear this snake-symbol. Secondly, the snake appears on the coins of individual kings of a line, and is not the general insigia of the dynasties. Thirdly, in six of the eight cases mentioned above the snake appears together with a bull. Only in two cases do we find it occurring without it, and along with *Chaitya*. In case of Nāgarāja Śeṣadatta, two serpents face each other with what looks like a post in between them and coiled up over a rectangular basement. We should also note that the known Kuṣāṇa and Gupta coins types too do not bear the snake design. This is another significant fact which helps us to reconstruct the history of the Nāga cult and tribe.

During the period 1st-4th century AD, Southern India seem to have come under considerable influence of the Nāgas. Ptolemy in Bk. VII, Pt. I, sections 91 and 92, of his *Geography* refers to the Coast of Soringoi with its capital Orthoura ruled over by Sornagos, and Arouarnoi with capital Malanga under King Basaronagos. As Dr. D.C. Sircar has pointed out in his *History of the Early Pallavas*, in *Journal of Indian History*, Vol. XIV, 1935, p. 154, this Soringoi no doubt represents the Coromandala and its capital Orthoura is most probably identical with Uragapur or Uraipur (Uraiyur on the Kaveri). Arouarnoi is supposed to have been identical with Kāñchī maṇḍala. It is difficult to arrive at actual names of the kings, but they would appear to be something like Śūryanāga and Vajra or Varṣanāga. Anyway, there is little doubt that in the time of the Greek geographer, this portion of the Deccan was under Nāga kings. M. Srinivasa Iyenger sponsored the Nāga origin of the Pallavas, vide his *Tamil Studies.* His theory is based on the Nāga alliance with the Choḷas mentioned in the *Manimekhalai* as well as the Nāga ancestry referred to in epigraphs like Talagunda inscriptions. Vincent Smith agrees with the view and holds that they might be somehow connected with the Kurumbas (*Oxford History of India*, 3rd ed., p. 220). Many more scholars have come forward to support the theory of the Nāga origin of the Pallavas of Kanchi[13] and close association of the Nāgas with the ancient Tamil land.[14]

That Andhradeśa and its neighbourhood was under the Nāgas during the early centuries of the Christian Era is suggested by evidence from more sources than one. The Sātavāhanas and their successors, the Chuṭu Kula

Sātakarṇīs drew their blood more or less from the Nāga stock. As Dr. H.C. Raychaudhuri has pointed out, the *Dvātriṁśatputtalikā* represents Śālivāhana, the mythological representative of the Sātavāhana dynasty, as of mixed Brāhmaṇa and Nāga origin.[15] This is amply attested to by the typical Nāga names which occur in their dynastic lists. That the Nāgas grew to be very powerful towards the end of the Sātavāhana rule is also proved by a number of facts. A chief called Skandanāga is found ruling in Bellarey district, in the reign of Pulumāvi, the king of the main Sātavāhana line. Secondly, Nāga Mūlanikā, the daughter of a Chuṭu king, is mentioned as making a gift of a Nāga, together with her son, who is called Śivaskanda-Nāga-Śrī. All the known kings of this line prove a close association with Nāgas. Thirdly, the name of Uragapura, the capital of Soringoi, suggests not an isolated reign of one Nāga king but a Nāga settlement in that locality of tolerably long duration. From the Buddhist traditions of Ceylon and Siam we also know that there was a Nāga country called Majerika near Kāñchī,[16] from whose king permission was once obtained to transfer a relic to Ceylon from Dantapura in the Andhradeśa. The difficulty is that while the Ceylonese tradition gives the date as 157 BC, the Siamese chronicle definitely puts it as AD 313. But though this might have been vitiated by the independent evidence of these traditions, they nevertheless help in establishing the conclusion, that during the first three centuries of the Christian Era, the Choḷa and Kāñchī maṇḍalas as well as part of Andhradeśa were under Nāga rulers.

That during the third and early part of the 4th century AD Northern India also was ruled by a number of Nāga kings is clearly proved by Pauranic as well as numismatic and epigraphic evidences. Three independent groups of Vidishā, Champāvatī or Padmāvatī and Mathurā are distinctly mentioned in such a way as to leave little doubt of their importance. Of all the Nāga dynasties of this period, the Bhāraśivas were the most prominent and historically the most tangible. We do not know whether Nāgabhaṭṭa and his son Mahārāja Maheśvara Nāga of the Lahore Copper Seal[17] belonged to any of the three groups or formed a separate Nāga family by themselves. Though this does not sufficiently justify the conclusion of Dr. H.C. Raychaudhuri that the Kuṣāṇa kingdom of Northern India disappeared in the 4th century AD having been conquered by the Nāgas, they had a major role to play along with other contemporary powers in the uproot of the Kuṣāṇas. These Nāgas must have been ruling over different portions of Uttarāpatha till they were themselves swept away before the conquering arms of Samudragupta.

As late as the time of Skandagupta, however, we find one Śarvanāga as the governor of Antarvedī.[18] In the neighbourhood of Surashtra and

Bharukachchha especially, the Nāgas seem to have held a prominent position down to the 6th century AD. From the Junagadh inscription, Skandagupta appears to have dealt severely with a Nāga rebellion.[19] In c. 570 AD Dadda I Gurjara uprooted the Nāgas,[20] who have been identified with the tribes ruled over by Nirihullaka of Broach.[21] Dhruvasena II's grant of G.S. 334 (654 AD) also mentions as Dūtaka the Pramātṛi Śrīnāga.[22]

The next important revival of the Nāgas particularly in Central India seems to date about the 8th century AD. Earlier in the second half of 7th century AD Mahārāja Tīvaradeva of Śrīpura in South Kosala most probably defeated a Nāga tribe.[23] Sometime after this period, we also note two references to Nāgas in the inscriptions of Bengal. The Ramganj record of Mahāmāṇḍalika Iśvaraghoṣa introduces us to a Ghoṣa Nāga family of Dhekkari, which was to be assigned to c. 11th century AD.[24] The *Bhubanesvara Praśasti* of Bhaṭṭa Bhavadeva, the minister of Harivarmadeva in c. 12th century AD,[25] also refers to the destruction of Nāga kings by him. The *Rāmacharita* mentions the conquest of Utkala, the kingdom of Bhavabhūṣaṇa-Santati, by Rāmapāla but it is not clear whether in this case the Nāgas were meant.

It was in the period 10th-12th century AD that the Chhindaka Nāga family who called themselves lords of Bhogavatī and Nāgavaṁśī had established themselves well over different portions Central India, particularly Bastar. If the evidence of *Navasāhasāṅkacharita* is accepted, then the Nāga king, whose daughter Śaśiprabhā was married to Sindhurāja Paramāra, must have been ruling in Ratnavatī on the Narmadā at about this period. As discussed above, the Nāgas of Kawardhā and Bhaṭṭigrāma were of still later date.

The history of the Nāgas in the Northern and North-Western provinces of Uttarāpatha, as far as traceable from literature and tradition, deserve a separate mention. We cannot be certain how far the legend of the invasion of the Tak or Takṣa – a Scythic tribe which worshipped serpents and, as suggested by some scholars, probably laid the foundation of the Nāgavaṁśī element the Rājput clan – might have been historically true. As discussed above, historically it is not true. Takṣaka is the name of a well known mythical Nāga to which the ancestry of the Takṣakas may be traced mythically without involving the foreign element. The Takṣakas might have had something to do with the foundation of Takṣaśilā. There is no doubt, however, that Kashmir from very early days, must have been a centre of the Nāgas. The *Rājataraṅgiṇī* has preserved a legendary account of the conflict between the followers of the Nāga cult and the Buddhists, immediately after the reign of the Kuṣāṇas. We also learn from the same source how Gonarda III revived the ancient rituals in accordance with the *Nīlamata Purāṇa* (Nīla was one of the chief mythic Nāgas). In AD 627 the Kārkoṭa Nāga dynasty was founded by Durlabha-Vardhana and lasted till AD 854. From the *Mahāvamsa*, again, we learn the conversion of as many as 84,000 Nāgas in the Himavanta region and of the Nāga king of Kashmir and Gandhāra. Hiuen Tsang also mentions that serpent-worship was known in Strīrājya.

But although we have many proofs of Nāga worship in the northern regions, we have no evidence of the political importance of the Nāgas here, except in Kashmir.

III

A careful examination of the data mentioned above reveals several very significant facts. In the first instance, a clear distinction must be made between kings or individuals who merely worshipped the Nāgas, and families or tribes who had come to be identified with the Nāgas themselves. Whether this was from long continued worship of the Nāgas or from having once been in the position of chief of the cult, must remain a matter of pure conjecture. But it is difficult to explain otherwise the occurrence of typical Nāga names in the dynastic lists of the royal families who are not known to have belonged to the Nāga race, nor the fact that out of hundreds of such dynasties, only five or six stand out as belonging to the Nāga *kula*. This would also explain the sporadic appearance of the Nāga symbol on the coins of individual rulers of Ayodhyā or Mālava referred to above. That the known Nāga coins bear only the humped bull and peacock designs, both emblems associated with the Śaiva cult, also confirms the theory that the people known as Nāgas had been serpent-worshippers in the long past, and had gradually changed their symbols along with the change in the very character of their own religion.

Thus at the very beginning we are hampered with the knowledge that (a) dynasties which described themselves as of Nāga *kulas* did not necessarily use the Nāga symbol, and (b) as the cases of the Ghoṣa dynasty of Bengal and the Nāgavaṁśīs of Bastar illustrate, might not even have used the word Nāga as part of their names. Therefore it must also be true that the mere use of Nāga symbols or the use of the appellation Nāga in their nomenclature does not justify the identification of any particular dynasty with the Nāga *kula*. It is therefore necessary to make a distinction between three probable cases: (1) An entire tribe or clan worshipping the Nāga might come to be known as the Nāgas, on semi-totemistic basis. The Pañchālas, the Kṛivīs and the Nāgas of Kashmir may be said to have belonged to this group; (2) Out of a religious hierarchy connected with the Nāga cult might be evolved ruling dynasties, who would at first use the Nāga as their emblem, but might in later ages, retain the designation 'Nāga *kula*', although actually worshipping only associated deities. This type is represented by the three Nāga dynasties of Vidishā, Mathurā and Champāvatī, the Chhindaka Nāgas of Bastar and the Ghoṣas of Bengal; (3) Then there might be the cases of new conversion, or of a revival of Nāga worship under individual kings of a dynasty, or an influence brought into the family through matrimonial alliances. This would explain the large number of names connected with Nāgas found in the majority of the dynasties, and the sudden appearance of the Nāga symbol on coins.

From an examination of the above facts, it appears that although we cannot infer the rise to political importance of the Nāga *kula* merely from the occurrence of Nāga names in the genealogies unless corroborated by some other evidences, it is possible to deduce a revival of Nāga or allied worship from a recurrence of such names. Two such revivals are clearly warranted by the data mentioned above. The first should be assigned to the period 1st-4th century AD, the second to the centuries 9th-11th AD. The latter is more interesting in the sense that it denotes a re-assertion of the non-Āryan elements in the cult with its earth-worship and human sacrifices before such goddesses as Danteswarī of Bastar, and that the sense of veneration felt for the Nāgas in this age is revealed by an attempt by the majority of the ruling dynasties to claim some connection, matrimonial or otherwise, with the Nāgas. It is noticed that most of the inscriptions containing traditions of Nāga alliance with royal families date from this period.

Such are the intricacies associated with the Nāga problem in Indian history. Any attempt to further highlight the role of the Nāgas in the political history of ancient India must keep these interesting features in mind.

REFERENCES

1. *IA*, VII, p. 134.
2. *EI*, XV, p. 246.
3. *SII*, II, p. 508.
4. Poona plates of Prabhāvatī Guptā, *EI*, XV, pp. 39-45; *CII*, V, pp. 5-9.
5. *EI*, XV, p. 249.
6. *IA*, XXII, pp. 144, 148.
7. Buhler, *EI*, I, p. 229.
8. Majumdar R.C. (ed.), *The Struggle for Empire*, 4th ed., 1989, pp. 104-5.
9. *JBORS*, XVI, p. 771. Also, Pt. B. Mishra, 'Orissa Under Bhauma Kings', 1934, pp. 14-17; *EI*, XXVIII, p. 213.
10. Chatterjee, *Indian Influence in Cambodia*, pp. 3ff.
11. *Ibid.*, p. 5.

12. Feurnal, *L'Empire Sumatranais de Srivijaya*, p. 11.
13. T.K. Venkatasubramanian, 'Nāga Origin of the Pallavas of Kanchi'; in *Indian History Congress Proceedings*, 38th Session, 1977, pp. 60-65.
14. C.S. Srinivasachri, *'The Ancient Tamils and the Nāgas'*, in *IHQ*, III, pp. 518-529.
15. *PHAI*, (1972 ed.) p. 365.
16. Cunningham, *Ancient Geography of India*; Sircar, D.C., *Journal of Indian History*, Vol. XIV, 1935, p. 156.
17. Fleet, *Gupta Inscriptions*, p. 283.
18. *Ibid.*, p. 68.
19. *Ibid.*, p. 59.
20. Kaira grant of Dadda III, *IA*, XIII, pp. 82ff.
21. *Bombay Gazetteer*, I, I, p. 115.
22. *EI*, I, p. 92.
23. Fleet, *Gupta Inscriptions*, Rajim Grant, p. 298, fn.1.
24. *Bhandarkar List*, No. 2100.
25. *Inscriptions of Bengal*, III, pp. 30ff.

SELECT BIBLIOGRAPHY

1. ARCHAEOLOGICAL SOURCES

a) Excavations and Explorations

Agrawal, D.P. : *Copper Bronze Age in India,* New Delhi, 1973.

Agrawal, D.P. and Chakravarty, D.K. (ed.) : *Essays in Indian Protohistory,* Delhi, 1979.

Bajpai, K.D. : *Archaeology in Uttar Pradesh,* Lucknow, 1953.

Mathura, New Delhi, 1980.

Barua, B.M. : 'Indus Script and Tantric Code', *Indo-Iranica,* Vol. I, 1946.

Bhan, Suraj : *Excavation at Mitathal and other Explorations in the Sutlej-Yamuna Divide,* Kurukshetra, 1975.

Chakravarty, D.K. : *Archaeology in the Third World,* New Delhi, 2003.

Dani, A.H. : *Indus Civilization, New Perspective,* Islamabad, 1981.

Excavations at Besnagar : Lake, 1910 in *JBBS,* pp. 135-46; *ASIAR,* 1913-14 pp. 186-226; 1914-15, pp. 66-68. *IAR,* 1963-

64 to 1965-66; 1975-77; Khare, M.D., *Vidisha*, Bhopal,1985.

Excavations at Mathura : *Indian Archaeology – A Review*, 1966-67 to 1972-73, 1973-74 to 1976-77.

Excavations at Pawaya : Gwalior Administration Report, 1924-25, p. 9, 1933-34. p. 9, 1939-40, p. 15, 1940-41, pp. 17-20; *ASIAR*, 1924-25, pp. 165-66, 1925-26, p. 190, 1915-16, pp. 101-09.

Grade, M.B. : *Archaeology in Gwalior*, 1934; *Padmavati*, Gwalior, 1952.

Gupta, S.P. : *Archaeology of Soviet Central Asia and the Indian Borderlands*, 2 Vols., Delhi, 1979.

Hertel, H. : *Excavations at Sonkh (Mathura District)*, 1966-67 to 1969-70, *Bulletin of the Museums and Archaeology*, U.P., No. 1 to 6.

Some results of the excavations at Sonkh; A Preliminary Report, National Museum, New Delhi, 1977.

Lal, B.B. : *Excavation at Hastinapur and other explorations in the Upper Ganga and Sutlej Basins*, 1950-52; *Ancient India*, No. 10-11, 1954-55: 5-151.

The Earliest Civilization of South Asia, Delhi, 1997.

India-1947-1997: New Light on the Indus Civilization, Delhi, 1999.

The Saraswati Flows On, Delhi, 2002.

Lal, B.B. (ed.) : *Indus Civilization: Problems and Issues*, Simla.

Mackay, E.J.H. : *Further Excavations at Mohenjodaro*, Delhi, 1938.

ChanhuDaro Excavations, 1935-36, New Haven, 1943.

Mahadevan, I. : *The Indus script: Text, Concordance and Tables*, Delhi, 1977.

Marshall, J. : *Mohenjodaro and the Indus Civilization*, London, 1931.

Misra, V.N. and Mate, M.S. (ed.) : *Indian Prehistory*, Poona, 1965.

Possehl, G. : *Ancient Cities of the Indus*, New Delhi, 1979.

Rao, S.R. : *Lothal and the Indus Civilization*, Mumbai, 1979.

Sankalia, H.D. : *Prehistory and Protohistory of India and Pakistan*, Poona, 1974.

Sankaranand, Swami : *The Rg Vedic Culture of the Prehistoric India*, Calcutta, 1943-44.

Sharma, R.K. : *Encyclopaedia of Art, Archaeology and Literature in Central India*, Vol. I-II, Delhi, 1998.

Trivedi, H.V. : *The Bibliography of Madhya Bharat Archaeology*, Gwalior, 1953.

Vats, M.S. : *Excavations at Harappa*, Delhi, 1940.

Vogel, J.Ph. : *Excavations at Mathura*, ASI, AR, 1911-12, pp. 120-33.

Wheeler, M. : *Indus Civlization*, Cambridge, 1968; *Civlization of the Indus Valley and Beyond*, London, 1966.

b) Inscriptions

Barua, B.M. and Sinha G. (eds.) : *Barhut Inscriptions*, Calcutta, 1926.

Bhandarkar, D.R. (ed.) : *List of Inscriptions of Northern India*, Appdx. *EI*, XIX-XXIII.

Dwivedi, H.N. (ed.) : *Gwalior Rajya Ke Abhilekh*, Gwalior, 1947.

Fleet, J.F. (ed.) : *Inscriptions of Early Gupta Kings and their Successors*, *CII*, III, Calcutta, 1988.

Hiralal, R.B. (ed.) : *Inscriptions of the Central Provinces and Berar*, Nagpur, 1932.

Hultzsch, E. : *Inscriptions of Asoka, Corpus Inscriptionum Indicarum*, (Reprint) Vol. I, London, 1925.

Lele, C.B. (ed.) : *Paramara Inscriptions in the Dhar State*, Dhar State Historical Series.

Luders (ed.) : *List of Brahmi Inscriptions upto 400 AD*, *EI*, X.

Mirashi, V.V. (ed.) : *Inscriptions of the Kalachuri Chedi Era, CII*, IV, I-II, Ootacumund, 1955.

Inscriptions of the Vakatakas, CII, Vol. VI, New Delhi, 1963.

Inscriptions of theSilaharas, CII, Vol. VI, New Delhi, 1977.

Shastri, A.M. (ed.) : *Inscriptions of the Sarabhapuriyas, Panduvamsis and Somavamsis*, pt. I-III, Delhi, 1995.

Trivedi, H.V. (ed.) : *Inscriptions of the Paramaras, Chandellas, Kachchhapaghatas etc*, pt. I-III, Delhi.

Also, *Epigraphia Indica*, Relevant Volumes.

c) Coins

Allan, J. : *Catalogue of Coins of Ancient India in the British Museum*, London, 1936.

Altekar, A.S. : *Coinage of the Gupta Empire. Catalogue of Gupta Gold Coins in the Bayana Hoard.*

'Some alleged Naga and Vakataka Coins', *JNSI*, Vol. V, 1943, pp. 111-134.

'Two Coins from Mathura', *JNSI*, Vol. VI, 1944, pp. 24-26.

Bajpai, Atima : *Madhya Pradesh Ke Nagvanshi Sikke*, (Hindi), Delhi, 1981.

Bajpai, K.D. : 'Braj-Mandal me upalabdha Naga, Gupta tatha Purva Madhya Kaleen Sikke', *The Researcher*, Vol. 12-13, 1972-73, pp. 25-28.

Chakravarty, S.K. : *A Study of Ancient Indian Numismatics*, Calcutta, 1931.

Chattopadhyaya, B. : *The Age of Kusanas – A Numismatic Study.*

Cunningham, A. : *Coins of Ancient India from the earliest times down to seventh century* AD, London, 1891 (Reprinted, 1963).

Coins of Medieval India from the seventh century down to the Muhammadan Conquest, London, 1894 (Reprinted, 1967).

Gupta, P.L. : *A Survey of Indian Numismatography*, Varanasi, 1964.

Bibliography of Indian Numismatics. Ancient Indian Silver Punch Marked Coins, Nasik, 1985.

Herzfeld, E. : *Kushaneo-Sassanian Coins, MASI*, Calcutta, 1930.

Jain, B.C. : *Inventory of the Hoards and Finds of Coins and Seals from M.P., NNM.*, No. 5, Varanasi, 1957.

Maity, S.K. : *Early Indian Coins and Currency System*, New Delhi, 1971.

Narain, A.K. : *Coin Types of Indo-Greek Kings.*

Rajguru, S.N. : 'New Hoard of Gold Coins of the Nagavansi Kings of Chakrakotya', *Orissa Historical Research Society Journal*, Vol. 8, pp. 75-82.

Rapson, E.J. : *Indian Coins*, Strassburg, 1897.

Roy, P.C. : *The Coinage of Northern India*, Delhi, 1980.

Sarma, I.K. : *Coinage of Satavahana Empire*, Delhi, 1980.

Satya, Sharva : *The Kusana Numismatics*, Delhi, 1985.

Singh, A.K. : 'Mathura ke Mitra evam Dutt Shashak', in T.P. Verma (ed.), *Yuga Yugina Vraja*, Varanasi, 1988, pp. 49-55.

Singhal, C.R. : *Bibliography of Indian Coins*, Bombay, 1950.

Smith, V.A. : *Catalogue of Coins in the Indian Museum, Calcutta*, Vol. I, Oxford, 1906.

Stein, M.A. : 'Notes on the Monetary System of Ancient Kashmir', NC, XIX, pp. 125-74.

Trivedi, H.V. : *Catalogue of Coins of the Naga Kings of Padmavati*, Gwalior, 1957.

Wright, H.N. : *Catalogue of Coins in the Indian Museum, Calcutta*, Vol. II, Oxford, 1907.

d) Art and Architectural Remains

Agrawal, R.C. : *Kashmir and its Monumental Glory*, Delhi, 1999.

Agrawal, Urmila : *Khajuraho Sculptures and their Significance*, New Delhi, 1964.

Agrawal, V.S. : *Gupta Art*, Lucknow, 1948.

Ali, R. : *Art and Architecture of the Kalachuris*, Delhi, 1980.

: *Pratihara Art in India*, Delhi, 1987.

Bajpai, K.D. : *Braj Ki Kala, Mathura*, Mathura, 1959.

Bandopadhyaya, B. : *Survey of Indian Metal Sculpture*, Delhi, 1987.

Banerjea, J.N. : *The Development of Hindu Iconography*, Calcutta, 1956 (Reprint).

Banerji, R.D. : *The Haihayas of Tripuri and Their Monuments*, Calcutta, 1931.

Barenes, E. : *Dhar and Mandu*, Bombay, 1907.

Barua, B.M. : *Barhut*, pt. I-III, Calcutta, 1934.

Bussagli M. and Sivaramamurti, C. : 5000 years of the Art of India, New York.

Chakravarty, K.K. and Sharma, R.K. (ed.) : *Art of the Kalachuris*, Bhopal, 1991.

Coomaraswamy, A.K. : *History of Indian and Indonesian Art*, New York, 1965.

Cunningham, A. : *Bhilsa Topes*, London, 1854.

Dhavalikar, M.K. : *Sanchi – A Cultural Study*, Pune, 1965.

Dwivedi, H.N. : *Tripuri-Vidisha, Padmavati and Bagh* (in Hindi), Gwalior, 1954.

Fabri, C.L. : *Discovering Indian Sculpture: A Brief History*, New Delhi, 1970.

Ganguli, O.C., Goswami, A. and Tarafdar, A. : *The Art of the Chandellas*, Calcutta, 1957.

Govt. of Madhya Bharat : *Descriptive and Classified List of Archaeological Monuments in Madhya Bharat*, Gwalior, 1952.

Haldar, A.K. : *Buddhist Caves of Bagh*, 1910-11.

Harle, J.C. : *The Art and Architecture of Indian Subcontinent*, Middlesex, 1986.

Havell, E.B. : *The Art Heritage of India*, Bombay 1964.

A Handbook of Indian Art, Varanasi, 1972.

Kak, R.C. : *Ancient Monuments of Kashmir*, London 1933.

Kramrisch, S. : *The Art of India*, London, 1965.

Indian Sculpture, Calcutta, 1933.

Krishnamurthy, K. : *Mythical Animals in Indian Art*, New Delhi, 1985.

Krishna Deva : *Temples of Khajuraho*, Delhi, 1965.

Temples of India, 2 Vols., Delhi, 1995.

Maisey, F.C. : *Sanchi and its Remains*, London, 1892.

Manwani, S.N. : *Evolution of Art and Architecture in Central India*, Delhi, 1988.

Marshall, Sir John : *The Bagh Caves*, (Reprint) Delhi, 1982.

Marshall and Foucher : *Monuments of Sanchi*, 3 Vols., Delhi, 1940.

Mishra, R.N. : *Sculptures of Dahala and Dakshina Kosala*, Delhi, 1987.

Patil, D.R. : *Monuments of Udayagiri Hills.*

The Cultural Heritage of Madhya Bharat, 1952.

Rao, T.A.G. : *Elements of Hindu Iconography*, 2 Vols., Madras, 1914, 1916, (Reprint, 1968).

Ray, N.R. : *Maurya and Post-Maurya Art*, New Delhi, 1975.

Maurya and Sunga Art, Calcutta, 1965.

Rowland, B. : *The Art and Architecture of India*, Middlesex, 1956.

Saraswati, S.K. : *A Survey of Indian Sculpture*, Calcutta, 1957.

Sharma, Mohanlal : *Padmavati*, (in Hindi), Bhopal, 1971.

Sivaramamurti, C. : *The Art of India*, New York, 1977.

Birds And Animals in Indian Sculpture, New Delhi, National Museum, 1974.

Smith, V.A. : *History of Fine Arts in India and Ceylon*, 3rd ed., Bombay.

Trivedi, R.D. : *Temples of Pratihara Period of Central India*, Delhi, 1990.

William, Jonna G. : *The Art of Gupta India, Empire and Province*, New Delhi, 1983.

Vidya, Prakash : *Khajuraho,* Delhi, 1967.

Zennas, E. and Auboyer, J. : *Khajuraho,* The Hague, 1960.

Zimmer, H. : *The Art of Indian Asia,* New York, 1960, 2 Vols.

2. TEXTS AND TRANSLATIONS

a) The Vedic Literature

Rg. Veda : Vedic Research Institute, Pune, 1993.

Atharvaveda : ed. S. Sarma, Bombay, 1940.

Samaveda : Ed. & tr. Th. Benfey, Leipzig, 1848.

Yajurveda : *Taittiriya Samhita*: Ed. A. Weber, Berlin, 1871-72.

Principal *Upanisads, Grihasūtras, Dharmasūtras* and *Brāhmaṇas* : Max Muller, *SBE,* I, II, XIV, XV, XXIX, XXX.

b) The Epics

Rāmāyaṇa : Eng. tr. M.N. Dutt, Calcutta, 1895-1905.

Mahābhārata : Eng. tr. M.N. Dutt, Calcutta, 1895-1905.

c) The Purāṇas

Agni Purāṇa : Eng. tr. M.N. Dutt, Calcutta, 1903.

Bhagavata Purāṇa : Ed. B.C. Bandopadhyaya, Calcutta, 1830.

Bhaviṣya Purāṇa : Venkatesvara Press, Bombay, 1910.

Brahma Purāṇa : Ed. V.N. Mandalika, Poona.

Brahmāṇḍa Purāṇa : Pub. Venkatesvara Press, Bombay, 1913.

Devībhāgavata Purāṇa : Tr. P. Tarkaratna, Calcutta, 1932.

Garuḍa Purāṇa : Eng. tr. M.N. Dutt, Calcutta, 1908.

Kālikā Purāṇa : Venkatesvara Press, Bombay, Sam. 1829.

Kūrma Purāṇa : Ed. N. Mukhopadhyaya, Calcutta, 1890.

Liṅga Purāṇa : Ed. Vidyasagar, Calcutta, 1876.

Matsya Purāṇa : Ed. Vidyasagar, Calcutta, 1876.

Mārkaṇḍeya Purāṇa : Eng. tr. Pargiter, Calcutta, 1888-1905.

Nārada Purāṇa : Tr. S. Sharma, Bareilly, 1971.

Nīlamata Purāṇa : Ed. R.L. Kanjilal and J. Zadoo, Lahore, 1924.

Padma Purāṇa : Ed. Mandalik, Poona, 1893-94.

Śiva Purāṇa : Ed. Raverkar, Bombay, 1909-11.

Skanda Purāṇa : Ed. Raverkar, Bombay.

Vāyu Purāṇa : Ed. R. Mitra, Calcutta, 1880-88.

Varāha Purāṇa : Ed. H. Sastri, Calcutta, 1893.

Viṣṇu Purāṇa : Tr. H.H. Wilson, 5 Vols., London, 1864-70.

d) Buddhist Literature

Dīghanikāya : Ed. T.W. Rhys Davids, London, 1890.

Divyāvadāna : Ed. Cowell and Neil, Cambridge, 1886.

Dhammapada : Ed. H.C.Norman, 5 Vols., London, 1906-15.

Mahāvaṁsa : Ed. W. Geiger, P.T.S., London, 1908, Eng. tr., W. Geiger, London, 1912.

Mahāvastu : Ed. Senart.

Majjhima Nikāya : Ed. V. Trenckner and R. Chalmer, P.T.S., London, 1888-1902.

Milinda Pañho : Tr. Rhys Davids, Cambridge, 1905.

Jātakas : Ed. Fousball, 7 Vols., London, 1877-97.

Eng. tr. E.B. Cowell, 7 Vols., Cambridge, 1895-1913.

Anguttaranikāya : Pali Text Society, ed. R. Morris, London, 1885-1900.

Vinayaa Piṭaka : Ed. Oldenberg, Edinburg, 1879-83.

e) Jaina Literature

Pauma Chariyam : Ed. H. Jacobi, Bhavnagar, 1914.

Grantha-traya : Ed. M.K. Shastri, Ahmedabad, 1939.

Āvaśyakacūrṇi : Ed. Jinadasa Jain, Rutlam, 1928.
Āvaśyakasūtraniryukti : Ed. Jina Bhadra Jani, Benaras, 1915.
Vividhatīrthakalpa : Ed. Jinaprabha Suri.

f) Sanskrit Literature

Arthaśāstra of Kauṭilya : Ed. R. Sama Sastry, Mysore, 1919.
Aṣṭādyāyī of Pāṇini : Ed. S.C. Vasu, Allahabad, 1891.
Amarakośa by Amarasiṁha : Ed. T. Ganapati Sastri, 4 parts, 1914-17.
Abhijñānaśākuntalam of Kālidāsa : Ed. S. Roy.
Bṛhatsaṁhitā of Varāhamihira : Ed. Kern, BI, Calcutta, 1865.
Bṛhajjātaka of Varāhamihira : Ed. Sitaram Jha, Benaras, 1934.
Bṛhatkathāmañjarī by Kṣemendra : Kavyamala series, Bombay, 1931.
Buddhacharita : By Asvaghosa.
Chaṇḍakauśika by Kṣemīśvara : Ed. J. Vidyasagar, Calcutta, 1884.
Daśakumāracharita of Daṇḍin : Ed. G. Bulhar, Eng. tr. M.R. Kal, Bombay, 1928.
Deśināmamāla by Hemachandra : Ed. Pischel, 1938.
Dvātriṁsatputtalikā (HOS)
Gāthāsaptaśati : Hala.
Harṣacharita of Bāṇa : Ed. K.P. Parab, Bombay, 1925.
Jayamaṅgalā : Commentary of Vātsyāyana's *Kāmasūtra* by Yaśodhara.
Kādambarī by Bāṇa : Ed. H. Siddhanta Vasiga, Calcutta.
Kathāsaritsāgara by Somadeva : Eng. tr. C.H. Tawney; ed. Penzer.
Kāvyamīmāṁsā of Rājaśekhara : G.O.S., No.1, Baroda, 1924.

Kumārasambhava of Kālidāsa : Eng. tr. Griffith, London, 1879.

Mālvikāgnimitra of Kālidāsa : Eng. tr. Tawney, Benaras, 1950.

Meghadūta of Kālidāsa : Ed. E. Hultzsch, London, 1911.

Mṛcchakaṭika by Śūdraka : Eng. tr. Ryder, Cambridge, 1905.

Nāmamālikā of Bhoja : Ed. R. Kulkarni, Poona, 1955.

Navasāhasāṇkacharita of Padmagupta : Ed. Islampurkar, Bombay, 1895.

Pṛithvīrāja Rāso of Chand Bardai : Pandia and Das, Benaras, 1913.

Prabodha Chandrodaya of Kṛṣṇamiśra : Eng, tr. J. Taylor, London, 1962.

Prabandhachintāmaṇi by Merutuṅga : Tr. C.H. Tawney, Calcutta, 1894-1901.

Raghuvaṁśa of Kālidāsa : Tr. G. Naudargikar, Bombay, 1897.

Rājamārtaṇḍa of Bhoja : Tr. R. Mitra, Calcutta, 1883.

Śālihotra of Bhoja : Ed. E.D. Kulkarni, Poona, 1953.

Sādhanamālā : Ed. B.T. Bhattacharya, Baroda, 1925.

Samarāṅgaṇa : Ed. T.G. Sastri, G.O.S., 2 Vols.,

Sutradhāra of Bhoja : Baroda, 1924-25.

Sṛṇgāra-Prakāśa of Bhoja : Ed. G.R. Josyer, Mysore, 1955.

Saraswatī Kaṇṭhābharaṇa of Bhoja : Ed. R. Barooha, Calcutta, 1883-84.

Tilakamañjarī of Dhanapāla : NSS, Bombay, 1903.

Vikramāṅkadevacharita : Ed. G. Buhlar, Bombay, 1875.

Yuktikalpataru of Bhoja : Ed. S. Sastri, Calcutta.

g) Greek and Chinese Sources

Hiuen Tsang : Tr. S. Beal (Buddhist Records of the Western World), London, 1884.

The Travels of Fa-hein	: H.S. Giles, Cambridge, 1923.
Indica: Fragments of Megasthenes	: Ed. E.A. Schwanbeck, Bonn, 1846.
Yuan Chwang	: Tr. T. Watters, London, 1904-5
Periplus Maris Erythaci	: Eng. tr. Schoff, London, 1912.
Records of the Buddhist Religion etc. by I-tsing	: Takakusu, J.A., Oxford, 1896.

h) Muslim Literature

'Āīn-i-Akbarī of Abūl'-l-Faẓl	: Eng. tr. Blochmann, Vol. I-III, Calcutta, 1868-94.
Kitab-ul-Hind and Atharal-Baquia of Al-Bīrūnī	: Eng. tr. (Alberuni's India) Sachau, London, 1914.
Tabaquāt-I-Akbarī of Nizāmuddin	: Eng. tr. B. Dey, Calcutta, 1931.
Tabaquāt-i-Nāsirī of Minhāj-ud-dīn	: Eng. tr. H.G. Raverty, London, 1881.
Tāj-ul Māśir of Hasan-un-Nizāmī	: Extr. tr. HIED, II, 204-43.
Tarikh-i-'Alāī of Amīr Khusrav	: Eng. tr. M. Habib, Bombay, 1931.
Ta'rīkh-i-Firishta	: Eng. tr. J. Briggs, Vol. I-IV, London, 1829.
Tarikh-i-Fīrūz-Shāhī of Ziā-ud-dīn Barni	: Ed. W.N. Leesele, Calcutta, 1860-62.
Ta'rikh-ī-Yamīnī of Al-'utbī	: Ed. eng. tr. by J. Raynolds, London, 1858.
Abd-u-lāh Wassāf	: Extr. tr. HIED, III, 24.
Wakiyāt-i-Kashmir	: Khwaja Mohammad Azam Dedamari Kashmiri, Srinagar.

3. MODERN WORKS

Agrawal, Ashwini	: *The Imperial Guptas*, Delhi.
Agrawal, K.L.	: *Vindhya Kshetra Ka Aitihasik Bhugol*, Satna, 1987.
Agrawal, R.C.	: *Kashmir and its Monumental Glory*, Delhi, 1998.

Aiyanagar, S.K. : *Ancient India*, Poona, 1941.

Altekar, A.S. : *Rashtrakutas and their Times*, Poona, 1934 (Reprint).

Agrawal, V.S. : *India as Known to Panini*, Allahabad, 1983.

Ancient Indian Folk Cults, Delhi, 1970.

Ali, S.M. : *Geography of the Puranas*, New Delhi, 1983.

Bagchi, P.C. : *Pre-Aryan and PreDravidian in India*, Calcutta, 1929.

Bailey, F.G. : *Tribe and Castes of India, Contribution to Indian Sociology*, No. V, 7-19, 1961.

Bamzai, P.N.K. : *History of Kashmir*, Delhi, 1962.

Banerji, R.D. : *Age of Imperial Guptas*, New Delhi, 1981.

Banerji, S.C. : *Cultural Heritage of Kashmir*, Calcutta, 1965.

Banerji, Sastri A. : *Asura India*, Patna, 1926.

Bapat, P.V. (ed.) : *2500 years of Buddhism*, New Delhi, 1959.

Bhandarkar, D.R. : *Ashoka*, Calcutta, 1932.

Bhandarkar, R.G. : *Early History of the Deccan*, 3rd ed., Calcutta, 1926.

Vaisnavism, Saivisim, and Minor Religious Systems, 1929.

Bhatia, P. : *The Paramaras*, New Delhi.

Bhattacharya, A. : *The Sun and the Serpent Lore of Bengal*, Calcutta, 1977.

Bhattacharya, P.K. : *Historical Geography of M.P.*, New Delhi, 1976.

Bhowmick, K.L. : *Tribal India*, Calcutta, 1971.

Bose, N.S. : *The Candellas*, Delhi.

Buddha, Prakash : *Rg.Veda and the Indus Valley Civilization*, Hoshiarpur, 1966.

Chandra, R.P. : *Indo-Aryan Races.*

Chakrabarty, C. : *Racial Basis of Indian Culture*, New Delhi, 1997.

Commisariat, M.S. : *History of Gujarat*, London, 1926.

Crooks, W. : *The Tribes and Castes of North-West Provinces and Oudh*, Calcutta, 1896.

Cunningham, A. : *The Ancient Geography of India*, (ed.) S.N. Majumdar, Calcutta, 1924.

Dandekar, R.N. : *A History of the Guptas*, Poona, 1947.

Dange, S.A. : *Towards understanding Hindu Myths*, New Delhi, 1999.

Myths from the Mahabharata, New Delhi, 1999.

Dasgupta, K.K. : *A Tribal History of Ancient India*, Calcutta, 1974.

Obscure Religious Cults, Calcutta, 1969.

Dasgupta, N. : "*Date of Lalitaditya Muktapida*", IC, XIV, pp. 11-ff.

Dash, N. : *Sarpayajna*, Cuttuck, 1962.

Datt, J.M. : "Population of India about 320 BC." *Man in India*, 42 (4), 1962.

Dikshit, R.K. : *The Candellas of Jejakabhukti*, New Delhi, 1997.

Dikhitar, V.R.R. : *The Purana Index*, 3 Vols., Madras, 1951-55.

Dey, N.L. : *Geographical Dictionary of Ancient and Medieval India*, London, 1927.

Deo, J.P.S. : *Cultural Profile of South Kosala*, Delhi, 1987.

Dwivedi, H.N. : *Madhya Bharat ka Itihas*, Gwalior, 1950.

Desai, A.R. : 'Tribes in Transition', in Romesh Thapar (ed.), *Tribe Caste and Religion in India*, Delhi, 1977.

Dubey, S.C. : *Tribal Heritage of India*, New Delhi, 1997.

Erdosy, George : *The Indo Aryans of Ancient South Asia*, Berlin, 1995.

Fergusson, James : *The Tree and Serpent Worship*, London, 1873.

Ganguly, D.C. : *History of the Paramara Dynasty*, Decca, 1933.

Ghosh, A. (ed.) : *Encyclopaedia of Indian Archaeology*, Delhi, 1989.

Ghoshal, U.N. : 'Dynastic Chronicles of Kashmir', *IHQ*, XVIII, pp. 195-207; 302-341; XIX, pp. 27-38; 156-72.

Goetz, H. : 'Conquest of India by Lalitaditya Muktapida', *JBBRAS*, XXVII, (1952), pp. 43ff.

Gupta, P.L. : *Prachin Chhattisgarh*, Raipur, 1973.

Gupta, S.P. : *Indus Saraswati Civilization, Origin Problems and Issues*, New Delhi.

Hastings, J. : *Encyclopaedia of Religion and Ethics*, Vol. 12, 1921.

Hopkins : *The Great Epics of India.*

Haimendorf C. Von Furer : *Tribes of India*, London, 1982.

Jain, J.C. : *Life in Ancient India as Depicted in Jain Canons*, Bombay, 1937.

Jain, K.C. : *Malwa through the Ages*, Delhi, 1972.

Jayaswal, K.P. : *History of India*, 150-350 AD, Lahore, 1993.

Imperial History of India, Lahore, 1934.

Andhakar Yugin Bharat (In Hindi).

Jonaraja : *Dvitiya Rajatarangini*, ed. by P. Peterson, Bombay, 1896; tr. J.C. Datt, Calcutta, 1887.

Joshi, J.P. : *Facets of Indian Civilization* (Essays in honour of Prof. B.B. Lal), Vol. I-III, Delhi, 2000.

Jha, V.D. : *Bastar Ka Murtishilpa*, Bhopal, 1989.

Khare, M.D. : *Vidisha*, (Hindi), Bhopal, 1985.

Kosare, H.L. : *Prachin Bharata til Nag*, (Marathi), Nagpur, 1989.

Kochhar, R. : *The Vedic People – Their History and Geography*, New Delhi, 2000.

Lahiri, B. : *Indigenious States of Northern India*, Calcutta, 1974.

Lama, Taranath : *History of Buddhism*, Petersburg, 1869.

Law, B.C. : *Tribes in Ancient India*, Poona, 1943.

Kshatriya Tribes in Ancient India, Calcutta, 1923.

Ancient Mid-Indian Kshatriya Tribes, Calcutta, 1924.

Historical Geography of Ancient India, Paris, 1954.

Lawrence : *The Valley of Kashmir*, London, 1895.

Levi, S. : *Pre-Aryan and pre-Dravidian in India*, Calcutta, 1929.

Mac Donell, A.A. and Keith, A.B. : *Vedic Index of Names and Subjects*, 2 Vols., London, 1912.

Maity, P.K. : *Historical Studies in the Cult of Goddess Manasa*, Calcutta, 1966.

Majumdar, A.K. : *Chaulukays of Gujarat*, Bombay, 1956.

Majumdar, D.N. : *Races and Cultures of India*, Delhi, 1961.

Majumdar, R.C. (ed.) : *The History and Culture of the Indian People*, Vol. 1-X, Bombay.

History of Bengal, Vol. I, Decca, 1943.

The Vakataka-Gupta Age, 1946.

Mankad, D.R. : *Puranic Chronology*, Anand (Gujarat), 1951.

Marmat, A.P. : *Ved Kaleen Nag Jatiyan, Rajaon Tatha, Sanskriti Ki Khoj*, (in Hindi), Ujjain.

Meena Nagvansha Kyon Aur Kaise, (in Hindi), Ujjain.

Mc. Crindle, J.W. : *Ancient India as Described by Megasthenes and Arrian*, London, 1877.

Ancient India as Described by Ptolemy, Calcutta, 1825.

Ancient India as Described in Classical Literature, West Minster, 1901.

Mitra, S.K. : *Early Rulers of Khajuraho*, Calcutta, 1958.

Mookerji, R.K. : *Chandragupta Maurya and His Times*, Madras, 1943.

The Gupta Empire, Bombay, 1948.

Harsha, Oxford, 1926.

Munshi, K.M. : *The Glory that was Gurjaradesa*, Part I-III.

The Imperial Gurjaras, Bombay, 1944.

Nair, R. : *Snake Worship in India*, New Delhi, 1993.

Niyogi, R. : *The History of the Gahadavala Dynasty*, Calcutta, 1959.

Oldham, F.C. : *The Sun and the Serpent*, London, 1905.

Ojha, G.H. : *History of the Rajputana*, Ajmer, 1936.

Panda, S.C. : *Naga Cult in Orissa*, Delhi, 1986.

Panikkar, K.M. : *Sri Harsha of Kanauj*, Bombay, 1922.

Pariter, F.E. : *Ancient Indian Historical Tradition*, London, 1922.

Dyansties of the Kali Age, London, 1913.

Patel, C.B. : *Dynastic History of the Nalas*, Calcutta, 1990.

Patil, D.R. : *The Cultural Heritage of Madhya Bharat*, Gwalior, 1952.

Petech, L. : *Northern India according to Shi-Ching-Chu*, Rome, 1950.

Pieres, E. : *The Maukharis*, Madras, 1934.

Pillai, V.G.S. : *Tree Worship and Ophiolatry*, Annamalai University, 1948.

Prasad, Ishwari : *History of Medieval India*, Allahabad, 1950.

Puri, B.N. : *India in the time of Patanjali*, Bombay, 1957.

The History of the Gurjara Pratiharas, Bombay, 1957.

Rajguru, S.N. : *Naga Itihasa* (Oriya), Bhubaneshwar, 1958.

Rapson, E.J. (ed.) : *Cambridge History of India*, Vol. I, Cambridge, 1922.

Ray, H.C. : *Dynastic History of Northern India*, 2 Vols. Calcutta, 1936 (Reprint).

Ray, S.C. : *Early History and Culture of Kashmir*, Calcutta, 1957.

Raychaudhuri, H.C. : *Political History of Ancient India*, 5th ed., Calcutta, 1950.

Rhys, Davids, T.W. : *Buddhist India*, London, 1923.

Risley, H.H. : *The People of India*, London, 1915.

Raza, M. and Ahmed, A. : *An Atlas of Tribal India*, New Delhi, 1990.

Ramkrishna Mission : *The Cultural Heritage of India*, 6 Vols., Calcutta.

Russell, R.V. and Hiralal, R.B. : *Tribes and Castes of Central Provinces of India*, 4 Vols., Reprint, Delhi, 1975.

S. Levi : *Le Nepal*, Vol. I-II.

Sampurnanada : *Samrat Harshavaradhana* (in Hindi), Bombay, V.S. 1977.

Sankaranand Swami : *Manasa Cult*, Calcutta, 1957.

Saran, P. : *Descriptive Catalogue of Non-Persian Sources of Medieval Indian History*, Bombay, 1965.

Sarkar, S.S. : *Aboriginal Races of India*, Calcutta, 1954.

Sastri, K.A.N. : *A Comprehensive History of India*, Vol. II, Calcutta, 1957.

Saxena, K.S. : *Political History of Kashmir*, Lucknow, 1974.

Sen, A. : *Animal Motifs in Indian Art*, Calcutta, 1972.

Sharma D. : *Early Chauhana Dynasties*, New Delhi, 1959.

Sharma, M.L. : *Padmavati*, (Hindi), Bhopal, 1971.

Sharma, R.K. : *The Kalchuris and their Times*, New Delhi, 1980.

Kalachuri Rajvansha Aur Unka Yug, (in Hindi), 2 Vols., New Delhi, 1999.

Tribal History of Central India, Vol. I-III, Delhi, 2002.

Shastri, A.M. : *India as seen in the Brhatsamhita of Varahamihira*, Delhi, 1969.

Shukla, Hiralal : *History of the People of Bastar*, Delhi, 1992.

Singh, Bhagwan : *Vedic Harappans*, New Delhi, 1995.

Singh, M.R. : *Geographical data in the Early Puranas*, 1972.

Singh, S. : *Kashmir Desa Aur Sanskriti*, (in Hindi).

Sinha, B.P. : *Decline of the Kingdom of Magadha*, Patna, 1954.

The Comprehensive History of Bihar, Vol. I, pt. I-II, Patna, 1974.

Sircar, D.C. : *Cosmography and Geography in Early Indian Literature*, Calcutta, 1967.

Successors of Satavahanas in Lower Deccan, Calcutta, 1939.

Soresen, S. : *An Index to the Names in the Mahabharata*, London, 1904.

Sankalia, H.D. : *The Prehistory and Protohistory of India and Pakistan*, Poona, 1974.

Shah, K.K. : *Ancient Bundelkhand*, New Delhi, 1974.

Sherring, M.A. : *Hindu Tribes and Castes*, New Delhi, 1974.

Smith, V.A. : *Early History of India*, 4th ed., Oxford, 1924.

Sriniwasan, M.S. (ed.) : *Mathura: The Cultural Heritage*, New Delhi, 1989.

Tarn, W.W. : *The Greeks in Bactria and India*, Cambridge, 1938.

Thakur, Upendra : *The Hunas in India*, Varanasi, 1967.

Tiwari, D.N. : *Primitive Tribes of India*, New Delhi, 1986.

Tiwari, S.K. : *Encyclopaedia of Indian Tribes*, New Delhi, 1994.

Antiquity of Indian Tribes, New Delhi, 1997.

Tripathi, R.S. : *History of Kanauj*, Benaras, 1937, (Reprint).

Tripathi, Vibha : *The Age of Iron in South Asia*, New Delhi, 2001.

Vaidya, C.V. : *Epic India*, Bombay, 1907.

History of Medieval Hindu India, Poona, 1921-26

Viyogi, N. : *Nagas – The Ancient Rulers of India*, New Delhi, 2002.

Vogel, J. Ph. : *Indian Serpent Lore*, London, 1926.

Wave, C.S. : *Serpent Worship and Other Essays*, London, 1888.

Wilson, H.H. : *Hindu History of Kashmir*, Calcutta, 1960.

Reports, Gazetteers and Journals

Ancient India
American Anthropology
Archaeological Survey of India Report by Cunningham
Bulletin of the Tribal Research Institute, Chhindwara
Bulletin of the Deccan College Post-Graduate and Research Institute, Pune
Current Anthropolgy
Critique of Anthropology

Epigraphia Indica
Gazetteers of M.P.
Indian Archaeology – A Review
Indian Antiquary
Indian Historical Quarterly
Indian Historical Review
Journal of Indian Anthropology
Journal of Indian History
Journal of Royal Asiatic Society
Memoirs of the Archaeological Suvery of India
Man and Environment
Puratattva
Science and Culture

INDEX